"Sacraments are at the heart of Catholic spirituality and liturgical life. They are celebrated in the context of the proclamation of God's Word. This excellent series will help Catholics appreciate more and more both the relationship between Word and Sacrament and how the sacraments are grounded in the riches of Scripture."

—**Thomas D. Stegman, SJ**, Boston College School of Theology and Ministry

"This series shows tremendous promise and ambition in laying out the multiple living connections between the Scriptures and the sacramental life of the Church. Taken together, these books could accomplish what Jean Daniélou's *The Bible and the Liturgy* accomplished for a previous generation of biblical and theological scholarship. And like that work, this series gives to students of the Bible a deeply enriched view of the mesh of relationships within and between biblical texts that are brought to light by the liturgy of the sacraments."

—**Jennifer Grillo**, University of Notre Dame

"In recent years, theological exegesis—biblical commentary by theologians—has made a significant contribution. This series turns the tables: explicitly theological reflection by biblical scholars. The result is a breakthrough. Theologically trained, exegetically astute biblical scholars here explore the foundations of Catholic sacramental theology, along paths that will change the theological conversation. This series points the way to the theological and exegetical future."

—**Matthew Levering**, Mundelein Seminary

"The sacraments come to us clothed in images that carry their mystery and propose it to our hearts. These images come from Scripture and are inspired by the Holy Spirit, who wills to transfigure us each into the full measure of Christ. The books in this series, by situating the sacraments within the scriptural imagery proper to each, will over time surely prove themselves to be agents in this work of the Spirit."

—**John C. Cavadini**, McGrath Institute for Church Life,
University of Notre Dame

CBTS A CATHOLIC BIBLICAL THEOLOGY OF THE SACRAMENTS

SERIES EDITORS

Timothy C. Gray
John Sehorn

The Bible and Baptism

The Fountain of Salvation

ISAAC AUGUSTINE MORALES, OP

B
Baker Academic
a division of Baker Publishing Group
Grand Rapids, Michigan

Published by Baker Academic
a division of Baker Publishing Group
PO Box 6287, Grand Rapids, MI 49516-6287
www.bakeracademic.com

Library of Congress Cataloging-in-Publication Data
Names: Morales, Isaac Augustine, 1976– author.
Title: The Bible and baptism : the fountain of salvation / Isaac Augustine Morales, OP.
Description: Grand Rapids, Michigan : Baker Academic, a division of Baker Publishing Group, [2022] | Series: A Catholic biblical theology of the sacraments | Includes bibliographical references and index.
Identifiers: LCCN 2021050608 | ISBN 9781540961785 (paperback) | ISBN 9781540965653 (casebound) | ISBN 9781493436835 (pdf) | ISBN 9781493436828 (ebook)
Subjects: LCSH: Baptism—Catholic Church. | Baptism—Biblical teaching. | Sacraments—Catholic Church.
Classification: LCC BX2205 .M595 2022 | DDC 234/.161—dc23/eng/20211207
LC record available at https://lccn.loc.gov/2021050608

Nihil obstat:
Rev. Jordan Schmidt, OP
Censor Librorum
August 16, 2021

Imprimi potest:
Very Rev. Kenneth R. Letoile, OP
Prior Provincial
August 16, 2021

Approbatio:
Most Rev. Thomas J. Tobin, DD
Bishop of Providence
October 6, 2021

Baker Publishing Group publications use paper produced from sustainable forestry practices and post-consumer waste whenever possible.

22 23 24 25 26 27 28 7 6 5 4 3 2 1

"With joy you will draw water
from the wells of salvation." (Isa. 12:3)

For my godchildren.
May you faithfully live out your baptismal calling
and so enter into the joy of the heavenly banquet.

Contents

Illustrations

Sidebars

Series Preface

> But one of the soldiers pierced his side with a spear, and at once there came out blood and water.
>
> —John 19:34 (ESV)

The arresting image of Jesus's pierced side has fed the spiritual imagination of countless believers over the centuries. The evangelist tells us that it "took place that the Scripture might be fulfilled" (John 19:36 ESV). Extending this line of thought, St. Thomas Aquinas goes so far as to compare the opened heart of Christ to the Scriptures as a whole, for the passion reveals the secret depths of God's trinitarian love latent in the Word, both written and incarnate. The Fathers of the Church—Latin, Greek, and Syriac alike—also saw in the flow of blood and water a symbol of the sacraments of Christian worship. From the side of Christ, dead on the cross, divine life has been dispensed to humanity. The side of Christ is the fount of the divine life that believers receive, by God's grace, through the humble, human signs of both Word and Sacrament.

Recognition of the life-giving symbiosis between Scripture and sacrament, so richly attested in the teaching of the Fathers of the Church, has proved difficult to maintain in the modern world. However much the Church has insisted upon the unity of Word and Sacrament, "the faithful are not always conscious of this connection," so "there is great need for a deeper investigation of the relationship between word and sacrament in the Church's pastoral activity and in theological reflection" (Benedict XVI, *Verbum Domini* 53).

This series seeks to contribute to that "deeper investigation" by offering a biblical theology of each of the seven sacraments.

One classic definition of theology is "faith seeking understanding." Catholic theology operates with the conviction that the deposit of faith—that which theology seeks to understand—has been brought to completion in Jesus Christ, is reliably transmitted in Scripture and Tradition, and is authentically interpreted by the Church's teaching office (see *Dei Verbum* 7–10). Accordingly, the teaching of the Catholic Church is the *initium fidei* or starting point of faith for theological reflection. The series does not aim primarily to demonstrate the truth of Catholic sacramental doctrine but to understand it more deeply. The purpose of the series, in short, is to foster a deeper appreciation of God's gifts and call in the sacraments through a renewed encounter with his Word in Scripture.

The volumes in the series therefore explore the sacraments' deep roots in the revelation of the Old and New Testaments. Since the study of Scripture should *always* be "the soul of sacred theology" (*Dei Verbum* 24), the expression "biblical theology" is used to indicate that the series engages in a theological reading of the Bible in order to enliven our understanding of the sacraments. The guidelines for such theological interpretation of Scripture are specified in *Catechism of the Catholic Church* 112–14 (cf. *Dei Verbum* 12): attention (1) to the entire content and unity of Scripture, (2) to the living Tradition of the whole Church, and (3) to the analogy of faith. A few words on each of these criteria are in order.

In keeping with the series' character as "biblical theology," the content and unity of Scripture is the criterion that largely governs the structure of each volume. The *Catechism* provides a helpful summary of the series' approach to this criterion. Following "the divine pedagogy of salvation," the volumes attempt to illuminate how the meaning of the seven sacraments, like that of all liturgical signs and symbols, "is rooted in the work of creation and in human culture, specified by the events of the Old Covenant and fully revealed in the person and work of Christ" (CCC 1145). Each volume explores (a) the Old Testament threads (including but not limited to discrete types of the sacraments) that (b) culminate in the ministry and above all in the paschal mystery of the incarnate Christ.

The series' acceptance of the Church's sacramental teaching ensures that the Church's Tradition plays an integral role in the volumes' engagement with the Bible. More directly, sidebars offer specific illustrations selected from the teaching and practice of the postbiblical Church, showing the sometimes surprising ways in which Tradition embodies the Church's ongoing reception of the biblical Word.

In the case of the sacraments, attention to the analogy of faith means, among other things, keeping always in mind their origin and end in the eternal life of the Blessed Trinity, their relationship to the missions of the Son and the Spirit, their ecclesial context, their doxological character, their soteriological purpose, their vocational entailments, and their eschatological horizon.

The series' intended readership is broad. While the primary audience is Catholics of the Roman Rite, it is hoped that others will find much to appreciate, particularly Catholics of the non-Roman rites as well as Eastern Christians who are not in full communion with the Bishop of Rome but whose sacramental theory and practice are very close. Protestant Christians, of course, vary widely in their views of sacramental worship, and their reception of the series is likely to vary similarly. It is our hope that, at the very least, the series will help Protestant believers better understand how Catholic sacramental teaching is born of Scripture and animated by it.

We pray that all those who read these volumes will together delight in the rich food of God's Word (cf. Isa. 55:2), seeking the unity in faith and charity to which we are called by our common baptism into the life of the Blessed Trinity. To him be the glory.

Timothy C. Gray
John Sehorn

Acknowledgments

I have been thinking and writing about baptism on and off for about ten years now, dating back to time spent at the Ludwig-Maximilians Universität in Munich in 2011–12, the year before I joined the Order of Preachers. Although this book looks very different from the project I proposed for the Alexander von Humboldt Fellowship that made that year possible, the book would have been much impoverished were it not for my time in Munich. I am grateful to the Humboldt Foundation for their generous support, as well as to the wonderful colleagues in Munich and elsewhere who gave me opportunities to test out some of my ideas during that year. I am particularly grateful to Prof. Dr. Knut Backhaus for his kindness, generosity, and hospitality.

I also wish to thank Tim Gray and John Sehorn, the series editors, for inviting me to write this volume. John has been a delight to work with as an editor, and this is a much better book as a direct result of his many helpful editorial suggestions. Thanks also to my Providence College colleague Stephen Long, who kindly read and commented on the four chapters on the Old Testament as well as other portions of the manuscript and was a frequent conversation partner throughout the writing process. I might have missed some important aspects of the biblical theology of baptism were it not for those conversations. For numerous stylistic improvements, I am indebted to Sister Agnes Maria of St. John, OP, of Our Lady of Grace Monastery, who generously read the entire manuscript, as well as to the editors at Baker Academic.

A special word of gratitude to Dr. Robin Jensen of the University of Notre Dame for giving me permission to use photographs she took of two ancient baptisteries from Naples and Henchir Sokrine. Her scholarship has shown the great value in studying architectural and artistic representations of baptism for mining the early Church's theology of the sacrament. The brief summaries of some of her work below are but the tip of the iceberg.

Biblical quotations throughout the work are from the NRSV unless otherwise noted. Italics in biblical quotations indicate my own emphasis.

Abbreviations

AB	Anchor Bible
ABD	*Anchor Bible Dictionary*. Edited by D. N. Freedman. 6 vols. New York: Doubleday, 1992.
AcT	*Acta Theologica*
ACW	Ancient Christian Writers
ANF	*Ante-Nicene Fathers*
AYBRL	Anchor Yale Bible Reference Library
BTS	Biblical Tools and Studies
BZNW	Beihefte zur Zeitschrift für die neutestamentliche Wissenschaft
CBET	Contributions to Biblical Exegesis and Theology
CBQ	*Catholic Biblical Quarterly*
CCC	*Catechism of the Catholic Church*
cf.	*confer*, compare
CTQ	*Concordia Theological Quarterly*
esp.	especially
ESV	English Standard Version
FC	Fathers of the Church
IBC	Interpretation: A Bible Commentary for Teaching and Preaching
ICC	International Critical Commentary
JBL	*Journal of Biblical Literature*
JSHJ	*Journal for the Study of the Historical Jesus*
JSNT	*Journal for the Study of the New Testament*
JSNTSup	Journal for the Study of the New Testament Supplement Series
JSOTSup	Journal for the Study of the Old Testament Supplement Series
JSPHL	*Journal for the Study of Paul and His Letters*
KJV	King James Version
LCL	Loeb Classical Library
LXX	Septuagint
NIGTC	New International Greek Testament Commentary
NovT	*Novum Testamentum*

NovTSup	Supplements to Novum Testamentum
NPNF[1]	*Nicene and Post-Nicene Fathers, Series 1*
NRSV	New Revised Standard Version
OTL	Old Testament Library
PNTC	Pillar New Testament Commentary
RSV	Revised Standard Version
SBT	Studies in Biblical Theology
SNTW	Studies of the New Testament and Its World
SP	Sacra Pagina
TNTC	Tyndale New Testament Commentaries
VT	*Vetus Testamentum*
WBC	Word Biblical Commentary
WUNT	Wissenschaftliche Untersuchungen zum Neuen Testament

Introduction

The Fountain of Salvation

You visit the earth and water it,
  you greatly enrich it;
the river of God is full of water;
  you provide the people with grain,
  for so you have prepared it.

—Psalm 65:9

Illumination . . . is the most beautiful and most magnificent of the gifts of God.

—Gregory of Nazianzus, *Oration* 40.3

Baptism was born in the land of Israel; we must interpret the material elements which it uses as a symbol according to the significance of these elements for the Jews of old. It is in a Jewish order of symbolism that we shall find the explanation of Baptism.

—Jean Daniélou, *The Bible and the Liturgy*

According to Aristotle, the ancient Greek philosopher Thales of Miletus, speculating on the nature of the universe, suggested that everything is made of water.[1] From our twenty-first-century perspective, it would be easy to mock

1. Aristotle, *Metaphysics* 1.983b.

this early attempt to make sense of the world. But if we stop to think about the importance of water, the idea, although still no doubt false, might appear less far-fetched. Around 70 percent of the human body is made of water. Roughly the same percentage of the earth's surface is covered by the water of the world's oceans, seas, and lakes. Every living organism on the planet depends on water for its life, whether directly or indirectly. Plants absorb it; animals drink it. In the natural realm, even if things are not made of water in the sense that Thales proposed, water is nevertheless the source of life. Little wonder, then, that this substance, so essential for every living thing, should also play a central role in God's plan of salvation.

The Scriptures and the liturgy abound with water imagery. From the first page of the Christian Bible to the last, water serves as a potent symbol, signifying life, death, purity, and, in one of the most famous accounts of the biblical narrative, the path to freedom. The Catholic Church's rite of blessing the baptismal waters draws on numerous accounts from both the Old and the New Testaments, appealing to a rich kaleidoscope of biblical symbols to illuminate the significance of baptism: the waters of creation, the flood, the crossing of the Red Sea, Christ's own baptism in the Jordan, and the water and the blood flowing from the side of Christ on the cross. All these elements of the biblical account shed light on this foundational sacrament.

A Biblical Theology of Baptism

Over the course of the past century, several major works have appeared on the topic of baptism from a biblical perspective. These works share one common feature: each of them focuses predominantly, if not exclusively, on the texts of the New Testament. In most cases they begin no earlier than Jewish practices related to washing and purification around the time of the New Testament.[2] The reason for this limitation should be obvious. The rite of baptism first appears in the New Testament, and the Old Testament says nothing explicitly about this foundational Christian sacrament.

Nevertheless, the approach of this study will be different, inspired by the writings of the Church Fathers as well as the Church's liturgy. The present

2. Although many studies of baptism discuss the phenomenon of "proselyte baptism," this one will not. I do not find the parallels particularly illuminating for a biblical theology of baptism. Those interested in the question may consult G. R. Beasley-Murray, *Baptism in the New Testament* (Grand Rapids: Eerdmans, 1962), 18–31.

work offers a broader understanding of the theology of baptism, drawing on numerous texts from the Old Testament. In his classic work *The Bible and the Liturgy*, Jean Daniélou writes, "If we wish to understand the true meaning of Baptism, it is quite clear that we must turn to the Old Testament."[3] The early Christians, following the lead of the New Testament writers, saw in several stories of the Old Testament prefigurations of baptism: creation, the flood and Noah's ark, the crossing of the Red Sea, and the washing of Naaman the Syrian in the river Jordan, to name a few. In this study of baptism, we will consider these and other texts from the Old Testament, even some that have not traditionally been associated with baptism. The rationale behind this approach is that the primary stock of images for understanding the significance of baptism should come from the Bible itself. As already noted, water imagery abounds in the Old Testament. Even texts that have not been explicitly associated with baptism can contribute to the significance of the sacrament.

Part 1 of this work will explore four aspects of water imagery in the Old Testament for the light they shed on baptism. To borrow a wonderful turn of phrase from Richard Hays, one might describe this part of the study as an exercise in "reading backwards"—that is, reading the texts of the Old Testament afresh in light of the new revelation God has made in Christ.[4] We will begin in chapter 1 by considering the connection between water, life, and salvation. The obvious starting point for this theme is the creation accounts of Genesis, but water frequently serves as an image of salvation in the prophetic texts of the Old Testament, especially, but not exclusively, in Isaiah. It is hardly surprising, then, that the first sacrament of Christian initiation should incorporate the use of water. Although water often connotes life in Scripture, it can also signify death. Chapter 2 will thus focus on some of the Old Testament texts in which the waters bring about death or at least threaten such destruction. The connection between this theme and Christian baptism should be obvious, particularly in light of the Pauline understanding of baptism as dying and rising with Christ (Rom. 6:1–11; Col. 2:11–12). One of the most famous episodes in all of Scripture, the crossing of the Red Sea, associates water with liberation, as God opens a path in the midst of the

3. Jean Daniélou, *The Bible and the Liturgy* (Notre Dame, IN: University of Notre Dame Press, 1956), 71.

4. Richard B. Hays, *Reading Backwards: Figural Christology and the Fourfold Gospel Witness* (Waco: Baylor University Press, 2014).

waters to lead the Israelites to freedom. Many early Christians, taking their cue from 1 Corinthians 10, saw in this event a type of baptism. The entry into the land described in the book of Joshua, moreover, evokes the image of this earlier crossing and fulfills the hope to which the Red Sea event points. These two episodes, as well as traditions stemming from them, will be the subject of chapter 3. Several baptismal texts in the New Testament also speak of baptism as a purification. In order to understand these texts better, chapter 4 will explore the Old Testament notion of purity, both ritual and moral, to see what light it can shed on the purificatory aspects of baptism. This typology of the symbolism of water is no doubt artificial, and as we will see, there is considerable overlap across categories. Nevertheless, it will be helpful to treat each theme separately before offering a synthesis.

In part 2, we will shift our attention to the New Testament, focusing primarily, but not exclusively, on explicit references to baptism. The first two chapters of this section, 5 and 6, will consider the Gospels, studying Christ's own baptism by John the Baptist and the ubiquitous water imagery in the Gospel of John. Chapter 7 will then explore the variations on the idea of being baptized "in the name," particularly as it relates to the Old Testament understanding of the name of the Lord. The association of baptism with the name of God, I suggest, implies that the rite relates to both the presence and the worship of God. Like all the sacraments, baptism draws its power from Christ's passion, death, and resurrection.[5] No one brings out this connection more clearly than Paul. His understanding of baptism as a union of the believer with these saving events will be the subject of chapter 8. In addition to the image of dying and rising with Christ, Paul draws on clothing imagery to describe what happens in baptism. Chapter 9 will examine this theme, looking at baptismal texts in Galatians and Colossians as well as other passages in which Paul uses clothing language as a mode of exhortation. The fluidity of this image suggests that there is a close connection between baptism and the Christian life. Chapter 10 focuses on the First Epistle of Peter, which some interpreters have suggested has a close connection with early baptismal liturgies. Whether or not this is the case, 1 Peter does make an important statement about baptism (1 Pet. 3:21), and it also elaborates the theme of new birth, which other New Testament texts associate with baptism. Additionally, this letter develops the understanding of the Church as a temple and a

5. CCC 1115.

royal priesthood. First Peter thus serves as a fitting transition to chapter 11, which discusses the New Testament understanding of purity as it relates to baptism. Whereas the law of Moses speaks broadly of two kinds of purity, ritual and moral, the New Testament texts about baptism seem to focus almost exclusively on purity as an ethical category. Nevertheless, the ethical understanding of purity still relates to ritual since baptism serves as the entrance to Christian worship. The final chapter of the study explores Paul's various depictions of baptismal unity. For Paul, baptism is ordered to unity—the healing of divisions between Jews and Gentiles and, indeed, between people of all sorts of backgrounds. Nevertheless, this is not a unity that flattens out differences. Rather, the unity that baptism brings about is characterized by a diversity of gifts and roles. All of these roles serve to further the Church's mission of bringing others into healing union with Christ.

Baptismal Anointing

The sacrament of baptism, both historically and as it is practiced in the Catholic Church today, incorporates a number of rites: exorcisms, clothing with a white garment, anointing with oil, and Scripture readings, among other acts. At the heart of the sacrament, however, lies the act of bathing with water, whether by pouring or by immersion. Although earlier studies of baptism with good reason include New Testament references to anointing or sealing, such as 2 Corinthians 1:22, I will limit this study primarily to the fundamental imagery of water. Nevertheless, we will see that even in texts that speak only of water, the idea of anointing is not far away. Christ's baptism is his royal anointing, and in our baptism we are joined to him, anointed to serve him and to reign with him as part of the new creation, of which he is the firstborn. The waters of baptism are an instrumental fountain of salvation, drawing their power from the true fountain, Christ, who paradoxically gives us new life through death, liberating us and preparing us to worship in his new temple.

PART 1

WRITTEN *for* OUR INSTRUCTION

Water in the Old Testament

1

The Waters of Life

> How fair are your tents, O Jacob,
> your encampments, O Israel!
> Like palm groves that stretch far away,
> like gardens beside a river,
> like aloes that the LORD has planted,
> like cedar trees beside the waters.
>
> —Numbers 24:5–6

The closing visions of the book of Revelation present an ambivalent picture of the role of water in the new heavens and the new earth. On the one hand, the waters of the sea, frequently interpreted in antiquity as the source of chaos and danger, will have no place in the new creation (Rev. 21:1).[1] On the other hand, the very next chapter draws on the imagery of water as a source of life (22:1–2). Both these images—the sea as a destructive force and the river as a source of life—appear in the opening book of the Bible. Water thus forms bookends around the Bible as a whole, suggesting its importance as a biblical image. The life-giving and destructive properties of water both play

1. The classic study on the chaotic portrayal of water and its relation to eschatology is Hermann Gunkel, *Schöpfung und Chaos in Urzeit und Endzeit* (Göttingen: Vandenhoeck & Ruprecht, 1921); for a recent criticism of some of Gunkel's ideas, see David Toshio Tsumura, *Creation and Destruction: A Reappraisal of the* Chaoskampf *Theory in the Old Testament* (Winona Lake, IN: Eisenbrauns, 2005).

an important role in the Christian understanding of baptism (see, e.g., Rom. 6:3–4). We will begin our study with the theme of water as a source of life.

The Waters of Creation

When it comes to the role of water in bringing about new life, the early chapters of Genesis provide fertile ground for the Christian imagination. At the beginning of the first creation account, in the chaotic conditions that precede God's ordering of the universe, there is only water and a "mighty wind" that sweeps across these primordial waters (Gen. 1:2 [NRSV marginal note]).[2] Not long after this description of the chaotic state of things, life begins to emerge from the waters. We read that, on the third day, God said, "'Let the waters under the sky be gathered together into one place, and let the dry land appear.' And it was so" (Gen. 1:9). Out of the waters appears the dry land, and from it the first life appears, various kinds of vegetation (1:11). The "fertility" of the waters reappears on the fifth day as God begins to fill the sea with inhabitants (1:20). Despite the initially menacing and chaotic appearance of the waters, under God's creative word, water becomes a source of life.

This connection between water and life continues in Genesis 2, with its description of the garden of Eden. Genesis describes this garden as a place of fertility and life, though also a place with the potential for disaster (as the reader soon discovers in Gen. 3). A passage that many modern interpreters see as perhaps an intrusion into the text identifies one of the important sources of life for the trees in the midst of Eden: the river flowing out of the garden (Gen. 2:10).[3] This river splits into four rivers, two of which (the Tigris and the Euphrates) are well known and the other two of which (the Pishon and the Gihon) are harder to pinpoint. The exact identity of the rivers does not matter for our purposes. The important point is that Genesis gives the impression that this river from Eden is the source of life. As some interpreters have

2. The language with which the text speaks of this wind is ambiguous, which for a variety of reasons led later readers to interpret the "wind" of Gen. 1:2 as a reference to the Spirit of God (indeed, the Hebrew phrase can be interpreted literally as "the Spirit of God," as older translations such as the RSV and the KJV do). As in many ancient languages, one word in Hebrew (*ruaḥ*) can mean "breath," "wind," or "spirit." The modifier *elohim* literally means "god" or "gods," but it can also be used as a superlative (hence the translation "a mighty wind").

3. For a brief discussion, see Claus Westermann, *Genesis 1–11: A Commentary*, trans. John J. Scullion (Minneapolis: Augsburg, 1984), 215–19.

The Life-Giving Power of Water

Many of the Church Fathers draw a connection between the creation account of Genesis 1 and baptism. Tertullian, for example, writes,

> What of the fact that waters were in some way the regulating powers by which the disposition of the world thenceforward was constituted by God? For the suspension of the celestial firmament in the midst He caused by "dividing the waters"; the suspension of "the dry land" He accomplished by "separating the waters." After the world had been hereupon set in order through its elements, when inhabitants were given it, "the waters" were the first to receive the precept "to bring forth living creatures." Water was the first to produce that which had life, that it might be no wonder in baptism if waters know how to give life.[a]

a. Tertullian, *On Baptism* 3 (*ANF* 3:670)

noted, the division into four rivers most likely symbolizes completeness, and so one can easily understand the river as the source of life for the whole world.[4]

The rest of the account of the events in the garden never mentions the river again; this is one of the reasons many interpreters see the description of the river as an insertion into the text.[5] Nevertheless, the association of water with life and salvation appears frequently throughout the Old Testament, especially in the Psalms and the Prophets.

The Waters of Life in the Psalms

The opening poem of the Psalter draws on this imagery to describe the one who meditates on the Torah.

> He is like a tree
>   planted by streams of water,

4. See Gordon J. Wenham, *Genesis 1–15*, WBC 1 (Waco: Word, 1987), 64–65; Westermann, *Genesis 1–11*, 217.

5. On the connection between rivers and the sanctuary, see Gordon J. Wenham, "Sanctuary Symbolism in the Garden of Eden Story," in *I Studied Inscriptions from before the Flood: Ancient Near Eastern, Literary, and Linguistic Approaches to Genesis 1–11*, ed. Richard S. Hess and David Toshio Tsumura (Winona Lake, IN: Eisenbrauns, 1994), 399–404.

> that yields its fruit in its season,
>   and its leaf does not wither.
> In all that he does, he prospers. (Ps. 1:3 ESV)[6]

The water imagery, of course, functions as a simile; the psalmist is not talking about literal water. Nevertheless, the juxtaposition of water with the notion of meditating on God's Word serves as a beautiful image for the close connection between baptism and the Word of God. Baptism is a sacrament of faith, one that combines word and physical action; it serves as the beginning of a life devoted to meditating on God's Word. Without such meditation, the baptized will wither like a tree planted in the desert.

One of the most famous and popular of the psalms also uses water to describe the refreshment that the Lord provides for his people:

> The Lord is my shepherd, I shall not want.
>   He makes me lie down in green pastures;
> *he leads me beside still waters*;
>   he restores my soul.
> He leads me in right paths
>   for his name's sake. (Ps. 23:1–3)[7]

As in Psalm 1, the water of which the psalmist speaks here is metaphorical. Nevertheless, and also as in Psalm 1, the imagery of Psalm 23 can shed light

Robin Margaret Jensen

Figure 1. Baptistery mosaic in a church in Henchir Sokrine, near Lamta (Leptis Minor)

6. The NRSV, striving to maintain inclusive language, uses plural pronouns to refer to the subject of the verbs. Unfortunately, this obscures the psalm's use of the gendered noun *ish*, which was later interpreted messianically.

7. Throughout this work italics in biblical quotations indicate my own emphasis.

The Biblical Theology of Baptisteries

The symbolism of ancient baptisteries offers a fascinating window into how early Christians interpreted the theology of baptism.[a] Many of these baptisteries include images from both the Old and the New Testaments, which also appear in some patristic writings on baptism. One of the most common motifs is drawn from the creation accounts of Genesis 1–2: fruit trees, birds, the four rivers flowing out from Eden (see figure 1). The Psalms also influenced the decoration of some of these baptisteries, especially those psalms that speak of water. Deer frequently appear in these spaces, alluding to Psalm 42 and the panting of the deer for water (v. 1). Some baptisteries include images of the Good Shepherd, reflecting a common representation of Jesus in the Gospels, as well as the famous Psalm 23. These baptisteries show that, from very early on, Christians drew on the Old Testament to flesh out the significance of the sacrament.

a. For a rich discussion of the symbolism of ancient baptisteries, see Robin Margaret Jensen, *Living Water: Images, Symbols, and Settings of Early Christian Baptism*, Supplements to Vigiliae Christianae 105 (Leiden: Brill, 2011), esp. 233–87.

on the significance of baptism. In the waters of baptism, the Lord restores the life of the baptized. He does so "for his name's sake," and the baptized receive the name of God in the sacrament.[8] Moreover, baptism is but the beginning of a life of walking in "paths of righteousness" (as Paul makes clear in Rom. 6).

Psalm 36, a meditation on the foolishness of the wicked and the faithfulness of God, also draws on the image of water to speak of God's care for his people. Describing the way that God preserves his people, the psalmist writes:

> How precious is your steadfast love, O God!
> All people may take refuge in the shadow of your wings.
> They feast on the abundance of your house,
> and *you give them drink from the river of your delights.*
> *For with you is the fountain of life*;
> in your light we see light. (Ps. 36:7–9)

8. See chap. 7 below.

It is possible that the psalm alludes to the garden of Eden, as the word "delights" in the phrase here translated "the river of your delights" literally refers to Eden (which in Hebrew simply means "delight").[9] The juxtaposition of water imagery with light ("With you is the fountain of life; in your light we see light") is also significant. One of the most common names for baptism among early Christians was "illumination" because of the enlightenment that the catechumens received with the gift of the Holy Spirit. One can see this connection between light and water in the imagery of John 8–9 and in the reference to being "enlightened" in Hebrews 6:2–4, as well as in other texts.[10]

Rejoicing over the gift of water and the life that it produces appears once more in Psalm 65, which speaks both of God's acts of deliverance (vv. 5–8) and of his basic provision of life (vv. 9–13). Whereas the middle stanza draws on water's destructive power—a point to which we will return in the next chapter—the final stanza emphasizes the life that water brings:

> You visit the earth *and water it*,
> you greatly enrich it;
> *the river of God is full of water*;
> you provide the people with grain,
> for so you have prepared it.
> *You water its furrows abundantly*,
> settling its ridges,
> *softening it with showers*,
> and blessing its growth. (Ps. 65:9–10)

No less than four times the psalmist explicitly underscores the importance of water in generating life, and the other blessings the people enjoy—grain, pastures, flocks (Ps. 65:12–13)—all depend on water for their existence.

One more psalm brings out the connection between water and life. Psalm 114 offers praise to God for the act of deliverance he accomplished for Israel by bringing the people out of Egypt. Most of this psalm reflects on God's control over the power of the sea, but the final verses point to another important episode in the Pentateuch:

9. L. Michael Morales, *Who Shall Ascend the Mountain of the Lord? A Biblical Theology of the Book of Leviticus*, New Studies in Biblical Theology (Downers Grove, IL: InterVarsity, 2015), 19.

10. See chaps. 6 and 11 below.

> Tremble, O earth, at the presence of the Lord,
> at the presence of the God of Jacob,
> *who turns the rock into a pool of water,*
> *the flint into a spring of water.* (Ps. 114:7–8)

Twice in the story of the exodus and Israel's wandering in the wilderness, the people grumble at their lack of water, fearing that they will die in the wilderness (Exod. 17; Num. 20). Twice, God provides water from a rock, sustaining their life. Although one might more commonly associate this image with the Eucharist (as St. Paul seems to do in 1 Cor. 10), the life-giving properties of water, which are shown forth in all the psalms considered in this section, also illuminate the significance of baptism, the sacrament that brings about entry into life and access to the Eucharist.

The Waters of Life in the Prophets

The life-giving property of water also appears frequently throughout the writings of the prophets. Water imagery pervades the book of Isaiah. The reason for this is not hard to find. For a people at the mercy of the rains for food, as the Israelites were—indeed, as nearly all inhabitants of the ancient Near East were—water naturally came to symbolize life and salvation. An important text in this regard appears toward the end of the first major section of Isaiah.[11] In fact, in this section we see two common uses of water in the Old Testament—one pointing backward to the exodus and the other drawing on the imagery of a wellspring to speak of salvation.

The oracles of Isaiah 11–12 bring together four significant themes throughout the book: the hope for a Davidic king, the evocation of Edenic imagery, the expectation of a new exodus, and the significance of the temple. Chapter 11 begins by describing Israel's hopes for a deliverer from the family of David (v. 1). In one of the most famous passages in Isaiah, the prophet describes the arrival of this figure as leading to Edenic conditions, including peaceful interactions between predator and prey (vv. 6–9). With verse 10 the prophet again takes up this hope for a Davidic king, referring once again to the "root of Jesse." This second oracle also expresses hope for an act of deliverance

11. Isaiah 1–12. This division is standard. For a brief discussion of the structure of Isaiah, especially the first half of the book, see Christopher R. Seitz, *Isaiah 1–39*, IBC (Louisville: John Knox, 1993), 7–10.

akin to the exodus from Egypt (v. 11). As at the first exodus the Lord parted the sea to make a path for the people of Israel, so he will do in this new act, the prophet writes:

> And the LORD will utterly destroy
> the tongue of the sea of Egypt;
> and will wave his hand over the River
> with his scorching wind;
> and will split it into seven channels,
> and make a way to cross on foot. (Isa. 11:15)

We will return to this imagery in chapter 3. For now, it merely serves the purpose of setting up another important use of water in this early section of Isaiah.

Isaiah 12 consists of a hymn of praise and thanksgiving to God for his forgiveness and salvation. This hymn continues to develop exodus motifs, referring to God as "my salvation" (12:2; cf. Exod. 15:2) and speaking of how the Lord acts "gloriously" (Isa. 12:5; cf. Exod. 15:2). At the heart of the hymn, the prophet shifts to a different symbolic use of water, speaking now of a fountain: "With joy you will draw water from the wells of salvation" (Isa. 12:3). In light of the Edenic imagery in Isaiah 11:6–9, this water imagery may also allude to the conditions of the garden. In support of such an interpretation, it is worth noting that the chapter ends with an exclamation of joy at God's presence in Zion (12:6). As God dwelt with human beings in the garden, a garden made fertile by the waters of the river of Eden, so now God dwells in Zion, and the people rejoice at the prospect of drawing water, here a symbol of life.[12] The connection between water imagery and Zion fittingly prefigures baptism, because baptism is the sacrament that introduces the believer into the Church's liturgical life. As we will see, the Old Testament frequently associates water symbolism with the worship of God.

Like the early chapters of Genesis, the song of praise in Isaiah 12 associates the life-giving property of water with life and salvation. Moreover, it situates that salvation in the sanctuary setting of Zion. This theme appears frequently throughout the book as well as in other parts of the Old Testament prophetic corpus.

12. For the temple imagery in the garden of Gen. 2–3, see again Wenham, "Sanctuary Symbolism"; Jon D. Levenson, *Sinai and Zion: An Entry into the Jewish Bible* (San Francisco: Harper & Row, 1987), 143–44.

The exuberance of Isaiah 12:1–6 finds a counterpart in Isaiah 35. This passage, the last prophetic oracle in the first half of Isaiah and one that can be viewed as a bridge to the second half of the book, describes the return of the exiles to Zion with joy.[13] Once again, one of the primary images for this act of redemption is fertility, a fertility made possible by the infusion of water into the desert.

The oracle begins on an exultant note, describing the joy and the new life that will come about in the wilderness (Isa. 35:1–2a). As is often the case in Isaiah, this new life in the midst of apparent aridity signals the presence of God with his people Israel. Those who experience this transformation are promised a vision of God (35:2b). The return of God and the people to Zion (35:10) brings about strength, salvation, and healing. The prophet exhorts the people to take confidence in God and his redeeming activity (35:3–4). The oracle then continues, describing this salvation as involving the healing of various ailments (35:5–6a). The salvation proclaimed by the prophet thus extends to the whole body.

In this context the prophet turns again to the imagery of water to symbolize the anticipated transformation of Israel's situation:

> For *waters* shall break forth in the wilderness,
> and *streams in the desert*;
> the burning sand shall become *a pool*,
> and the thirsty ground *springs of water*;
> the haunt of jackals shall become a swamp,
> the grass shall become reeds and rushes. (Isa. 35:6b–7)

The connection between the various forms of water appearing in the wilderness and the healings described in the preceding verses is no doubt a poetic one. Nevertheless, this connection contributes to the multifaceted imagery of water in the Old Testament. Water serves as a potent symbol for Israel's hopes, a sign of God's healing and redemption. The rest of the oracle proceeds to describe God's act of creating a highway for the exiles and bringing them back to Zion (Isa. 35:10). New life, salvation, joy—these are the conditions symbolized by the flow of running waters in the wilderness. Moreover, the reference to Zion would also evoke Israel's hopes for a return to the worship of God in the temple. Many of these images reappear in the second half of Isaiah.

13. On the connection between this oracle and Isa. 40, see Brevard S. Childs, *Isaiah*, OTL (Louisville: Westminster John Knox, 2001), 299–300.

As is well known, the second major section of Isaiah (chaps. 40–55) begins with words of comfort (Isa. 40:1), as God promises to bring the Jewish exiles back from Babylon. In a famous passage the prophet announces, "In the wilderness prepare the way of the Lord, make straight in the desert a highway for our God" (40:3). The image of a highway reflects the oracle of Isaiah 35 just considered (35:8–10). More important for our purposes, however, is the wilderness motif, which appears several times in Isaiah 40–55.

Isaiah 41 bears a number of resemblances to Isaiah 35. Like the earlier text, Isaiah 41 speaks of reversal and redemption for Israel. God promises the people that their enemies will be put to shame and brought to nothing (41:11–12). Despite Israel's apparent insignificance (41:14), God will make them capable of cutting through mountains and hills, leading them to glory in him (41:16).

In this context the prophet once again promises that there will be water and refreshment in the wilderness. As they pass through the wilderness, the Lord will transform it, providing water for the Israelites and turning the desert into a fertile place (Isa. 41:17). As in Isaiah 35, the water God provides for the people takes on various forms, thus underscoring the abundance of the supply:

> I will open *rivers* on the bare heights,
> and *fountains* in the midst of the valleys;
> I will make the wilderness *a pool of water*,
> and the dry land *springs of water*. (Isa. 41:18)

Some interpreters take this description to refer to literal water in a dry land.[14] While that may be the case, the literal fulfillment of this promise would nevertheless still point to the symbolic significance of water as a source of salvation and new life. The subsequent verses, in fact, connect this water supply with garden imagery, speaking of the growth of an abundance of trees in the wilderness (Isa. 41:19–20). Once again, God appears as the source of the waters of life and the fertility that they generate.

The desert imagery that predominates in the second part of Isaiah serves once again as the setting for God's provision of water for his people in chapter

14. Joseph Blenkinsopp, *Isaiah 40–55: A New Translation with Introduction and Commentary*, AB 19A (New York: Doubleday, 2002), 203.

43. Exodus imagery functions as the paradigm for the act of redemption by which God promises to bring the people out of Babylon. Two different aspects of water imagery play an important part in this promise.

First, the prophet appeals again to the great act of deliverance God brought about at the Red Sea, rescuing the people from the Egyptians. Moreover, the prophet introduces the Lord as Israel's king, an image that has resonances with the crossing of the Red Sea (Isa. 43:15; cf. Exod. 15:18). He then identifies the God of Israel more explicitly as the one who brought about the exodus:

> Thus says the LORD,
>   who makes a way in the sea,
>   a path in the mighty waters,
> who brings out chariot and horse,
>   army and warrior;
> they lie down, they cannot rise,
>   they are extinguished, quenched like a wick. (Isa. 43:16–17)[15]

This earlier act of deliverance serves as the foundation for a new act that God is about to accomplish for Israel. This new act is in continuity with other aspects of Israel's escape from Egypt, too, and water plays a second important role in this deliverance.

Just as the Lord provided water for the Israelites during their time in the wilderness (Exod. 15:22–25; Num. 20:2–13), so now he promises to provide rivers of water even in apparently desolate places:

> I am about to do a new thing;
>   now it springs forth, do you not perceive it?
> I will make a way in the wilderness
>   and rivers in the desert.
> The wild animals will honor me,
>   the jackals and the ostriches;
> *for I give water in the wilderness,*
>   *rivers in the desert,*
> *to give drink to my chosen people,*
>   the people whom I formed for myself
> so that they might declare my praise. (Isa. 43:19–21)

15. We will return to this text in chap. 3 to consider it from the perspective of the exodus.

Life-giving water in the midst of a wasteland functions as a symbol of the miraculous nature of God's act of deliverance.[16] Moreover, the "way in the wilderness," as some interpreters suggest, most likely corresponds to the highway described in Isaiah 40:3.[17] This imagery reappears not long after this oracle, but with the added elements of God's Spirit and the blessing.

The prophet returns to the theme of redemption in Isaiah 44. Once again the Lord acts on behalf of his chosen people (44:1–2). As in Isaiah 41 and 43, here the prophet symbolizes salvation as an outpouring of water (44:3a). Thus far, the oracle resembles the earlier promises of water in the desert in an unremarkable way. In the words that follow, however, the prophet adds a new element, interpreting the water as a symbol of the gift of God's Spirit and his blessing: "I will pour my spirit upon your offspring, and my blessing on your offspring" (44:3b). In some texts of the Old Testament, God's Spirit is portrayed as the source of life (Gen. 2:7; Ezek. 37:1–14). Other texts, most famously the book of Deuteronomy, closely associate blessing and life (Deut. 30:15, 19–20). The water imagery of this oracle from Isaiah, then, symbolizes two of the most prized possessions for the ancient Israelite—God's Spirit and blessing, which are also closely related to the promise of life that God made to Israel on the cusp of their entering the promised land.

The prophet proceeds to describe this blessing in terms of fertility (Isa. 44:4). Once again, water serves as the source of fertility and life. The prophet also describes this blessing as the particular relationship God has with his people Israel (44:5). A personal relationship with the Lord, the true source of all life, forms the substance of the blessing promised to the Israelites, the blessing God will give them by the gift of his Spirit. Whether intentional or not, this conjunction of water, life, blessing, and garden imagery (44:4) resembles the garden of Eden, where a river flowed out to give life to the garden and the first man and woman lived in communion with God, the source of blessing. One could see this prophetic promise as offering an initial reversal of the curse human beings experienced for their transgression in Eden.[18]

Even texts that lament Israel's disobedience use water imagery to describe the good life the people might have enjoyed had they obeyed. Toward the end

16. John T. Willis, *Images of Water in Isaiah* (Lanham, MD: Lexington Books, 2017), 98.

17. See Bernard W. Anderson, "Exodus Typology in Second Isaiah," in *Israel's Prophetic Heritage: Essays in Honor of James Muilenburg*, ed. B. W. Anderson and W. Harrelson (New York: Harper & Brothers, 1962), 177–95, esp. 181–84.

18. On the connection between death and exile, see Kenneth J. Turner, *The Death of Deaths in the Death of Israel: Deuteronomy's Theology of Exile* (Eugene, OR: Wipf & Stock, 2010).

Baptismal Water Everywhere

Early Christians frequently saw water in the Old Testament as prefiguring baptism. St. Cyprian of Carthage writes of Isaiah 43,

> But as often as water is named alone in the Holy Scriptures, baptism is referred to, as we see intimated in Isaiah: "Remember not," says he, "the former things, and consider not the things of old. Behold, I will do a new thing, which shall now spring forth; and you shall know it. I will even make a way in the wilderness, and rivers in the dry place, to give drink to my elected people, my people whom I have purchased, that they might show forth my praise." There God foretold by the prophet, that among the nations, in places which previously had been dry, rivers should afterwards flow plenteously, and should provide water for the elected people of God, that is, for those who were made sons of God by the generation of baptism.[a]

a. Cyprian of Carthage, *Epistle* 62.8 (*ANF* 5:360).

of Isaiah 48 the prophet recalls Israel's disregard for the commandments, by which the Lord sought to teach them for their own well-being (48:17). Grieving over their disobedience, God says through the prophet:

> O that you had paid attention to my commandments!
> Then your prosperity would have been *like a river*,
> and your success *like the waves of the sea*. (Isa. 48:18)

Israel's stubbornness prevented them from receiving God's blessing, but even so, the prophet holds out hope that the Lord will now fulfill his promises. As in Isaiah 43, the text describes Israel's return from exile in Babylon by drawing on exodus imagery—specifically, God's provision of water during the people's wandering in the wilderness:

> *They did not thirst* when he led them through the deserts;
> *he made water flow for them from the rock*;
> he split open the rock and *the water gushed out*. (Isa. 48:21; cf. Exod. 17:1–7)

Over and over again, water serves as a symbol of redemption.

Indeed, in the subsequent chapter, Isaiah once again uses the images of thirst and of water to describe the salvation God is about to accomplish for his people. Announcing the imminent day of salvation, God calls the imprisoned out of their captivity (Isa. 49:8–9). The prophet goes on to describe their return:

> They shall not hunger *or thirst*,
>   neither scorching wind nor sun shall strike them down,
> for he who has pity on them will lead them,
>   and *by springs of water will guide them.* (Isa. 49:10)

Water—the difference between life and death in a wilderness—will be readily available to those returning to the land. As is so often the case throughout this section of Isaiah (see, e.g., Isa. 40:3), God's act of salvation consists of making a road for the people in the wilderness (49:11–12). The provision of water along such a road assures the people of continued life on the way.

One of the final oracles of Isaiah 40–55 returns briefly once again to the image of water. The prophet's description of prosperity and abundance begins with the imagery of thirst:

> Ho, everyone who thirsts,
>   come to the waters;
> and you that have no money,
>   come, buy and eat!
> Come, buy wine and milk
>   without money and without price. (Isa. 55:1)

Because it is readily available in contemporary Western society, it might not occur to modern readers just how costly water could be in antiquity.[19] In addition to the financial burden, one also ought to consider the physical toil involved in carrying water from its source to one's home. In this light, one can understand how appealing the promises of guidance beside springs of water and of obtaining water without cost would be, as well as why such promises would symbolize salvation and life.

Water is only the first of a list of nourishments offered by God through the prophet. He also offers wine and milk as well as rich food (Isa. 55:2). All these supplies indicate the fullness of life that God is offering. In a way, however,

19. See Willis, *Images of Water in Isaiah*, 102.

they also serve as pointers to the ultimate source of life, God himself. As John Willis suggests, the invitation to come to the waters and drink seems to parallel God's call to draw near to him: "Incline your ear, and *come to me* [cf. "come to the waters" in 55:1]; listen, *so that you may live*" (Isa. 55:3a). As water maintains people in deserted places, so the Lord's instruction functions as a source of life. Indeed, from a biblical perspective, one could say that the Lord himself is *the* source of life, a life mediated through things like water. The connection between water and the Lord's instruction is unsurprising in light of the way other Old Testament texts portray God. Psalm 36 describes the Lord as "the fountain of life" (v. 9), and the prophet Jeremiah twice refers to him as "the fountain of living water" (Jer. 2:13; 17:13).[20] Just as God brought forth the waters of creation, so he provides for the needs of those who call upon him, offering literal water for their physical needs and, even more importantly, spiritual water welling up to eternal life (John 4:14). The use of water in the rite of baptism fittingly brings these two realities together, as God provides spiritual life through the use of physical water.

Isaiah 55 offers one more reference to the life-giving power of water. In a famous image, the prophet compares the power of the rain and the snow to bring fertility with the power of God's word:

> For as the rain and the snow come down from heaven,
>   and do not return there until they have watered the earth,
> making it bring forth and sprout,
>   giving seed to the sower and bread to the eater,
> so shall my word be that goes out from my mouth;
>   it shall not return to me empty,
> but it shall accomplish that which I purpose,
>   and succeed in the thing for which I sent it. (Isa. 55:10–11)

Once again, the juxtaposition of water and word is a potent symbol for baptism, in which physical water and the power of God's word together bring new life to the baptized.

One final oracle, from the third part of Isaiah (chaps. 56–66), draws on both water and garden imagery to describe the state of the redeemed. In Isaiah 58 the prophet explains why the people's acts of piety—specifically, fasting and observing the sabbath—go unheeded. Without acts of justice, the prophet

20. Willis, *Images of Water in Isaiah*, 103.

says, fasting and sabbath observance remain empty. Fasting that does not result in compassion for one's neighbor is worthless. In the context of this exhortation, the Lord describes how their situation will change if they care for the needy and comfort the sorrowful:

> The LORD will guide you continually,
> and satisfy your needs in parched places,
> and make your bones strong;
> and you shall be *like a watered garden,*
> *like a spring of water,*
> *whose waters never fail.* (Isa. 58:11)

The combined reference to both a spring of water and a watered garden underscores the gift of fertility and life.

Water imagery as a sign of salvation also appears in two texts from the Minor Prophets. More specifically, these passages identify the temple as the source of this water. The last oracle of Joel describes the salvation of Judah in language resembling the oracle of Isaiah 55, combining the symbols of milk, wine, and water:

> In that day
> the mountains shall drip sweet wine,
> the hills shall flow with milk,
> and *all the stream beds of Judah*
> *shall flow with water;*
> *a fountain shall come forth from the house of the LORD*
> *and water the Wadi Shittim.* (Joel 3:18)

Judah's salvation is to be characterized by the sources of life and joy. The rest of the oracle suggests that water lies at the heart of the promise. In contrast to the salvation and prosperity that God will bring about for his people, the prophet speaks of the desolation of Egypt and Edom (Joel 3:19–20). Fertility and life result from the water flowing from the house of the Lord, implicitly making the land of Judah like a garden in contrast to the desolation of the lands of Egypt and Edom.

A much briefer instance of the same motif appears toward the end of the book of Zechariah: "On that day living waters shall flow out from Jerusalem, half of them to the eastern sea and half of them to the western sea; it shall continue in summer as in winter" (Zech. 14:8). Zechariah does not explicitly connect the water with the temple, but in light of this prophetic motif it seems likely that the house of the Lord once again serves as the source of this living and (implicitly) life-giving water.

The clearest and most extensive example of this imagery of life-giving water appears in a famous vision toward the end of Ezekiel, which recapitulates the language of Eden. The last nine chapters of the book (Ezek. 40–48) present a lengthy description of a new temple, which is a promise of hope to the Jews living in exile after the destruction of Solomon's temple by the Babylonians in the sixth century BC. Toward the end of that vision Ezekiel describes the outpouring of a stream of water from the temple.

Following an extensive account of the dimensions of the temple and its sacrifices, Ezekiel returns to the entrance of the temple, where he has a vision similar to the ones described in Joel and Zechariah, only more elaborate: "Water was flowing from below the threshold of the temple toward the east (for the temple faced east); and the water was flowing down from below the south end of the threshold of the temple, south of the altar" (Ezek. 47:1b). Over the course of the vision, Ezekiel is brought further along this stream, and the flow of water becomes deeper and stronger. As he moves down the stream, the water reaches Ezekiel's ankles, then his knees, then his waist (47:3–4). Eventually, the water becomes a river so deep that it cannot be crossed on foot, one in which a person can swim (47:5).

More important than the depth of the river, however, is the effect the river has on its surroundings. Much like the waters of creation under God's directive word, the river becomes a source of life, bearing fruit and giving life to a variety of living creatures (Ezek. 47:8–9, 12). Although the waters of the river give life, it is important to note what the source of this life is. Their life-giving power is not intrinsic to the waters themselves but rather stems from the place of their origin: "because the water for them flows from the sanctuary," as the Lord tells Ezekiel (47:12). The vision thus describes the water of the river as an instrument of God's own life-giving power.

"For with You Is the Fountain of Life"

Baptism is the sacrament of new life; through baptism believers are joined to Christ and given new birth. In light of the abundant evidence of the connection between water and life in the Old Testament, it is hardly surprising that physical water came to serve as an instrumental means of God's grace in the sacrament. Many of the texts above make clear, however, that the waters receive their life-giving power from another source. As Lawrence DiPaolo rightly points out with respect to the Psalms, God is the one who makes the waters life-giving.[21] In the order of grace, the power of baptism comes not from any natural properties of water but rather from the God who uses his creation as a means of imparting life.

Life is not the only effect of the waters of baptism, however. As Paul teaches, baptism brings about life through death and burial with Christ (Rom. 6:3–11). The life-giving power of water, so amply attested throughout the Old Testament, is also balanced by its destructive power. To this aspect of water we now turn.

21. Lawrence DiPaolo Jr., "Images of Water in the Psalms," *The Bible Today* 53 (2015): 207–12, here 209.

2

The Waters of Death

> You cast me into the deep,
> into the heart of the seas,
> and the flood surrounded me;
> all your waves and your billows
> passed over me.
>
> —Jonah 2:3

Although water often serves as a symbol of life in the Old Testament, many biblical texts also associate it with death. Narratives describe the destructive power of water, and poetic texts use water as an image for being overwhelmed. Additionally, water is frequently depicted as the dwelling place of deadly creatures such as Leviathan or the dragon. In light of all these associations between water and death, it is hardly surprising that baptism, which in the early Church frequently involved full immersion, was associated not only with new life but also with a passage through death into that new life. Indeed, many early Christians describe the baptismal font in terms of death. St. Ambrose, for example, characterizes baptism as participating in Christ's crucifixion.[1] Likewise, St. Cyril of Jerusalem understands the rite of baptism as symbolizing Christ's death and burial.[2] St. John Chrysostom describes baptism as entering

1. Ambrose, *The Sacraments* 2.23.
2. Cyril of Jerusalem, *Mystagogical Lectures* 2.4–6.

a grave and emerging into new life: "For when we immerse our heads in the water, the old man is buried as in a tomb below, and wholly sunk forever; then as we raise them again, the new man rises in its stead."[3] In each of these cases, the imagery of death comes primarily from St. Paul's teaching in Romans 6, which explicitly speaks of baptism as burial with Christ. Nevertheless, there is good reason to think that the Old Testament associations of water with death informed the New Testament understanding of baptism, even if only indirectly.

In a passage we will consider more carefully in the second part of this study, Jesus alludes to his impending passion as a kind of baptism: "Are you able to drink the cup that I drink, or be baptized with the baptism that I am baptized with?" (Mark 10:38b). In context Jesus speaks not of an actual baptism but rather of the overwhelming nature of the death he was to face. In doing so he draws on imagery that appears frequently in the book of Psalms. The use of such baptismal terminology must have had some influence on early Christian understandings of baptism—Paul's description of baptism as being buried and rising with Christ is hardly accidental. It is therefore worth examining the destructive nature of water in the Old Testament as a remote background to a biblical theology of baptism.[4]

The Waters of Death in the Pentateuch

One of the most frequently cited precursors to baptism among the Church Fathers is the Genesis account of the flood.[5] In appealing to this episode, the Fathers are simply following the lead of the New Testament, which already draws a connection between baptism and the flood. First Peter 3, referring to the time when "God waited patiently in the days of Noah, during the building of the ark," proceeds to present the salvation of Noah and his family as a foreshadowing of baptism: "And baptism, which this prefigured, now saves you—not as a removal of dirt from the body, but as an appeal to God for a good conscience, through the resurrection of Jesus Christ" (1 Pet. 3:20–21).

3. John Chrysostom, *Homilies on the Gospel of John* 25.2 (*NPNF*[1] 14:89).

4. In some traditions, the connection also may not be so remote. For a discussion of some of these themes as they appear in Eastern Orthodox practice regarding baptism, see C. Oancea, "*Chaoskampf* in the Orthodox Baptism Ritual," *AcT* 37 (2017): 125–42.

5. Jean Daniélou, *The Bible and the Liturgy* (Notre Dame, IN: University of Notre Dame Press, 1956), 75.

Jean Daniélou offers the basic pattern of the typology: "This [the theological idea of the flood] may be reduced to its essential lines: the world is filled with sin; the judgment of God destroys the sinful world; one just man is spared to be the principle of a new creation."[6] Many patristic writers take the connection between baptism and the flood introduced by 1 Peter and develop it in a number of directions.

Before we examine those developments, however, we should first consider the flood as it stands in the narrative of Genesis. The motivation behind the flood appears clearly in the first conversation between God and Noah. Seeing the violence and corruption that pervades the earth, God decides to destroy the human race and start over with Noah and his family (Gen. 6:13–18). The destructive power of water is directed, then, to the elimination of wickedness and corruption. As St. Paul notes in Romans, one of the consequences of baptism is the destruction of the "old self" as well as the "body of sin" (Rom. 6:6).[7] Baptism reflects on a personal level, then, what the flood was intended to accomplish on a grand scale. In this regard, it is worth noting that the Genesis story refers to the corruption of "all flesh" (Gen. 6:12). Intriguingly, two of Paul's baptismal texts (Rom. 6:1–11; Gal. 3:27) appear in close proximity to his discussions of not giving in to the "flesh" (Rom. 7; Gal. 5). Perhaps the account of the flood helped shape Paul's characterization of the flesh.

First Peter also notes that "eight persons" were saved from the flood (1 Pet. 3:20). Several of the Church Fathers, drawing on the symbolism of the number eight, connect the flood not only with death but also with the resurrection.[8] Indeed, in some writings the flood takes on a cosmic significance. The number of persons (eight) is frequently associated with the "eighth day," a designation that ancient Christians gave to the day of Jesus's resurrection, which was the first day of the new creation and which followed the sabbath, the seventh day. While this numerical connection might strike modern readers as fanciful, it is not as arbitrary as it appears at first sight. Many interpreters have noted a number of parallels between the account of the flood in Genesis 6–9 and the first creation story of Genesis 1:1–2:3.

6. Daniélou, *The Bible and the Liturgy*, 75–76.

7. A similar idea seems to be behind the understanding of baptism that underlies Colossians (see Col. 2:11–12; 3:9–10). The phrase that the NRSV usually translates as "old self" is more literally the "old human being" (*anthrōpos*).

8. For the following, I have relied on Daniélou, *The Bible and the Liturgy*, 77–85.

As one scholar has noted, the flood serves as a return to the precreation state of things, when all was a watery chaos (Gen. 1:1–2).[9] The waters of the flood subside, and the dry land appears, as it did on the third day of creation (1:9–13; 8:13–14). The earth is then repopulated with many of the same animals created in the first creation account—namely, animals, birds, and creeping things (8:17, 19; cf. 1:20, 24). Finally, God gives Noah and his family the same commission he had given to the first human beings: "Be fruitful and multiply on the earth" (8:17b; cf. 1:28).

One final point regarding the flood bears mentioning. The first thing Noah does after he leads his family and the animals out of the ark once the waters have subsided is to build an altar and offer sacrifices (Gen. 8:20). In other words, we see a pattern of God destroying or purifying the earth by water, and people subsequently having communion with God through worship. This sequence serves as a fitting type for the later Christian practice whereby baptism serves as the gateway to the other sacraments, especially the Eucharist. As we will see, the pattern of passing through the waters into new life and worship is common, with one of the most famous examples appearing in the book of Exodus.

The destructive power of water features prominently in two places in the book of Exodus, one at the beginning of the book, describing the oppression of the Israelites at the hands of the Egyptians, and the other at the culmination of their liberation from slavery.[10] In the first instance, Pharaoh attempts to have all the newborn Israelite boys drowned in the Nile, but through God's providential care one of them is saved from the destructive waters, foreshadowing the deliverance of the people. In the second instance, the Egyptians themselves suffer the death-dealing force of the waters of the sea.

Near the very beginning of Exodus, the ominous power of water, present at the beginning of creation and once again at the time of the flood, reappears, this time in the form of the Nile. Exodus opens with language reminiscent of the book of Genesis, noting the Israelites' fertility in the midst of the land (Exod. 1:7). This sign of God's blessing upon the people indicates God's faithfulness to the promises he made to the patriarchs (Gen. 17:2–6; 26:2–5;

9. David L. Petersen, "The Yahwist on the Flood," *VT* 26 (1976): 438–46, here 441.

10. For a recent study that connects these two episodes with the flood, see Joshua Joel Spoelstra, *Life Preservation in Genesis and Exodus: An Exegetical Study of the* Tēbâ *of Noah and Moses*, CBET (Leuven: Peeters, 2020).

35:11–12). At the same time, the new pharaoh, who does not "know" Joseph (Exod. 1:8), perceives this fertility as a threat to his power and so takes action to oppress the Israelites. When enslavement and forced labor fail to curtail their multiplication (1:12), Pharaoh proceeds to an even crueler tactic, commanding the midwives to kill the newborn Israelite boys immediately as they emerge from the womb. When the midwives refuse to cooperate, he turns to the destructive power of water, commanding that all his people toss the male infants of the Israelites into the Nile (1:22). In one of the book's many great ironies, the Nile, which served as the source of life for the ancient Egyptians, becomes a source of death for the Israelites.

Into this dire situation comes Moses, born to a Levite couple unwilling to comply with the barbarous edict of Pharaoh. Seeking to preserve the life of their child, the mother puts Moses in a *tebah* plastered with bitumen and pitch (Exod. 2:3). Most translations render the Hebrew word *tebah* in this verse as "basket." While such a translation makes sense in context, it also hides an important connection with another part of the Pentateuch. This word appears in only one other passage in the entire Old Testament: it is used for the ark that Noah builds to escape the waters of the flood. As Noah passes through the destructive waters of death in an ark, so the baby Moses survives Pharaoh's decree by the providential guidance of a mini-ark. Moreover, in another great irony, Moses passes through the waters of death to a new life, a life in the very household of Pharaoh.[11]

As already noted, Moses's narrow escape from the waters of the Nile foreshadows Israel's passage through the waters of the Red Sea, one of the most famous examples in the Old Testament of water's destructive power. Exodus offers two accounts of the Red Sea crossing, a prose description in chapter 14 and a poetic retelling in chapter 15. While both chapters recount the death of the Egyptians, each version offers a different perspective on the significance of the event.

Like the story of the flood, the crossing of the Red Sea has several parallels with the first creation account.[12] As the Lord stands between the Israelites and the Egyptians, Exodus notes that there is both darkness and light (Exod. 14:20; cf. Gen. 1:3–5). Moreover, when Moses stretches out his hand over the waters

11. Spoelstra, *Life Preservation*, 335.

12. The ancient writer known as Pseudo-Philo compares the crossing of the Red Sea to the creation account in his *Liber antiquitatem biblicarum* (*Biblical Antiquities*) 15.6. I owe this reference to Daniélou, *The Bible and the Liturgy*, 87n5.

of the sea, the Lord drives back the waters by a strong wind (Exod. 14:21).[13] As the wind blows the waters back, the dry land appears (cf. Gen. 1:9–10). Some interpreters have taken these images to suggest that the crossing of the Red Sea functions as a new creation.[14] Further support for this interpretation can be seen in Exodus 16, where the Lord insists that the Israelites observe the sabbath, even before the people have received the Decalogue (16:22–26). Just as the first creation account culminates in God's rest on the seventh day (Gen. 2:1–3), so Israel's escape from Egypt through an act of new creation culminates in the observance of the sabbath.

Already in the centuries leading up to the birth of Christ, some Jewish interpreters saw the crossing of the Red Sea as a new creation. The Wisdom of Solomon, for example, describes Israel's escape as a new fashioning of creation:

> For the whole creation in its nature was fashioned anew,
> complying with your commands,
> so that your children might be kept unharmed.
> The cloud was seen overshadowing the camp,
> and dry land emerging where water had stood before,
> an unhindered way out of the Red Sea,
> and a grassy plain out of the raging waves,
> where those protected by your hand passed through as one nation,
> after gazing on marvelous wonders. (Wis. 19:6–8)

In between the prose description of the crossing of the sea in Exodus 14 and the account of the manna in Exodus 16, the book interjects a poetic celebration of Israel's deliverance. Commonly known as the Song of the Sea, this hymn praises God for his great act of deliverance. Much could be said about this famous text, but for our purposes it will suffice to point out two aspects of the poem. First, while the prose account in Exodus 14 describes the waters of the sea falling back upon the Egyptian charioteers and horses, the song describes God throwing the Egyptian army into the sea (Exod. 15:1, 4). A common modern explanation of this discrepancy is to appeal to different

13. Cf. Gen. 1:2, though the phrase is not identical in Hebrew. Genesis refers to a *ruaḥ elohim*, which can be translated in a number of ways. Exodus, on the other hand, refers to a "strong" (*'azzah*) wind.

14. William H. C. Propp, *Exodus 1–18: A New Translation with Introduction and Commentary*, AB 2 (New York: Doubleday, 1999), 523, 560–61.

"Why Fear to Cross the Red Sea?"

The crossing of the Red Sea was a popular image for baptism in the early Church. St. Augustine offers one example of some of the correspondences between Israel's deliverance and baptism:

> The journey through the sea was a type of the sacrament received by the baptized, and of nothing else but this; the pursuing Egyptians represent our hordes of past sins, and nothing else. The mysteries are plain for you to see. The Egyptians are pressing hard, harrying us, just as sins are hot on our heels, but only as far as the water's brink. Why then are you afraid to approach Christ's baptism, you who have not come yet, why fear to cross the Red Sea? Why is it red? Because the Lord's blood has hallowed it. Why are you afraid? Perhaps the consciousness of some heinous sins pierces you and tortures your soul within you, telling you that the sin you have committed is so great that you must despair of being forgiven. In that case, fear indeed that some remnant of your sins may linger, but fear it only if even one of the Egyptians survived![a]

a. Augustine, *Exposition of the Psalms* 80.8, in Augustine of Hippo, *Saint Augustine: Expositions of the Psalms 73–98*, ed. John E. Rotelle, trans. Maria Boulding, The Works of Saint Augustine III/4 (Hyde Park, NY: New City, 2002), 158.

sources for the two accounts. Source criticism may be useful in this instance, but another explanation also lies to hand—namely, the use of poetic license. The image of tossing the Egyptians into a body of water would naturally evoke Pharaoh's decree at the beginning of Exodus that the people should throw the newborn Israelite boys into the waters of the Nile (Exod. 1:22), and it serves as a complement to the prose account of the crossing of the Red Sea.[15] Seen in this light, the death of the Egyptians becomes an act of poetic justice, a fitting retribution for their mistreatment of the Israelites.

Second, and perhaps more important than this notion of judgment, is the song's basic orientation toward worship. The whole song is itself an act of worship, praising God for his powerful deeds. It also points forward to the goal of the exodus, Israel's encounter with God on the mountain. Indeed, the song comes to its climax in a meeting with God in the sanctuary:

15. See Joshua A. Berman, *Inconsistency in the Torah: Ancient Literary Convention and the Limits of Source Criticism* (Oxford: Oxford University Press, 2017), 54–60.

> You brought them in and planted them on the mountain of your own possession,
> the place, O Lord, that you made your abode,
> the sanctuary, O Lord, that your hands have established.
> (Exod. 15:17)

Through the waters of the Red Sea, God leads the Israelites not into an abstract freedom of autonomy but rather into a relationship of worship with himself, continuing the pattern seen in the story of Noah.[16] This movement through the waters of death to worship serves as a fitting symbol of baptism. The crossing of the Red Sea leads to Israel's first act of observing the sabbath as well as to their receiving the manna to eat. Already in the writings of the New Testament, manna serves as a type foreshadowing the early Christian practice of the Eucharist (see John 6, esp. vv. 48–58). Moreover, in an important sense the exodus culminates in Israel's encounter with God on Mount Sinai. There God enters into a covenant with his people, one ratified by the "blood of the covenant" in a sacrificial ritual that also contributed to the early Christian understanding of the Eucharist (Exod. 24:1–11; cf. Matt. 26:28 and parallels).

The Waters of Death in the Psalms

In the texts we have considered thus far, although water is presented as a destructive force, God's chosen people do not always experience death. Noah and his family survive the deluge; the infant Moses is drawn out of the Nile alive; the Israelites walk through the midst of the Red Sea on dry land, with only the Egyptians drowning in the waters. There are other texts, however, that express the danger of water in a much more pressing way, as a threat not simply to Israel's enemies but to the Israelites themselves. The Psalms are filled with many such references, illustrating another dimension of the power that water had on the ancient Israelite imagination.

One of the most important psalms to consider in this regard is Psalm 69, which features prominently in the Gospels in connection with Jesus's passion and death. The New Testament writers cite or allude to at least three

16. For an excellent discussion of this aspect of the exodus as it relates to liturgy more generally, see Joseph Cardinal Ratzinger, *The Spirit of the Liturgy*, trans. John Saward (San Francisco: Ignatius, 2000), 13–23.

different parts of the psalm in passages concerning Jesus's death. In one of the farewell discourses of John's Gospel, Jesus quotes this psalm to explain the animosity he experiences from the Jewish leaders: "More in number than the hairs of my head are those who hate me without cause" (Ps. 69:4a; cf. John 15:25). Earlier in the same Gospel, John interprets Jesus's action in the temple in light of the psalm: "It is zeal for your house that has consumed me" (Ps. 69:9; cf. John 2:17). Finally, all four Gospels at least allude to this psalm with respect to the soldiers offering Jesus wine to drink: "They gave me poison for food, and for my thirst they gave me vinegar to drink" (Ps. 69:21; cf. Matt. 27:48 and parallels; John 19:28–29). In light of this psalm's influence on the passion traditions and of the prominence that the threat of water plays in the psalm, it seems at least possible that Psalm 69 helped shape Jesus's interpretation of his death as a kind of baptism (see Mark 10:38–39; Luke 12:50).

The psalm begins with a plea for deliverance from an agony characterized as the overpowering effects of water. Whatever the trial the psalmist is experiencing, he describes it with the imagery of waters that have reached his neck (Ps. 69:1). The flood, a powerful symbol of destruction, threatens to overwhelm the psalmist, causing him distress as he waits to see whether God will deliver him (69:2–3). After a shift from the poetic description of his situation to a more straightforward account of his enemies (69:4–12), the psalmist returns once more to the image of water to describe his enemies:

> Rescue me
>   from sinking in the mire;
> let me be delivered from my enemies
>   and from the deep waters.
> Do not let the flood sweep over me,
>   or the deep swallow me up,
>   or the Pit close its mouth over me. (Ps. 69:14–15)

The parallelism of these verses underscores the close association between floodwaters and death, as the psalm moves progressively through references to the flood, the deep, and the pit.[17]

17. In the Old Testament the pit often serves as a synonym for Sheol, the place of the dead (see, e.g., Ps. 16:10). For an excellent discussion of Sheol and its relation to the pit, see Jon D. Levenson, *Resurrection and the Restoration of Israel: The Ultimate Victory of the God of Life* (New Haven: Yale University Press, 2006), 35–66.

The plea for deliverance continues, describing the plight of the psalmist for several more verses before ending on a note of praise and thanksgiving for God's saving action (Ps. 69:20–36). The final call to praise subtly highlights God's control over the waters, as the psalmist calls on heaven, earth, and the seas to praise him (69:34).

This imagery of water as a symbol for the powers of death pervades the Psalter. Space does not permit, nor does the nature of this work require, a detailed study of each instance of the image, but a brief survey of other examples is in order. Twice in Psalm 18, water is presented as an agent of death. In verses 4–5, the "torrents of perdition" are put in parallel with the "cords of death" and the "cords of Sheol." Several verses later the psalm celebrates God's rescue, once again drawing on water imagery: "He reached down from on high, he took me; he drew me out of mighty waters" (18:16). The "mighty waters" appear again in Psalm 32, describing that from which God will preserve the psalmist (32:6; see also 144:7).[18] Psalm 42 likewise describes the experience of abandonment by God as being overwhelmed by water:

> Deep calls to deep
> at the thunder of your cataracts;
> all your waves and your billows
> have gone over me. (Ps. 42:7)

Psalm 88, one of the gloomiest of the Psalms, expresses a lament with similar water imagery at two different points. Early on, the psalmist compares his circumstances to death, speaking both of the grave and of the overwhelming power of water:

> For my soul is full of troubles,
> and my life draws near to Sheol.
> I am counted among those who go down to the Pit;
> I am like those who have no help,
> like those forsaken among the dead,
> like the slain that lie in the grave,
> like those whom you remember no more,
> for they are cut off from your hand.

18. Although the translations differ in Pss. 18:16 ("mighty waters") and 32:6 ("great waters"), the Hebrew phrase underlying both translations (*mayim rabbim*) is the same. (The Hebrew phrase appears in v. 17, which the NRSV renders as v. 16.)

You have put me in the depths of the Pit,
  in the regions dark and deep.
Your wrath lies heavy upon me,
  and *you overwhelm me with all your waves.* (Ps. 88:3–7)

Toward the end, the psalmist returns to water imagery to describe his situation:

They surround me like a flood all day long;
  from all sides they close in on me.
You have caused friend and neighbor to shun me;
  my companions are in darkness. (Ps. 88:17–18)

In contrast, Psalm 124 rejoices over God's protection, noting how the situation might have been had the Lord not watched over the psalmist and his companions:

Then the flood would have swept us away,
  the torrent would have gone over us;
then over us would have gone
  the raging waters. (Ps. 124:4–5)

Most of these instances of water imagery are just that—imagery. But one of the stanzas of Psalm 107 speaks of the literal danger posed by the waters of the sea. This section of the psalm, which may serve as a brief retelling of an episode from the book of Jonah, uses the phrase "mighty waters" to refer to the actual sea (107:23). A voyage taken for business purposes quickly devolves into a scene of terror, as storm winds stir up the waves, threatening to destroy the ship and bring the sailors down into the depths (107:25–27). Faced with impending calamity, the sailors cry out to God, who demonstrates his power over the sea, calming the storm and returning the sea to a more peaceful condition (107:28–29).

The Old Testament also speaks of the death-dealing power of water in more cosmic, even mythical language.[19] Several passages in the Psalms emphasize God's control over the waters and the flood. Twice Psalm 29 depicts

19. To speak of "mythical language" in the Bible is simply to acknowledge that the writers of Scripture engaged with the ideas in their surrounding cultures. For an older but still useful study of the question, see Brevard S. Childs, *Myth and Reality in the Old Testament*, SBT 27 (London: SCM, 1960).

the Lord as reigning over water. In fact, the first description of the Lord's might concerns water:

> The voice of the Lord is over the waters;
>   the God of glory thunders,
>   the Lord, over mighty waters. (Ps. 29:3)

The psalmist continues, expounding God's power over the cedars of Lebanon and the various regions that surround the land, but toward the end he returns once more to the waters: "The Lord sits enthroned over the flood; the Lord sits enthroned as king forever" (Ps. 29:10). This control reappears at several points in the Psalms. Psalm 33 refers to the Lord gathering up the waters (33:7). Psalm 93 describes the Lord's power as mightier than that of the floods and the sea (93:3–4). Psalm 104, most likely alluding to the account of the flood in Genesis 6–9, recounts God's control over the waters: how he first allowed them to rise up to cover the mountain, then caused them to recede, and finally set a boundary for them (104:6–9). Psalm 106, one of many retellings of the crossing of the Red Sea, once again acknowledges God's power over the waters, a power both to save (106:9–10) and to destroy (v. 11).

At least two of the Psalms go further than the ones we have just considered, implicitly associating the danger of water with mythical creatures. Like the other psalms discussed, Psalm 74 describes God's control over the waters, but in a more vivid manner. The description of God's power resembles both the first creation account of Genesis and the crossing of the Red Sea, recounting God's parting of the waters (74:13). In describing this power, the psalmist also refers to God's power over "dragons" and "Leviathan":

> You divided the sea by your might;
>   you broke the heads of the dragons in the waters.
> You crushed the heads of Leviathan;
>   you gave him as food for the creatures of the wilderness.
>   (Ps. 74:13–14)

According to the psalmist, the Lord's power extends to all kinds of waters, first and foremost the sea with its terrifying monsters, but also springs, torrents, and streams (74:15).

The Sign of Jonah

One of the most vivid images of water as a threatening power appears in the story of Jonah. The prayer Jonah offers from the belly of the fish seems to imply that he has undergone a kind of death:

> The waters closed in over me;
>   the deep surrounded me;
> weeds were wrapped around my head
>   at the roots of the mountains.
> I went down to the land
>   whose bars closed upon me forever;
> yet you brought up my life from the Pit,
>   O Lord my God. (Jon. 2:5–6)

In the Gospel of Matthew, Jesus refers to the sign of Jonah, comparing his own time in the tomb to the three days Jonah spent in "the belly of the sea monster" (Matt. 12:40). This juxtaposition of the imagery of Jonah being tossed into the sea (a body of water) with Jesus's resurrection may have played some part in the way the early Christians interpreted baptism as a kind of death and resurrection.

The other famous mythological creature of the Old Testament, Rahab, also features in several texts describing God's control over the waters. Psalm 89, which focuses on the covenant with David and its apparent failure, includes a lengthy description of the Lord's might (89:5–18). Among the many characteristics the psalmist praises, he notes God's control over the waters and, more specifically, over the beast Rahab:

> O Lord God of hosts,
>   who is as mighty as you, O Lord?
>   Your faithfulness surrounds you.
> You rule the raging of the sea;
>   when its waves rise, you still them.
> You crushed Rahab like a carcass;
>   you scattered your enemies with your mighty arm.
>   (Ps. 89:8–10)

Despite the terror that Rahab represents, this beast is as nothing compared to the Lord's strength.

Rahab makes an appearance in two other texts emphasizing God's control over the waters, one in Job and one in Isaiah. In one of Job's final speeches, he recounts God's power in language reminiscent of the Psalms. Twice he notes the way God sets limits to the waters (Job 26:8, 10). Finally, Job describes God's conquest of Rahab: "By his power he stilled the Sea; by his understanding he struck down Rahab" (26:12). Similarly, Isaiah 51 appeals to God's control over Rahab, this time in the context of a retelling of the crossing of the Red Sea:

> Was it not you who cut Rahab in pieces,
>   who pierced the dragon?
> Was it not you who dried up the sea,
>   the waters of the great deep;
> who made the depths of the sea a way
>   for the redeemed to cross over? (Isa. 51:9c–10)

In both these texts, water's threatening power is personified in the creature Rahab. At the same time, both writers put this threat within the context of God's control over water.

Arrogant Kings and Watery Deaths in the Prophets

The personification of water's power in the Old Testament is not limited to cosmic creatures like Leviathan and Rahab. Ezekiel also associates the destructive power of water with some of Israel's enemies. The prophet portrays the king of Tyre and the Egyptian pharaoh as destructive powers like the seas and the Nile—the king of Tyre is said to claim, "I am a god . . . in the heart of the seas" (Ezek. 28:2), and the Lord addresses Pharaoh as "the great dragon" in the Nile (29:3)—and emphasizes God's control over the power of the waters. Both rulers are described as pictures of arrogance, setting themselves up with absolute sovereignty over their domains—but in fact subject to the humbling judgment of God.

Ezekiel 27 and 28 focus primarily on the people of Tyre and their king, emphasizing their connection with the waters of the sea. Both chapters follow a common pattern: first the people, then the king make an arrogant statement about themselves. In response to these words, the Lord brings punishment upon them, in both cases describing their death as related in some way to the seas on which they traded.

Chapter 27 begins by recounting the people's role as sea merchants. Living on the edge of the sea, they boast of their beauty, which the prophet proceeds to describe with reference to their sea craft, built of materials from the surrounding cities and nations (Ezek. 27:5–9). The prophet then enumerates the goods the people traded in, ranging from slaves (v. 13) to ebony and ivory (v. 15) to precious stones and linen (v. 16) to wine (vv. 18–19). Ezekiel notes that the ships are full of these goods, an ominous backdrop to what is to follow (v. 25b).

The amassing of this great wealth sets up the people for a precipitous fall. In the following verse, the prophet continues:

> Your rowers have brought you
> into the high seas.
> The east wind has wrecked you
> in the heart of the seas. (Ezek. 27:26)

The seas, the indirect source of their wealth and pride, become their undoing. Rather than returning home with their earnings, they end up at the bottom of the seas with their wealth (27:27), prompting a lament from all those who traded with them (27:28–32). This lament emphasizes the death-dealing power of the seas, which brings to an end not only their trading but also their very lives (27:32–34).

In the following chapter, Ezekiel prophesies against the king of Tyre, underscoring his arrogance and pronouncing a fitting end to his life because of it. The pride of the king reflects Tyre's prowess on the seas (Ezek. 28:2). In punishment, God pronounces the king's impending death. Among the various things the prophet says about this death, he describes it as taking place in the seas:

> They shall thrust you down to the Pit,
> and you shall die a violent death
> in the heart of the seas. (Ezek. 28:8)

The pit and the seas serve, then, as the burial place for Tyre's arrogant leader.

Ezekiel offers a similar, though briefer, description of Pharaoh in the subsequent chapter. Like the king of Tyre, Pharaoh speaks arrogant words, provoking the Lord to judgment. These arrogant remarks, like the king of Tyre's, concern a body of water—in this case the Nile:

> Thus says the Lord God:
>
> I am against you,
>   Pharaoh king of Egypt,
> the great dragon sprawling
>   in the midst of its channels,
> saying, "My Nile is my own;
>   I made it for myself." (Ezek. 29:3)

Just as the people of Tyre and their king boasted about their mastery over the waters, so Pharaoh claims absolute control over the river Nile.

The form of punishment that the Lord declares for Pharaoh differs from that of the king and people of Tyre, but it still reflects his mastery over water. Rather than drowning Pharaoh in the Nile in the same way that he brought the Tyrians to their end in the depths of the sea, God announces that he will drag Pharaoh and his people ("the fish of your channels") out of the river and toss them into the desert, where they will die and not receive a proper burial (Ezek. 29:4–5). Arrogance and pride result in death for ruler and people alike.

All of this may seem far removed from the sacrament of baptism. What does the punishment of ancient rulers have to do with a Christian ritual developed centuries later, primarily with reference to the death and resurrection of Jesus Christ? At least two aspects of these texts can shed light on Christian baptism. First, the oracles against the king of Tyre and against Pharaoh emphasize God's authority over water and God's use of water to bring about death. Second, both the king of Tyre and Pharaoh serve as types of the primary malady that afflicts human beings and that baptism is meant to remedy: pride. In the punishment of these ancient rulers one can see a foreshadowing of the kind of death baptism brings about, a death to the "old human being," as Paul puts it (see Rom. 6:6). This "old human being" was one characterized by arrogance and pride, exemplified in the king of Tyre (Ezek. 28:2, 17).

The Baptismal Waters of Death

As we will see in chapter 8, death serves as one of the primary images of what baptism accomplishes. The main source for this image is, of course,

Christ's death and resurrection, through which Paul interprets baptism (see, e.g., Rom. 6:1–11; 1 Cor. 1:13), and he rarely, if ever, gives any indication that the Old Testament may contribute to this understanding of baptism as a kind of death (for one possible implicit exception, see 1 Cor. 10:1–5). Nevertheless, the association between water and death in these Old Testament passages sheds important light on the sacrament of baptism. Three aspects of these texts contribute to a biblical theology of baptism.

First, in some passages the death symbolized by water also serves as a path to new life or new creation. The story of the flood echoes the first creation story of Genesis, with the primal chaos of the waters, the emergence of the dry land, and the repopulation of the land by Noah's family and the animals on the ark. The crossing of the Red Sea reflects a similar pattern. These descriptions of a passage from death to life on a grand scale illustrate what takes place on a personal level for all those who receive baptism.

Second, both the story of the flood and the crossing of the Red Sea culminate in acts of worship. Once the waters of the flood have subsided and God instructs Noah to leave the ark, Noah's first act is to offer burnt offerings (Gen. 8:20). But even before this act, the story of the flood emphasizes the importance of worship through the description of the ark. The dimensions and arrangement of the ark resemble the design of the tabernacle and the temple.[20] Moreover, Genesis describes Noah with adjectives used to describe the qualifications for entering God's presence in the temple.[21] Similarly, the crossing of the Red Sea leads, first, to God feeding the Israelites with manna in the wilderness (Exod. 16) and, later, to the establishment of the covenant through a sacrificial ritual (Exod. 24). Both stories, then, serve as another fitting symbol of baptism, insofar as this rite is the entryway to the other sacraments, especially the Eucharist.

Finally, the oracles against the king of Tyre and Pharaoh illustrate another important dimension of baptism, the putting to death of the "old human being" (see Rom. 6:6; Col. 3:9–10). Both these rulers function as types of arrogance and pride. The king of Tyre in particular reflects characteristics of Adam. He is said to have been in "Eden, the garden of God," and he was

20. See L. Michael Morales, *Who Shall Ascend the Mountain of the Lord? A Biblical Theology of the Book of Leviticus*, New Studies in Biblical Theology (Downers Grove, IL: InterVarsity, 2015), 59, and the sources cited in nn. 56 and 57 on the same page.

21. "Righteous" and "blameless." See again Morales, *Who Shall Ascend the Mountain of the Lord?*, 58–59.

covered with precious stones and metals (Ezek. 28:13). But due to his "iniquity," he was expelled from the "mountain of God" (28:14–15). Ezekiel describes the king's punishment with a variety of images—being expelled from the sanctuary, being exposed out in the open, being consumed with fire (28:15–18)—but earlier in the chapter, he meets his demise "in the heart of the seas," the very place where he displayed his arrogance (28:2, 8). Similarly, Colossians closely associates baptism with death and the destruction of various vices. In baptism, believers are buried with Christ (Col. 2:12), and in living out their new baptismal life, they are called to put to death various vices associated with the "old human being" (see Col. 3:5–10). Again, it is unlikely that Paul alludes to these passages from Ezekiel. Nevertheless, they serve as a useful image for what baptism does.

As already noted, the death-dealing power of water in the Old Testament often serves as a path of transition rather than an end in itself. Nowhere is this clearer than in the crossing of the Red Sea, which features prominently in patristic interpretations of the sacrament of baptism. This crossing marks a transition from slavery to freedom, a freedom oriented to possessing a land in which God will dwell with Israel. We turn now to various Old Testament images of water as the path to freedom.

3

The Waters of Freedom

> Why is it, O sea, that you flee?
> O Jordan, that you turn back?
> —Psalm 114:5

In the popular imagination, the central point of the story of the exodus is the political liberation of the Israelites from Egyptian slavery. While freedom certainly plays an important part in the story, the biblical account of the exodus is far more nuanced and paradoxical. It is true that the Lord acts with a mighty hand to bring the Israelites out of Egypt. Nevertheless, the goal of that liberation is more complex. One of the leitmotifs of the early chapters of Exodus is the question of service: Whom will the Israelites serve? God repeatedly sends Moses to Pharaoh with the message "Let my son go *that he may serve me*" (Exod. 4:23 ESV; see also 8:1, 20; 9:1, 13; 10:3).[1] Pharaoh wants to keep the people in Egypt so that they may serve him in forced labor, but God demands that Pharaoh let the people go so that they may serve him in worship. In other words, the question is not one of freedom as autonomy. Rather, it is a question of what kind of service will actually free the Israelites. Some baptismal texts in the New Testament reflect this paradox. For example,

1. The NRSV obscures the contest between the Lord and Pharaoh by rendering the Hebrew word *'ebed* as "worship" when referring to God and as "serve" when referring to Pharaoh. While it is true that the service the Israelites render to God is worship, the NRSV translation has the disadvantage of losing the conflict at the heart of the story.

in Romans 6, soon after Paul's appeal to baptism, he contrasts two kinds of slavery: slavery to sin and slavery to righteousness (6:17–23). Slavery to righteousness, however, is not the opposite of freedom but rather its precondition, as other parts of Paul's Letters show (see Rom. 8:2; Gal. 5:1). In other words, true freedom comes through serving God. This paradoxical connection between service and freedom lies close to the heart of the theology of baptism.

The fundamental liberating act in the Old Testament is the crossing of the Red Sea, which shaped the imagination of the ancient Israelites as well as patristic understandings of baptism. The pharaoh serves as a type of the devil or sin, and the crossing of the sea serves as a type of liberation from the powers of sin.[2] Crucial to this liberation, though, is the goal of worship. In this chapter we will consider this connection between water, liberation, and worship as it first appears in Exodus and then as it is developed in the Psalms and other portions of the Old Testament.

Bound for Freedom: Slavery in the Exodus Tradition

The motif of slavery is a central aspect of the exodus tradition throughout the Old Testament. In both versions of the Decalogue, God identifies himself as the one who brought the Israelites out of "the house of slavery" (Exod. 20:2; Deut. 5:6). In fact, throughout the book of Deuteronomy and much of the Old Testament, the Lord frequently identifies himself by this act of deliverance for Israel.[3]

Even before it narrates how the Lord actually brings the people out of Egypt, however, the book of Exodus offers a foreshadowing of the events to come in the story of Moses's birth. Moses's trajectory anticipates what the Israelites as a people will undergo through the exodus. It is a movement from slavery into freedom. Born to an enslaved people, from the first breath Moses takes he faces the prospect of death, thanks to the pharaoh's decree that all

2. On the influence of the crossing of the Red Sea on patristic interpretations of baptism, see Jean Daniélou, *The Bible and the Liturgy* (Notre Dame, IN: University of Notre Dame Press, 1956), 86–98.

3. Deuteronomy uses the phrase "the house of slavery" six times when speaking of God as the liberator of the Israelites. In addition to the reference in the Decalogue, see also Deut. 6:12; 7:8; 8:14; 13:5, 10. Both Joshua (24:17) and Judges (6:8) also use this phrase in the same way, and it appears in the Prophets as well (Jer. 34:13; Mic. 6:4). I owe this point to Brian M. Britt, "Exodus Tradition in the Bible," Bible Odyssey, accessed July 2, 2020, https://www.bibleodyssey.org/en/passages/related-articles/exodus-tradition-in-the-bible.

the newborn Israelite boys should be cast into the Nile (Exod. 1:22). As noted in the previous chapter, through the guiding hand of providence the actions of Moses's parents preserve his life. He passes through the waters meant for destruction and comes out of them alive. Not only does he survive the threat of the death-dealing waters, however. He also becomes a free man, raised not just in any household but in the household of the one who is trying to destroy Moses's people (Exod. 2:5–10). Unlike his fellow Israelites, Moses no longer suffers under the harsh treatment of Egyptian taskmasters. Perhaps more importantly, though, Moses's new royal status prefigures the vocation to which God will call the whole people of Israel. At the crossing of the Red Sea, the Israelites, too, are to pass from Egyptian slavery into freedom. The purpose of this liberation, however, is even more profound. The Israelites do not simply become royalty. Rather, God calls the Israelites to be his royal priesthood and a holy nation (Exod. 19:6).[4]

A similar movement from slavery to freedom can be seen in one of Paul's baptismal texts. Romans 6 describes baptism both as a passing from death to life (6:3–5) and as a liberation from slavery to sin (6:6, 17–23). In fact, there is another, more subtle connection between Romans and Exodus. Paul describes the liberation of Christians not in an absolute sense but rather as a transfer from one lordship to another. Whereas formerly the baptized were enslaved to sin, now they are enslaved to God (6:22). Passing through the waters of the Red Sea leads the Israelites into a new kind of service, the service of worship. Similarly, through baptism believers are brought into a relationship of worship and holiness, in which they present themselves to God in service (6:12–14).

The context of the crossing of the Red Sea emphasizes its relation to the Israelites' liberation. Shortly before the people's escape, they receive the festivals of Passover and of Unleavened Bread. In the institution and the ritual of the latter feast, Exodus twice emphasizes the Israelites' liberation. Moses exhorts them, "Remember this day on which you came out of Egypt, *out of the house of slavery*, because *the Lord brought you out from there* by strength of hand; no leavened bread shall be eaten" (Exod. 13:3). Moses also instructs them to recall these events for future generations, instructing their children about the purpose of the feast: "When in the future your child asks you, 'What does this mean?' you shall answer, '*By strength of hand the Lord brought us out of Egypt, from the house of slavery*'" (13:14). The imagery

4. It is significant that 1 Peter, which many interpreters see as at least in part a reflection on baptism, draws on this language of a royal priesthood (1 Pet. 2:9–10).

of a "strong hand" appears several times throughout the early chapters of Exodus.[5] God shows his strength through the signs and wonders that he works against Egypt. The culminating act of God's mighty hand, however, is the parting of the Red Sea, at which point the people of Israel definitively escape from Egypt.

The book of Exodus speaks of God's deliverance of Israel in a number of ways. With respect to Israel's slavery, perhaps the most important language the book uses is that of "redemption." Because it has become part of the common stock of religious vocabulary in the Christian tradition, many people are unaware of the origins of the word.[6] Redemption language in the ancient Near East came from the realm of economics. One can see examples of this original use in the book of Leviticus, which speaks of the practice of "redeeming" or buying back either a piece of property (Lev. 25:25) or relatives who have fallen into misfortune and sold themselves into slavery (25:47–49).[7] Twice the book of Exodus uses this language to speak of God's deliverance of the Israelites from the Egyptians, once toward the beginning of the contest between God and Pharaoh and a second time in the account of the crossing of the Red Sea.

After Pharaoh's initial refusal to let the people of Israel go, God recommissions Moses and Aaron to bring the same message to Pharaoh again. Sending them also to their own people, God commands them, "Say therefore to the Israelites, 'I am the Lord, and I will free you from the burdens of the Egyptians and deliver you from slavery to them. *I will redeem you with an outstretched arm* and with mighty acts of judgment'" (Exod. 6:6). The images of redemption and of an outstretched arm reappear in the description of the crossing of the Red Sea, suggesting that this event is the definitive redemption of the Israelites from their slavery. When Moses cries out to God at the sea, the Lord commands him, "But you lift up your staff, and *stretch out your hand* over the sea and divide it, that the Israelites may go into the sea on dry ground" (14:16). The Lord's outstretched arm, by which he promises to redeem his people, is symbolized by Moses's own hand stretched out over the sea. This final act of judgment on the Egyptians accomplishes what God had promised toward the beginning of the book.

The Song of the Sea (Exod. 15:1–18) celebrates the event explicitly as an act of redemption, drawing once again on the image of God's outstretched hand:

5. See Exod. 3:19–20; 6:1; 13:3, 9, 14, 16.

6. For a brief discussion, see Jeremiah Unterman, "Redemption (OT)," *ABD* 5:650–54.

7. See also the laws concerning the "redeeming" of a house in Lev. 25:29–34.

You *stretched out your right hand*,
the earth swallowed them.
In your steadfast love you led the *people whom you redeemed*;
you guided them by your strength to your holy abode.
(Exod. 15:12–13)

A few points in this song deserve comment. First, there is the obvious connection between the parting of the sea and God's promise to the people in Exodus 6. Here at last the Lord has delivered the people from slavery to the Egyptians with arm outstretched, using the very same language of the promise. This helps to explain why the song puts so much emphasis on God's name, which occurs ten times in the song itself and five times in the opening three verses of Exodus 15 (including the introduction of the song). It is only at the crossing of the Red Sea that the Israelites come to an initial knowledge of the meaning of God's name as it relates to his redeeming activity (see Exod. 20:2).[8] In a similar way, baptism into the name of God is entry into knowing God and his saving work.

Second, and equally important, is the emphasis in the latter part of the song on the liturgical goal of the exodus. Twice the song speaks of the Israelites coming to God's dwelling place (Exod. 15:13, 17). In other words, the purpose of Israel's liberation is not simply to leave Egypt.

Third, the song as it stands in Exodus anticipates further aspects of Israel's journey to the promised land. Moses speaks of the amazement that seizes the surrounding nations, who look on as the Lord leads the people into this land (Exod. 15:13–17). This description makes clear that there is more to the exodus than simply escaping from Egyptian slavery. If the Israelites do not also enter the land God promised to Abraham, Isaac, and Jacob, the exodus will be incomplete (see Exod. 3:8, 17).

The purpose of obtaining the land, however, is not simply to secure a place for the Israelites to live. Rather, as the song indicates, its ultimate end is to establish communion between God and the Israelites. They are to come to his holy mountain, to the sanctuary, to the place where heaven and earth meet (Exod. 15:17). This liturgical goal pervades the book of Exodus. As noted above, the contest between God and Pharaoh is one of service: Will

8. On the revelation of the divine name in Exodus, see Christopher R. Seitz, *Word without End: The Old Testament as Abiding Theological Witness* (Grand Rapids: Eerdmans, 1998), 229–47, esp. 235–45.

the Israelites continue to perform hard labor for Pharaoh, or will he let them go to offer God proper worship? From the time God calls Moses on Mount Horeb, he emphasizes the centrality of worship. When Moses asks for a sign that God has sent him, the Lord points to a future act of worship on that same mountain (Exod. 3:12). God initially sends Moses to demand an opportunity for the Israelites to worship him (3:18), and toward the end of their conversation God returns to the theme of service: "And I say to you, 'Let my son go *that he may serve me*'" (4:23a ESV). Even the structure of the book points to the centrality of worship. As others have noted, the shape of Exodus reflects God's twofold command to Pharaoh, "Let my people go, that they may serve me" (8:1 ESV).[9] The first fifteen chapters of the book focus on the act of redemption. The rest of Exodus then focuses on the laws of the covenant and especially on the design and building of the tabernacle, which takes up nearly half of the book (Exod. 25–40).

The structure of the Pentateuch as a whole further underscores the importance of the covenant and of worship.[10] In Exodus 19 the people arrive at Mount Sinai, where God gives them their priestly and royal vocation (19:6). The Israelites remain at Mount Sinai for the rest of Exodus, all of Leviticus, and the first ten chapters of Numbers. At the heart of the Pentateuch are the stipulations for the covenant relationship between God and Israel. This suggests that the crossing of the Red Sea, impressive though it was, served as just the beginning of the relationship between God and the Israelites, a relationship characterized by worship and obedience to his commandments. In a similar way, Christian baptism initiates people into an entire way of life, a life of service to the God who redeems them through waters made powerful by the blood of Christ.

The Afterlife of a Motif

It would be hard to overstate the influence that the exodus tradition exercised on the ancient Israelite imagination. From the description of Joshua leading

9. Joseph Cardinal Ratzinger, *The Spirit of the Liturgy*, trans. John Saward (San Francisco: Ignatius, 2000), 13–23.

10. On the structure of the Pentateuch and the centrality of Leviticus within that structure, see L. Michael Morales, *Who Shall Ascend the Mountain of the Lord? A Biblical Theology of the Book of Leviticus*, New Studies in Biblical Theology (Downers Grove, IL: InterVarsity, 2015), 23–38.

the people into the promised land to the various prophetic appeals to the exodus as the paradigm of God's redeeming activity, this event plays a central role in the Old Testament vision of God and his relationship to his people. Given the emphasis on the importance of worship in Exodus in particular and in the Pentateuch as a whole, it is not at all surprising to see that the crossing of the Red Sea plays a prominent role in the Psalter, which frequently recounts the events of the exodus in poetic form. In many of the Psalms, the events of the exodus serve as the basis for the people's praise of God and often culminate, as the exodus itself does, in the establishment of a place for the people to worship the Lord.

One clear example of this connection between the crossing of the Red Sea and the offering of sacrifice appears in Psalm 66, which begins by calling all creation to worship the Lord for his powerful deeds (66:1–4). The psalmist goes on to specify a particular deed, the parting of the waters for the people of Israel. Both the crossing of the Red Sea and the parting of the Jordan seem to be in mind (66:5–7), which is unsurprising given the many connections between these two events.[11] From these stories, the psalmist then moves on to God's activity in his own life. Even here, however, the psalmist describes his experience in language drawn from the exodus:

> You let people ride over our heads;
>   we went *through fire and through water*;
> yet you have brought us out to a spacious place. (Ps. 66:12)

Immediately following this description of God's deliverance, the psalmist promises to enter the temple to offer sacrifices (Ps. 66:13–15). Redemption leads inescapably to acts of worship that reaffirm the communion between the psalmist and God. The psalm closes with a recounting of God's faithfulness to the psalmist, once again praising God for his answer to the psalmist's prayer and for his continued steadfast love (66:16–20).

Psalms 77 and 78 also recall the crossing of the Red Sea. The former psalm consists of a meditation on God's saving deeds in the past. It begins with a cry for help, expressing the psalmist's dire situation. In the midst of this trial, he wonders aloud whether God has abandoned him (77:4–10). Beginning in verse 11, however, the psalmist calls to mind God's past deeds of faithfulness.

11. See below for a discussion of these connections.

Unsurprisingly, he focuses on the paradigmatic event of the exodus, when God parted the waters for the people. Extolling God's greatness over all other gods, the psalmist sings, "With your strong arm you redeemed your people, the descendants of Jacob and Joseph" (77:15). The language of God's "arm" and of "redemption" is the same as that found in Exodus 6:6 and would naturally evoke the crossing of the Red Sea. The following verses confirm that the psalmist has this event in mind:

> When the waters saw you, O God,
>   when the waters saw you, they were afraid;
>   the very deep trembled. (Ps. 77:16)

Describing the cosmic phenomena that characterized Israel's redemption, the psalmist concludes by making explicit the connection to the exodus:

> Your way was through the sea,
>   your path, through the mighty waters;
>   yet your footprints were unseen.
> You led your people like a flock
>   by the hand of Moses and Aaron. (Ps. 77:19–20)

The psalm ends on this note, with no mention of worship or a holy abode. Nevertheless, by its very genre as a hymn, the psalm associates the redemption from Egypt with the praise of God.

Psalm 78 recounts Israel's history of infidelity through the time of David. Rather than give an exposition of the whole psalm, I will focus on those parts of the text that reflect Israel's redemption from Egypt. After describing Israel's tradition of instructing their children about God's saving deeds, the psalmist recalls the many wonders associated with Israel's escape. Among these marvels—which include the plagues, the pillar of cloud and the pillar of fire, and the water flowing from the rock—the psalmist recounts the crossing of the sea: "He divided the sea and let them pass through it, and made the waters stand like a heap" (78:13). Despite these acts of kindness, the Israelites repeatedly rebelled, with constant complaints and doubts about God's care for them (78:17–41). In response to this incessant rebellion, the psalmist again evokes the events of the exodus, describing the plagues in detail (78:42–51). This account, too, culminates in the parting of the Red Sea, but this time the psalmist adds an important element:

> He led them in safety, so that they were not afraid;
>   but the sea overwhelmed their enemies.
> And *he brought them to his holy hill,*
>   *to the mountain that his right hand had won.* (Ps. 78:53–54)

As in the book of Exodus, the goal of Israel's redemption is not simply autonomy but rather worship. The end of the psalm underscores this point, noting God's choice of Mount Zion as the place of his sanctuary (78:67–69).

Like Psalm 78, Psalm 106 recounts God's deeds in the context of Israel's repeated infidelity, but the latter psalm narrates Israel's history through the time of the people's exile among the nations. Twice the psalmist appeals to the crossing of the Red Sea as an example of God's faithfulness to his people. After an initial word of praise for God's steadfast love (106:1–3) and an appeal to God to remember his people (106:4–5), the psalmist hearkens back to Israel's time in Egypt. Despite the power God had shown in the plagues, the people rebelled when they came to the Red Sea (106:6–7). Nevertheless, the Lord brought them through its waters despite their rebelliousness: "He rebuked the Red Sea, and it became dry; he led them through the deep as through a desert" (106:9). By contrast, Israel's enemies were overwhelmed by the waters of the sea (106:11). This saving act resulted in a brief period of faith on the part of the people and, once again, an act of worship, as they praised the Lord for their deliverance (106:12). A few verses later, recounting Israel's act of idolatry at Mount Sinai ("Horeb," 106:19), the psalmist appeals once more to the crossing of the sea:

> They forgot God, their Savior,
>   who had done great things in Egypt,
> wondrous works in the land of Ham,
>   and awesome deeds by the Red Sea. (Ps. 106:21–22)

The juxtaposition of Israel's idol worship with their passing through the Red Sea suggests that the purpose of their redemption was proper worship. The psalm ends with a plea for deliverance from the people's state of exile:

> Save us, O LORD our God,
>   and gather us from among the nations,
> *that we may give thanks to your holy name*
>   *and glory in your praise.* (Ps. 106:47)

Just as the exodus was ordered to worship and fellowship with God, so God's future act of redemption is to serve the purpose of reestablishing communion between the people and God.

Psalms 77, 78, and 106 have an important feature in common. All three psalms appeal to God's saving act in the past in order to address a present concern. In this respect, the Psalms anticipate Paul, who appeals to the exodus tradition—retold with baptismal language—to warn his audience to avoid falling into idolatry (1 Cor. 10). Both the Psalms and Paul offer us a fruitful approach to the Christian life. Baptism is the touchstone of Christian existence, and in times of both joy and trial we do well to think back to God's saving act in the sacrament.

One of the shorter hymns in the Psalter, Psalm 114, also briefly recounts the exodus from Egypt, uniting this event with Israel's entry into the land. The psalm focuses on God's control over the sea and the river Jordan, both of which flee at the presence of God. Most importantly, though, the psalm begins by highlighting the liturgical purpose of the exodus:

> When Israel went out from Egypt,
> the house of Jacob from a people of strange language,
> *Judah became God's sanctuary,*
> *Israel his dominion.* (Ps. 114:1–2)

Once again, we see the combination of priestly and royal themes to describe Israel's identity as God's chosen people.

The Exodus in Isaiah

While the exodus plays a prominent role in much of the prophetic literature, references to the crossing of the Red Sea appear with particular frequency in Isaiah. As in many of the Psalms, in Isaiah this event serves as a model for God's future act of redemption. Twice in Isaiah 10–11 the prophet describes Israel's hoped-for redemption with reference to the Red Sea. Promising the Israelites that God will do to the Assyrians as he did to the Egyptians, Isaiah appeals to the saving events of the exodus, describing a deliverance similar to the crossing of the Red Sea (Isa. 10:26). Israel's future liberation will reflect her past. The following chapter, which offers hope for a Davidic heir endowed with the Spirit (11:1–5), once again draws on the crossing of the Red Sea as the paradigm for Israel's future deliverance:

The Song of Souls to Be Purified

In the second part of Dante Alighieri's *Divine Comedy*, the *Purgatorio*, the poet weaves together images reminiscent of baptism. The souls to be purified reach the mountain of purgatory by crossing the sea of death in a vessel (canto 2, lines 37–51). As they approach the shore, they sing the psalm that begins "When Israel went out from Egypt" (Ps. 114:1 [113:1 in Dante's Vulgate]). The imagery of crossing the waters of death while singing a song of Israel's deliverance from Egypt brings together the ideas of baptism as both death and liberation. Moreover, the content of the psalm points to its ultimate end—namely, worship—as the second verse of the psalm reads, "Judah became God's sanctuary, Israel his dominion" (Ps. 114:2). In Dante's vision, the healing administered in purgatory completes the liberation begun through dying with Christ in baptism, thus preparing the soul to enter into the glorious worship described in the *Paradiso*.

And the LORD will utterly destroy
  the tongue of the sea of Egypt;
and will wave his hand over the River
  with his scorching wind;
and will split it into seven channels,
  and make a way to cross on foot;
so there shall be a highway from Assyria
  for the remnant that is left of his people,
as there was for Israel
  when they came up from the land of Egypt. (Isa. 11:15–16)

As we saw in chapter 1, this act of redemption leads seamlessly into an act of worship (Isa. 12:1–6). Redemption through the waters goes hand in hand with worship.

A similar pattern appears in Isaiah 43, another chapter that describes God's future redemption of Israel as a new exodus. Since we already considered part of Isaiah 43 in chapter 1, our comments here will be brief. The prophet draws on exodus imagery twice in the chapter. In the opening verses, the Lord reaffirms his election of Israel as his people (Isa. 43:1) and promises that they will pass through water and through fire without being harmed

(43:2). He goes on to speak of the return of the people from east, west, north, and south, "from far away" and "from the end of the earth" (see 43:5–6). Toward the end of this first section, the Lord describes Israel as "everyone who is called by my name, *whom I created for my glory*, whom I formed and made" (43:7). Much like the first exodus, this latter act of redemption has worship as its goal.

A little later in the same chapter, the exodus imagery becomes more pronounced. First, the prophet makes a clear allusion to the crossing of the sea, describing the Lord's act of parting the waters for his people and then drowning their enemies in the sea (Isa. 43:16–17). Then the oracle describes how God will provide for his people in the wilderness, as he did once before (43:18–20). The end of the oracle explains the purpose for which God chose the Israelites, describing them as "the people whom I formed for myself so that they might declare my praise" (43:21). Once again, we see a close connection between passing through the waters and praising God. Freedom comes through worship.

Another passage we have already considered likewise promises a future redemption reminiscent of the crossing of the Red Sea. The deadly power of the sea, personified in the great monster Rahab, gives way to the "arm of the Lord." The prophet first makes a plea (Isa. 51:9–10) drawing on several images from the exodus: a reference to God's arm, a description of the drying up of the sea, and an identification of Israel as the "redeemed." This plea points forward to the prophet's expectation of a future act of redemption—one that, once again, will result in an act of worship:

> So the ransomed of the Lord shall return,
> and come to Zion with singing;
> everlasting joy shall be upon their heads;
> they shall obtain joy and gladness,
> and sorrow and sighing shall flee away. (Isa. 51:11)

Yet again, we see that Israel's redemption through the waters leads to an act of worship, the truest expression of freedom.

Isaiah makes one more allusion to the crossing of the Red Sea in chapter 63. The passage is part of a lengthy communal lament over Israel's misfortunes, in which the people ask for God's mercy in light of his past acts of redemption (Isa. 63:7–64:12). As is common among laments, the song alternates between

God's fidelity and Israel's unfaithfulness. Following a description of Israel's rebellion that resulted in their punishment, the prophet writes,

> Then they remembered the days of old,
> of Moses his servant.
> Where is the one who brought them up out of the sea
> with the shepherds of his flock?
> Where is the one who put within them
> his holy spirit,
> who caused his glorious arm
> to march at the right hand of Moses,
> who divided the waters before them
> to make for himself an everlasting name,
> who led them through the depths? (Isa. 63:11–13a)

The exodus imagery is once again unmistakable: the Lord's arm, the hand of Moses, and the parting of the sea. On the basis of this past act of redemption, the people once again plead with God to rescue them from their current crisis. We need not examine the details of this plea here. For our purposes, one of the most important aspects of the lament is the way in which it ends:

> *Our holy and beautiful house,*
> *where our ancestors praised you,*
> *has been burned by fire,*
> and all our pleasant places have become ruins.
> After all this, will you restrain yourself, O LORD?
> Will you keep silent, and punish us so severely? (Isa. 64:11–12)

At the culmination of Israel's lament, we find once again a reference to the temple and to Israel's worship. Liberation is not an end in itself but rather finds its fulfillment in worship.

The Waters Stood Still: The River Jordan and the Red Sea

From the first encounter between the Lord and Moses in Exodus, the Lord announces that he will bring the people back to the land he had promised to Abraham, Isaac, and Jacob (Exod. 3:8). The Pentateuch, however, ends in Deuteronomy with the people still on the cusp of entering the promised land. The book of Joshua recounts the completion of God's promise, and many features of the book tie it closely to the Pentateuch. The Lord chooses Moses's successor well before the end of the Pentateuch (Num. 27:12–23), and the early chapters of Joshua closely connect the events of the book with the Pentateuch. Joshua begins with a reference to Moses's death and with God commanding Joshua to lead the people across the Jordan into the promised land (Josh. 1:1–9). When Joshua sends spies to scout out the land, some of the inhabitants they encounter have already heard of the wonders that the Lord did for Israel, particularly the parting of the Red Sea (2:10). Joshua later compares the crossing of the Jordan to the crossing of the Red Sea (4:23). Although the entrance into the land did not shape the imagination of early Christians as much as the crossing of the Red Sea did, a few patristic authors interpret baptism in light of the main event of the early chapters of Joshua.[12] Several features of these early chapters serve as a fitting symbol of baptism.

From start to finish, the crossing of the Jordan has a liturgical dimension. The Levitical priests and the ark of the covenant play a central role in the event, leading the people across the river. Joshua interprets the ark as an indication of God's presence among the people (Josh. 3:10–11). As we will see, once the people finish crossing the river, they commemorate the event with a liturgical celebration (5:2–12).

The crossing of the river also has numerous connections with the exodus tradition. The Lord assures Joshua that he will be with him, just as he was with Moses (Josh. 3:7), and the text notes that the people respect Joshua just as they had respected Moses (4:14). Moreover, these events are twice connected with the commandments that Moses had given to Joshua and to the Reubenites, the Gadites, and the half-tribe of Manasseh (4:10, 12). The account of these events also repeatedly emphasizes the significance of the twelve tribes. Joshua is to choose twelve men, one from each tribe (3:13; 4:2), who are to set up twelve stones in the Israelite camp from the midst of the Jordan as a memorial of what God did there (4:2–9). This emphasis on the twelve tribes recalls the twelve pillars Moses set up on Mount Sinai at the ceremony establishing the covenant (Exod. 24:4).

The most obvious connection between the exodus and the crossing of the Jordan is, of course, the parting of the river. The Lord tells Joshua that

12. See Daniélou, *The Bible and the Liturgy*, 102–4.

Entering the Promised Land through Baptism

The fact that "Joshua" and "Jesus" are different versions of the same name has led many interpreters to draw connections between Moses's successor and Christ. Origen of Alexandria writes,

> Indeed you who long to draw near to the hearing of the divine law have recently forsaken the darkness of idolatry and are now for the first time forsaking Egypt. When you are reckoned among the number of the catechumens and have undertaken to submit to the precepts of the Church, you have parted the Red Sea and, placed in the stations of the desert, you daily devote yourself to hearing the Law of God and to looking upon the face of Moses, through which the glory of the Lord is revealed. But if you also have entered the mystic font of baptism and in the presence of the priestly and Levitical order have been instructed by those venerable and magnificent sacraments, which are known to those who are permitted to know those things, then, with the Jordan parted, you will enter the land of promise by the services of the priests. In this land, Jesus receives you after Moses, and becomes for you the leader of a new way.[a]

a. Origen, *Homily* 4.1, in *Homilies on Joshua*, ed. Cynthia White, trans. Barbara J. Bruce, FC 105 (Washington, DC: Catholic University of America Press, 2002), 52–53.

when the priests stand in the river with the ark, the waters will be cut off and stand in a heap (Josh. 3:13). While the waters stand in this way, the people cross over on "dry ground" (3:17), just as they did at the Red Sea (Exod. 14:29).[13] Once the people have finished crossing the river, Joshua explains the significance of the memorial of the twelve stones: "For the Lord your God dried up the waters of the Jordan for you until you crossed over, *as the Lord your God did to the Red Sea, which he dried up for us until we crossed over*, so that all the peoples of the earth may know that the hand of the Lord is mighty, and so that you may fear the Lord your God forever" (Josh. 4:23–24). The many connections between the crossing of the Jordan and the exodus, especially the events at the Red Sea, suggest that the Israelites' liberation is incomplete until they enter the land God had promised to them. Indeed, shortly after the crossing of the river, God

13. Although the Hebrew words are different, the basic idea is the same.

says to Joshua, "Today I have rolled away from you the disgrace of Egypt" (Josh. 5:9).[14]

One final connection to the exodus appears in the Israelites' first actions after crossing the river. At the Lord's direction the people perform two rites essential to the covenant. First, Joshua has all the men of Israel circumcised (Josh. 5:2–7). In addition to being the sign of God's covenant with Abraham (see Gen. 17), circumcision is a requirement for celebrating the Passover (Exod. 12:48), the second rite the Israelites observe on the other side of the Jordan. The celebration of this festival serves as a fitting bookend to God's liberation of Israel from Egypt. The Israelites celebrated the first Passover while still in the land of Egypt, shortly before God led them through the waters of the Red Sea to freedom (Exod. 12). Now in the land of Canaan, with that liberation officially complete (note the reference to the cessation of the manna in Josh. 5:12), the Israelites celebrate their freedom with another Passover. The crossing of the Red Sea led immediately to Israel's first observance of the sabbath (Exod. 16) and more remotely to the establishment of the covenant by sacrifice (Exod. 24), two liturgical actions. Israel's freedom did not mean simple autonomy; rather, it was ordered to the worship of and communion with their God. The same can be said for the crossing of the river Jordan. Passing through the water leads to worship.[15] In this regard, the entrance of the Israelites into the land serves as a fitting prefiguration of the practice of baptism, which initiates the believer into the Church's life of worship and communion with God.[16]

Freedom through Worship

The crossing of the Red Sea is one of the most iconic events of the Old Testament. It appeals to one of the most fundamental human desires: the desire for freedom. As many of the Church Fathers saw it, the story of the crossing of the Red Sea represents a liberation from Satan (personified in Pharaoh) and from sin. Likewise, the New Testament at times speaks of baptism as

14. On the importance of Joshua as the culmination of various strands in the Pentateuch, see Joseph Blenkinsopp, "The Structure of P," *CBQ* 38 (1976): 275–92, esp. 287–91.

15. It is perhaps also worth noting the connection between the crossing of the river and circumcision as the prerequisite to participating in the Passover. Perhaps a New Testament text such as Col. 2:11–12, which speaks of baptism as akin to circumcision, may be offering a faint echo of Israel's entrance into the promised land.

16. See CCC 1244.

liberation from slavery to sin (see Rom. 6). But closely related to the liberation from sin is the exodus tradition's emphasis on the importance of worship. God liberates the Israelites so that they can worship ("serve") him and enjoy communion with him. The connection between liberation from sin and liberation for worship is not hard to see. According to some Jewish traditions, idolatry is the primordial sin (see Rom. 1:18–32; Wis. 11:15–12:2). Freedom from sin, then, logically leads to proper worship.

Sin and worship also both relate to the ancient Israelite understanding of purity, which had both ritual and moral dimensions. In the following chapter we will explore images of purity and impurity as a final Old Testament prefiguration of baptism.

4

The Waters of Purity

> Wash me thoroughly from my iniquity,
> and cleanse me from my sin.
>
> —Psalm 51:2

An obvious symbolic meaning of water, stemming from one of its most common uses, is that of cleansing. Water is a powerful purifying agent, and many have interpreted baptism primarily in these terms.[1] Despite this interpretation, we will see in the next part of this work that cleansing or purification is only one among many aspects of the New Testament's vision of baptism. Indeed, it is not even the most common interpretation of the rite. Nevertheless, purity does play a role in the New Testament's portrayal of baptism, and the roots of the concept lie in the Old Testament.

Most Christians today associate purity with the heart, and frequently they limit its significance to the realm of sexual morality. We need not consider the reasons for this narrow view here, but it is an unfortunate one. The Old Testament understanding of purity is far richer, encompassing both regulations concerning the worship of God in the temple and the whole of the moral life, not just sexuality.[2] Ritual purity and the rites associated with it

1. Thomas Aquinas, for example, emphasizes the cleansing power of water several times in his discussion of baptism. See *Summa Theologiae* III q. 66.

2. On the relationship between sin and impurity in ancient Israel, see Jonathan Klawans, *Impurity and Sin in Ancient Judaism* (New York: Oxford University Press, 2000), on which I rely for much of this chapter.

regulate admission to God's presence and participation in Israel's liturgical life. This kind of purity has less to do with what modern people commonly call "ethics" than with the proper way to approach God in worship.[3] The Old Testament does speak of moral purity; however, this kind of purity extends far beyond the sexual realm. An example of this kind of purity can be found in the first chapter of Isaiah:

> Wash yourselves; make yourselves clean;
> remove the evil of your doings
> from before my eyes;
> cease to do evil,
> learn to do good;
> *seek justice,*
> *rescue the oppressed,*
> *defend the orphan,*
> *plead for the widow.* (Isa. 1:16–17)

The purity God calls for can be summed up in the word "justice," which in the Old Testament entails caring for the widow and the orphan, among other things.

Both aspects of purity, the ritual dimension and the moral dimension, contribute to a proper understanding of baptism. As shown in the previous chapters, the various connections in the Old Testament between water and worship prefigure baptism's role as the initiation into the Church's worship, the gateway to the other sacraments. In this regard, it functions in a way that is analogous to the ritual washings of the Old Testament. But baptism also serves as a remedy for sin. As I argued in chapter 2, God's condemnation and punishment of Pharaoh and the king of Tyre symbolize baptism's destruction of the sin of pride. A consideration of the Old Testament concept of purity will add another important dimension to a biblical theology of baptism.

A Typological Introduction: Naaman the Syrian

Before we consider purity in the Old Testament more generally, let us look at a narrative example of cleansing that several patristic authors use as an

3. For a recent argument that there may have been an ethical dimension even to the laws of ritual purity, however, see Leigh M. Trevaskis, *Holiness, Ethics and Ritual in Leviticus* (Sheffield, UK: Sheffield Phoenix, 2011).

illustration and type of baptism: the healing of Naaman the Syrian (2 Kings 5:1–19).[4] On its surface, this story would seem to be unrelated to other Old Testament conceptions of purity. Although Naaman does suffer from a skin disease, which defiles a person (see Lev. 14), as a pagan he would not have sought to participate in Israel's temple cult.[5] Moreover, although as a pagan he would be seen as an idolater, there is no explicit mention of any sins related to impurity in his case. Despite these obvious differences, a few aspects of the story nevertheless serve as a fitting illustration of purity, particularly as it relates to baptism.

Even if Naaman had no intention of participating in Israel's worship, the very disease from which he suffered would have conjured up associations with ritual impurity. Though the disease was painful and isolating, for an ancient Israelite exclusion from the temple would have been equally so. In Naaman's case, however, early in the story the emphasis falls squarely on his physical condition, as his Israelite servant girl notes how the prophet Elisha could "cure" him of the illness (2 Kings 5:3). In response to this promise, Naaman travels to the king of Israel to seek a cure, presuming that the prophet would be under the king's control (5:5b–7). When Elisha hears of the man's arrival and the king's response, he sends for him, promising that Naaman will see the power of the Israelite prophet (5:8).

Rather than receive Naaman, however, Elisha simply sends a messenger with instructions that the Syrian should bathe seven times in the river Jordan, and afterward he will be "clean" (2 Kings 5:10). Notice that the prophet does not say, "You shall be cured," but rather, "You shall be clean." From the prophet's perspective purity has a greater priority than physical well-being. At this Naaman becomes angry, once again expressing his desire to be "cured" (5:11). But from that point on, the emphasis shifts to cleansing. Even Naaman himself suggests that the rivers of Damascus could make him "clean" (5:12). At the urging of his servants, however, he relents and immerses himself in the river seven times, as the prophet has commanded. As promised, Naaman's skin is healed, and he becomes "clean" (5:14).

4. For a brief discussion of this tradition as well as other connections between some important events at the Jordan and baptism, see Jean Daniélou, *The Bible and the Liturgy* (Notre Dame, IN: University of Notre Dame Press, 1956), 105–12.

5. Although frequently translated as "leprosy," the disease from which Naaman suffered was not Hansen's disease, as actual leprosy is known today. See Matthew Thiessen, *Jesus and the Forces of Death: The Gospels' Portrayal of Ritual Impurity within First-Century Judaism* (Grand Rapids: Baker Academic, 2020), 43–54.

Like the Samaritan "leper" in the Gospel of Luke (Luke 17:11–19), Naaman returns to express his gratitude to Elisha for his healing. The Syrian acknowledges the power of the God of Israel and offers the prophet a gift. When Elisha refuses the gift, Naaman decides on another course of action: he will take some of the dirt of the land of Israel back to his home so that he can worship the Lord with sacrifices and burnt offerings (2 Kings 5:17). Even though, as a Syrian, Naaman will not participate in Israel's worship, he has nevertheless been converted to the God of Israel. His "baptism" leads to his worship of the one true God.

Several features of this story make it a fitting image of baptism. The most obvious connection with baptism is Naaman's act of bathing himself (in the Septuagint, he literally "baptized himself") in the river. As some of the Fathers note, the story of Naaman points forward to the welcome of the Gentiles into God's people.[6] The "conversion" of Naaman to the God of Israel foreshadows the role of conversion in the practice of baptism, and the healing of Naaman symbolizes the healing that the sacrament effects.[7]

Before we move on to consider texts more obviously concerned with ritual purity, it is worth lingering over the interplay between "curing" and "cleansing" in this episode. As noted above, Naaman comes to Israel hoping that he will be cured of his condition. When Elisha calls for him, the prophet bids him to wash in the river and be "clean." Elisha sees Naaman's problem as deeper than a skin disease. More important than physical healing is reconciliation with the God of Israel and the ability to worship him, which is how the story ends.[8] What this suggests is that the deepest healing we need is this reconciliation, a restoration to a proper relationship with God. As the story of Naaman illustrates symbolically, baptism serves as the beginning of this renewed relationship, a relationship that requires continual nourishment in acts of worship for the rest of a person's life.

Impurity and Israel's Liturgical Life

As noted in the introduction to this chapter, the concepts of purity and impurity had at least two different meanings in ancient Israel. The first had to

6. See the summary in Daniélou, *The Bible and the Liturgy*, 111–12.

7. See CCC 1263.

8. We see a similar point in the famous story of Jesus healing the leper (Mark 1:40–45 and parallels). Although most people focus on the miraculous cure that Jesus performs for the man, his request is that Jesus make him "clean"—that is, that he might be welcomed back into Israel's liturgical life.

do with Israel's liturgical practices, and it is commonly referred to as "ritual purity."[9] The adjective "ritual" in this phrase has a twofold signification. First, it indicates that this kind of purity relates to the rituals performed in the temple. Those Israelites who were "ritually impure" were forbidden from participating in the various rites of the temple during the time of their impurity. The term also points to the fact that rituals played a part in restoring an Israelite to a state of purity.

With respect to ritual impurity, it is important to emphasize that it is in no way the result of sin. Although many Christians today think of purity primarily in moral terms, this kind of purity relates to actions or even experiences that do not necessarily have any moral implications. The kinds of things that "defile" a person—that is, render that person ritually impure—are listed primarily in the book of Leviticus (Lev. 11–15) as well as in one chapter in the book of Numbers (Num. 19). Most sources of this kind of impurity involve direct or indirect contact with largely natural substances or activities, such as certain animals deemed "unclean," childbirth, certain skin diseases, and bodily discharges.[10]

In his masterful study of the relationship between impurity and sin in ancient Judaism, Jonathan Klawans notes three characteristics of ritual impurity: "(1) The sources of ritual impurity are generally natural and more or less unavoidable. (2) It is not sinful to contract these impurities. And (3) these impurities convey an impermanent contagion."[11] It is obvious that some of the sources of this contagion are avoidable.[12] The chances of an average Israelite coming across the carcass of a shrimp or lobster (Lev. 11:9–12), much less touching it (11:24–25), are relatively slim. Other sources of impurity, however, are clearly unavoidable. A woman cannot prevent her body from menstruating (15:19), nor can a man perfectly control the fluids that escape his body (15:2).

9. For a good discussion of some of the problems with this term as well as its usefulness despite these problems, see Klawans, *Impurity and Sin*, 22–23. David Wright prefers the terminology of "tolerated" and "prohibited" impurity rather than "ritual" and "moral" impurity, respectively, because it underscores the fact that purity falls on a continuum, thus showing a closer connection between impurities stemming from amoral acts and impurities stemming from sin. See David P. Wright, "The Spectrum of Priestly Impurity," in *Priesthood and Cult in Ancient Israel*, ed. Gary A. Anderson and Saul M. Olyan, JSOTSup 125 (Sheffield, UK: Sheffield Academic, 1991), 150–81. See also Jay Sklar, *Sin, Impurity, Sacrifice, Atonement: The Priestly Conceptions*, Hebrew Bible Monographs 2 (Sheffield, UK: Sheffield Phoenix, 2005), 139–59.

10. For the details, see Lev. 11–15 and the discussion in Klawans, *Impurity and Sin*, 23.

11. Klawans, *Impurity and Sin*, 23.

12. Klawans, *Impurity and Sin*, 23–24.

Likewise, childbirth (12:1–8) and skin diseases (Lev. 13–14) are natural occurrences largely beyond the control of those who experience them.

Even a moment's reflection on some of the things that convey ritual impurity shows that they are not sinful. As already noted, many of these causes are beyond the control of most people. In fact, some of these activities are the subject of positive commandments, such as childbearing (see Gen. 1:28).[13] The mere fact of contracting some kind of impurity, then, is not a sin.[14] The Israelite's primary duty was to be aware of his or her state of purity or impurity in order to avoid bringing anything unclean into the holy place (Lev. 15:31).[15]

The effect of these impurities was temporary, lasting anywhere from less than a day to several weeks. Those in a state of ritual impurity were to refrain from visiting the temple and, in some cases, to remain isolated from the rest of society (Lev. 13:45–46).[16] Nevertheless, this kind of exclusion was not permanent. Following the prescribed rituals and waiting the designated amount of time would result in the reintegration of the impure person into the community.

Leviticus and Numbers stipulate various rituals for restoring a person to purity, many of which involve water. In the case of a man healed of a skin disease, the priest and the one to be cleansed performed two rites involving water (Lev. 14:1–32). First, taking two birds, the priest would kill one of them over a jar of fresh water (14:5). Dipping the living bird in the blood of the dead bird, he would then sprinkle the blood on the "patient" seven times. Following this rite, the man shaved himself and bathed in water twice, once on the same day and a second time seven days later (14:8). Following the second bath, the man was welcomed back into the community, and he would bring an offering to the priest, indicating his reintegration into Israel's life of worship (14:9–10).

13. As Klawans (*Impurity and Sin*, 24) notes, even Israelite priests, who were responsible for the care of the sanctuary, were expected to beget and rear children.

14. It is worth noting, however, that a few texts do speak of the inadvertent contraction of ritual impurity as sinful. See Num. 6:9–12 and the discussion of the passage in Jay Sklar, "Sin and Impurity: Atoned or Purified? Yes!," in *Perspectives on Purity and Purification in the Bible*, ed. Baruch J. Schwartz et al. (London: T&T Clark, 2008), 18–31, here 27n44.

15. Klawans, *Impurity and Sin*, 25. Klawans goes on to note two cases in which impurity can lead to sin—namely, the refusal to purify oneself after contracting corpse impurity (Num. 19:13, 20) and entering the holy place while in a state of impurity (Lev. 7:20–21; 15:31; 22:3–7). In each of these cases, the person is cut off from the people and/or from the presence of the Lord.

16. Klawans, *Impurity and Sin*, 26.

The removal of impurity related to bodily discharges (Lev. 15) also involved cleansing with water. This kind of impurity affected not only the one who suffered from it but also, indirectly, those who came into contact with beds or chairs on which the impure person had lain or sat, or through other forms of indirect contact (15:5, 8–11). In all of these cases, those who had become impure through contact had to wash their clothes, bathe with water, and remain unclean until the evening, a ritual mentioned six times in a span of seven verses (15:5–11). As for the man who himself contracted the impurity, the procedure was the same (washing clothes and bathing in water), but the man first had to wait seven days (15:13). Once his purity was restored, the man would approach the tent of meeting, where he brought offerings for the priest to offer up in sacrifice (15:14–15). As with the cleansing after skin diseases, the purification of the man with the discharge restored him to participation in Israel's liturgical life. Similar regulations applied to a man who came into contact with a woman during the time of her menstrual period (15:21–22).

Miqva'ot in First-Century Israel

The number of people who received baptism on the day of Pentecost—three thousand persons in one day (Acts 2:41)—might seem astounding. How did the apostles find enough water to perform so many baptisms? It is possible that the numbers are inflated in keeping with literary conventions of the time. However, the availability of water would not have caused a problem for performing so many baptisms. Archaeological digs have uncovered numerous baths in and around Jerusalem from the time of the New Testament. It seems likely that at least some of these functioned as *miqva'ot*—that is, baths used for ritual immersions related to the purity legislation in Leviticus and elsewhere. Regardless of the actual function of these baths, which is disputed, their mere existence points to the ready availability of water for many purposes, including baptism.[a]

a. For a balanced discussion of the archaeological evidence, see Benjamin G. Wright, "Jewish Ritual Baths—Interpreting the Digs and the Texts: Some Issues in the Social History of Second Temple Judaism," in *The Archaeology of Israel: Constructing the Past, Interpreting the Present*, ed. Neil Asher Silberman and David B. Small, JSOTSup 237 (Sheffield, UK: Sheffield Academic, 1997), 190–214.

Although every form of ritual impurity was the result of something natural, not every source of impurity was something strictly biological or physiological. Leviticus seems to imply that some of the rites involved with sacrifice in the temple, particularly the Day of Atonement, led to impurity, but for an ancient Israelite this activity would be seen as "natural" since it was a normal part of the people's day-to-day life.[17] The text nowhere explicitly states that the priests become unclean through their activity, but the rite calls for washing with water three times. As the high priest prepared to enter the holy of holies to offer the sacrifice for the Day of Atonement, he was to wash his body with water before putting on his priestly vestments (Lev. 16:4). After performing the rite in the holy of holies, upon leaving the sanctuary, the priest would remove his linen garments and bathe in water once again before offering additional sacrifices for himself and for the people (16:24). Similarly, before he could return to the camp, the man who drove the goat "for Azazel" into the wilderness (another part of the ritual) had to wash his clothes and his body in water (16:26). Likewise, the one responsible for burning the remains of the bull and the goat offered in sacrifice had to wash his clothes and body in water before returning to the camp (16:28).

Numbers 19 describes another ritual that conferred impurity on the priest: the ceremony of the red heifer. As with the impurity (implicitly) contracted on the Day of Atonement, the removal of this impurity involves bathing with water. Both the priest and the one who burns the heifer during the rite are instructed to wash their clothes and bathe in water, remaining unclean until the evening (Num. 19:7–8). This chapter also prescribes rites for purification after contact with a corpse, another source of impurity for the ancient Israelites. Whoever touched a dead body became unclean for seven days. In order to remove this impurity, the person had to bathe with water on the third day and on the seventh day (19:12). Similar regulations applied to persons who were present in a tent when another person died or who entered a tent with a corpse in it, as well as those who touched a corpse in the open field (19:14–16). The purification of these persons involved sprinkling with water on the third day and the seventh day as well as washing their clothes and themselves in water on the seventh day (19:19). At the end of that day they became clean once again.

There are obvious differences between baptism and the rites for ritual impurity in Leviticus. The rites in Leviticus were repeated as frequently as

17. See Klawans, *Impurity and Sin*, 23–24.

necessary, whereas baptism is performed only once. Nevertheless, the rites of purification share two characteristics with baptism. First, and most obviously, both involve the use of water. Second, and perhaps more importantly, just as the rites of purification rendered an Israelite fit to participate once again in the temple liturgy, so baptism is the gateway to the sacraments, the initiation of a person into the Church's liturgical life.

Some might wonder why God would insist on these rituals for admitting people into his presence, particularly when many of the things that render a person impure are unavoidable—and in some cases mandatory—natural actions or processes. One intriguing proposal is that the ritual system was a part of God's pedagogy to teach the Israelites about the weakness of the flesh.[18] The things that defile ancient Israelites are closely associated with the "flesh," a word that occurs more than twenty times in Leviticus 12–15.[19] Similarly, as we will see in the next section, certain sins bound up with the flesh could also defile the land and lead to exile. Idolatry, violence, and sexual immorality all in some way relate to the flesh and bring pollution to the land.[20] They belong to the expanded category that Paul would later develop: the "works of the flesh" (Gal. 5:19–21). The ritual system, then, is meant to call God's people to become more like him by renouncing the works of the weakened flesh. The problematizing of literal flesh points to the deeper, much more serious problem of the works of the flesh.[21]

Impurity and Sin

Alongside the ritual understanding of purity and impurity, one finds in the Old Testament the language of purity or washing used with reference to certain sins. It is important to note that there are many differences between ritual impurity and moral impurity.[22] Ritual impurity, as we have seen, stems

18. See Peter J. Leithart, *Delivered from the Elements of the World: Atonement, Justification, Mission* (Downers Grove, IL: IVP Academic, 2016), 91–121, esp. 97–104.

19. Leithart, *Delivered from the Elements*, 99–100. The repetition of the Hebrew *bāśār* is lost in many translations, which often render the word with synonyms such as "body."

20. Genesis 6:11–13 explicitly associates the flesh with violence.

21. This is not to deny the goodness of embodied existence but rather to underscore the corrupting influence of sin. The Hebrew word *bāśār* can have a range of meanings, from neutrally referring to the body (Gen. 2:23; 2 Sam. 5:1) to referring in a darker way to the corruption of the flesh (e.g., Gen. 6:11–13).

22. See Klawans, *Impurity and Sin*, 26–27. The following contrast between ritual and moral impurity is a slightly modified summary of Klawans's discussion.

from natural activities that are not sinful per se. Ritual impurity is impermanent but contagious and precludes a person from entering the holy place and participating in Israel's worship (at least until the person performs the proper rites to remove the impurity). By contrast, moral impurity, as the name suggests, comes from immoral acts, especially heinous sins such as murder and idolatry.[23] Moral impurity lasts much longer than ritual impurity, and it cannot be passed on to another person—one does not contract moral impurity by consorting with sinners. Moral impurity also does not preclude one from participating in Israel's rituals. In fact, one ritual performed in the sanctuary presumes that one of the participants in the rite may have committed an offense (Num. 5:11–31).[24] Finally, moral impurity pollutes the offender and, by extension, the land. When such moral impurity builds up beyond a certain undefined limit, the Israelites suffer punishment, particularly in the form of exile from the land (see, e.g., Lev. 18:24–30).[25]

Despite these important differences, there are also similarities between ritual and moral impurity, most obviously in the language of impurity.[26] Moreover, as we will see, even though sins do not result in the kind of ritual impurity that precludes a person from participating in temple worship, various Old Testament texts suggest that Israel's collective guilt renders that worship ineffective. The expulsion of Israel from the land because of moral impurity serves as a kind of analogy to the effect of ritual impurity, because one of the primary purposes of entering the land was so that Israel would have a place where God would dwell with them and they could worship him. Rather than offer an exhaustive analysis of this phenomenon, let us consider a few examples of moral impurity in the Old Testament.

One of the most poignant expressions of the desire for moral purity appears in Psalm 51.[27] Purity imagery permeates this psalm, and it closely associates this purity with God's mercy and a return to worship in the temple. The psalm begins with a plea for God's mercy and quickly moves into the language of purity: "Wash me thoroughly from my iniquity, and cleanse me

23. See Ps. 106:36–38 and Ezek. 36:17–18 as well as the discussion of these texts below.

24. Klawans, *Impurity and Sin*, 27.

25. I owe this reference to Klawans, *Impurity and Sin*, 30.

26. It is worth noting, though, as Klawans (*Impurity and Sin*, 26) points out, that there are some terminological differences between moral and ritual impurity.

27. For a recent discussion of this and other passages in the Old Testament that use the imagery of washing, see Lesley R. DiFransico, *Washing Away Sin: An Analysis of the Metaphor in the Hebrew Bible and Its Influence*, BTS 23 (Leuven: Peeters, 2016).

The Purifying Waters of Baptism

Early Christians applied the Old Testament's imagery of ritual cleansing to baptism and its effects on sin. In his oration on baptism, St. Gregory of Nazianzus writes,

> Let us be baptized, then, that we may be victorious. Let us participate in the purifying waters, which cleanse more than hyssop, and purify more than blood prescribed by the Law. They are more holy than the ashes of a heifer that sprinkles the partakers and brings a temporary cleansing of the body but not a complete removal of sin.[a]

a. Gregory of Nazianzus, *Oration* 40.11, in *Festal Orations*, trans. Nonna Verna Harrison (Crestwood, NY: St. Vladimir's Seminary Press, 2008), 107.

from my sin" (Ps. 51:2). The psalmist then laments his sins, acknowledging their gravity and the way that he has offended God. Returning to his plea for purity, the psalmist prays, "Purge me with hyssop, and I shall be clean; wash me, and I shall be whiter than snow" (51:7). This imagery is most likely a metaphorical use of one or more of Israel's purification rites, which often involved the use of hyssop. A few verses later the psalmist renews his plea, asking God for inward purity: "Create in me a clean heart, O God, and put a new and right spirit within me" (51:10). Even though most instances of moral impurity do not exclude the offender from participating in Israel's worship, Psalm 51 closely associates the sinner's offense with exclusion from the presence of God (51:11). It would be tempting to take all of this language metaphorically, without reference to Israel's temple. After all, the psalmist suggests that a contrite heart is the truly acceptable sacrifice (51:17). However, the psalm ends with an expression of hope for the revival of Israel's temple offerings:

> Do good to Zion in your good pleasure;
> rebuild the walls of Jerusalem,
> then you will delight in right sacrifices,
> in burnt offerings and whole burnt offerings;
> then bulls will be offered on your altar. (Ps. 51:18–19)

In at least this instance, moral purity seems to be a prerequisite for the proper offering of sacrifice and worship in the temple.[28]

A similar connection on a national scale can be seen in Psalm 106, which recounts the people's sins—namely, the offenses of idolatry, human sacrifice to demons, and the shedding of innocent blood (106:36–38)—resulting in their expulsion from the land (106:40–41). On a national level, the sins of the people lead to their exile. Nevertheless, even in the midst of their exile, the psalmist expresses hope for a return to the land and, even more importantly, to worshiping the Lord:

> Save us, O Lord our God,
> and gather us from among the nations,
> *that we may give thanks to your holy name*
> *and glory in your praise*. (Ps. 106:47)

Again, although moral impurity on an individual level does not necessarily exclude one from worship in the temple, the collective guilt of Israel eventually does lead to the removal of the people from their place of worship.

This connection between sins that defile and unacceptable worship appears frequently in the prophetic literature as well. Although it is true, as Klawans rightly notes, that moral impurity did not prevent an ancient Israelite from participating in temple liturgy on a day-to-day basis, the prophets do seem to suggest that the collective moral impurity of the people can render their sacrifices unacceptable.[29] We see this, for example, in Isaiah. In the opening chapter of the book, God brings a lawsuit against Israel for the people's many sins.[30] Because of these sins, the Lord despises their offerings:

> What to me is the multitude of your sacrifices?
> says the Lord;
> I have had enough of burnt offerings of rams
> and the fat of fed beasts;

28. Some interpreters see these verses as an addendum to the original psalm. See the discussion in DiFransico, *Washing Away Sin*, 89n37, and the sources cited there. Nevertheless, the point remains that either the psalmist or a later editor connected moral purity with proper sacrifice.

29. Klawans makes an important and useful distinction: "Moral impurity does indeed affect the sanctuary (e.g., Lev. 20:3), but its effect does not reach the sanctuary by the entrance of sinners *into* the sanctuary" (*Impurity and Sin*, 29, emphasis in the original).

30. For a recent discussion of this passage in context, see DiFransico, *Washing Away Sin*, 36–52. DiFransico notes that the language of cleansing here differs from Old Testament notions of cultic purity (44–45).

I do not delight in the blood of bulls,
  or of lambs, or of goats. (Isa. 1:11)

The prophet proceeds to elaborate the futility of Israel's offerings, scorning their incense, their festivals, the raising of their hands, and their prayers (Isa. 1:12–15). The prophet then gives the reason for the unacceptability of Israel's worship, calling for their purification. The context makes clear that this is not a ritual purification but rather a conversion of heart, a turning away from their misdeeds against the poor and the marginalized:

Wash yourselves; make yourselves clean;
  remove the evil of your doings
  from before my eyes;
cease to do evil,
  learn to do good;
seek justice,
  rescue the oppressed,
defend the orphan,
  plead for the widow. (Isa. 1:16–17)

Texts like this one, then, suggest that ritual purity, though important, is not enough. In order for Israel to offer sacrifices acceptable to God, the people must also be morally pure, especially in their treatment of the poor and the oppressed.

One of the most important prophetic passages with respect to moral purity appears in Ezekiel 36, which includes a series of oracles describing both the reasons for Israel's punishment and their eventual redemption and restoration to the land. The prophet draws an analogy between ritual impurity and moral impurity in order to explain Israel's exile:

> Mortal, when the house of Israel lived on their own soil, they defiled it with their ways and their deeds; *their conduct in my sight was like the uncleanness of a woman in her menstrual period.* So I poured out my wrath upon them for the blood that they had shed upon the land, and for the idols with which they had defiled it. (Ezek. 36:17–18)

Israel's misdeeds—specifically, their shedding of blood and their idolatry—result in the defilement of the land. Significantly, the prophet compares their actions to menstrual impurity. In light of the discussion of ritual impurity above, it should be clear that the comparison cannot have anything to do with the nature of the acts. Menstruation is a natural, biological process, not a sin. The comparison, then, must refer instead to the effects of ritual impurity. Just as menstruation prevents a woman from entering into God's presence in the temple, so Israel's sins result in their expulsion from the land. The following verse describes their punishment as a scattering among the nations (Ezek. 36:19). The comparison with the effects of menstrual impurity suggests that the most important aspect of Israel's expulsion is their loss of the temple, the dwelling place of God in their midst.

Following this description of Israel's sins and consequent punishment, the Lord promises to redeem Israel by bringing them back to the land. According to Ezekiel's oracle, however, the redemption is not a simple return. Rather, it will entail a transformation, described as a purification from sin. Through the prophet, the Lord promises:

> I will sprinkle clean water upon you, and you shall be clean from all your uncleannesses, and from all your idols I will cleanse you. A new heart I will give you, and a new spirit I will put within you; and I will remove from your body the heart of stone and give you a heart of flesh. I will put my spirit within you, and make you follow my statutes and be careful to observe my ordinances. (Ezek. 36:25–27)

Once again, purity has a moral dimension: it consists in obeying God's commandments. This obedience comes about not by the simple effort of the people but rather by God's action of purifying the people, giving them a new heart, and implanting his own Spirit within them.

A little later the same oracle describes the transformation of the land itself, such that people will compare it to the garden of Eden (Ezek. 36:35). Because the temple symbolized a return to Eden for the ancient Israelites, this reference to the garden subtly underscores the importance of the temple for this return.[31] In this regard, it is worth recalling that Ezekiel closes with a lengthy description of the prophet's vision of a new temple (Ezek. 40–48), a temple

31. See Gordon J. Wenham, "Sanctuary Symbolism in the Garden of Eden Story," in *I Studied Inscriptions from before the Flood: Ancient Near Eastern, Literary, and Linguistic Approaches to Genesis 1–11*, ed. Richard S. Hess and David Toshio Tsumura (Winona Lake, IN: Eisenbrauns, 1994), 399–404.

reminiscent of Eden.[32] This liturgical theme can be seen in the comparison the prophet makes between the people and the flocks for temple worship: "Like the flock for sacrifices, like the flock at Jerusalem during her appointed festivals, so shall the ruined towns be filled with flocks of people. Then they shall know that I am the LORD" (Ezek. 36:38). These references to festivals and the temple should come as no surprise. Purity and the temple go together, and even though an Israelite's sins did not prevent him or her from participating in temple worship, the people's collective sin could and did result in their exile.

The Ordination Rite: A Priestly Baptism

Two passages in the Pentateuch describe the rite of ordination for Aaron and his sons in a way that manifests important similarities with Christian baptism and also involves elements of purification (Exod. 29:1–35; Lev. 8). We will briefly mention four aspects of the rite.[33] First, ordination is the only ritual in the Old Testament in which one person bathes another: the Lord commands Moses to wash Aaron and his sons with water (Exod. 29:4; Lev. 8:6). Second, Moses clothes them in a new garment (Exod. 29:5–9; Lev. 8:7–13). Third, there is a purification ritual for the altar (Exod. 29:10–14; Lev. 8:14–17).[34] Finally, unlike the other ritual washings described in Leviticus, the washing of the ordination rite takes place only once. In these four respects—its administration by another, the vesting with a new garment, the purificatory nature of the rite, and its once-for-all character—Old Testament ordination serves as a fitting anticipation of the Christian rite of baptism, which, as I will argue in chapter 11, has a priestly dimension.

Images of Baptism in the Old Testament

As we come to the end of the first part of this study, let us review the various images we have considered. Many of these do not play an explicit part in the New Testament's descriptions of baptism. Nevertheless, insofar as the texts

32. See also the discussion of this passage in chap. 1 above. The temple vision at the end of Ezekiel serves as a fitting bookend, mirroring earlier chapters of the book, which announce the departure of God's presence from the Jerusalem temple (see esp. Ezek. 8–11).

33. I owe the following points to Peter J. Leithart, *The Priesthood of the Plebs: A Theology of Baptism* (Eugene, OR: Wipf & Stock, 2003), 95–96.

34. Leviticus is more explicit than Exodus about the purificatory nature of the ritual.

we have explored contribute to the biblical symbolism of water, they can contribute to an understanding of the sacrament of baptism. Several passages we have considered reflect a pattern at the heart of the Church's understanding of baptism, and there has been significant overlap across some of the images.

The most important aspect of water imagery in the Old Testament for understanding baptism is its role as the source of life. In the New Testament, baptism is the gateway to eternal life (see, e.g., John 3:1–15). The connection between water and life, prominent in Genesis, also appears throughout the Old Testament. Frequently we see water presented as a symbol of spiritual life, at times even associated with the gift of God's Spirit (see, e.g., Isa. 44:1–6). Significantly, the life-giving power of water also has close associations with Israel's hope for a new temple. This suggests that the true source of life is to be found in worshiping God and dwelling in his presence.

One of the great paradoxes of the gospel, however, is that life comes through death, through giving one's life away.[35] This is especially true of Paul's account of baptism (Rom. 6:1–11). In addition to portraying water as the source of life, the Old Testament frequently plays on water's destructive, death-dealing power, as in the accounts of the flood and the crossing of the Red Sea. Significantly, both of these stories of redemption through water culminate in an act of worship, with Noah offering sacrifices on Mount Ararat (Gen. 8:20) and God establishing a covenant with the people on Mount Sinai through a sacrificial meal (Exod. 24). Throughout these and other texts, the Old Testament also emphasizes that the destructive power of water is subject to God's control. He brings about the flood and drowns Pharaoh's army in the sea. He conquers the beasts Leviathan and Rahab (Ps. 74; Isa. 51). He humbles the king of Tyre and the pharaoh (Ezek. 27–29), men who in their arrogance claim to have dominion over the waters.

In addition to putting Pharaoh's army to death, the waters of the Red Sea also serve as a symbol of the Israelites' redemption from slavery. This story has left a deep impression on the Old Testament, resounding throughout the Psalms and the Prophets, especially Isaiah. The freedom God gave to the Israelites, however, did not consist in mere autonomy. Rather, as I have argued, the freedom God gave the people of Israel found its fulfillment in their obeying his commandments and, even more importantly, worshiping him. One can see this reflected in the crossing of the river Jordan into the promised land, cul-

35. This theme pervades the New Testament. Among the many texts that attest to this pattern, see Matt. 10:38–39 and parallels.

minating in the celebration of the Passover, the sacrifice that commemorated Israel's redemption from Egypt. The primary purpose of obtaining the land was to establish a place where God would dwell in their midst.

Essential to approaching God's presence in the tabernacle, and later in the temple, was the concept of purity. Only those who were ritually pure could participate in the liturgical celebrations without fear, and one commonly recovered this purity through rites that involved bathing with water. Purity and impurity also were associated with sin. Certain heinous sins defiled the land, resulting eventually in the expulsion of the people; the collective sin of Israel brought about the people's exile. Thus, the prophet Isaiah exhorts the people to cleanse themselves from their sins of oppression and idolatry (Isa. 1:16–17), and the prophet Ezekiel conveys God's promise to purify the people from their sins (Ezek. 36:25–27). This purification would lead to the reestablishment of communion between God and Israel, symbolized most clearly in the gift of a new temple (Ezek. 40–48).

From this survey of Old Testament images of water, we can outline some contours of a biblical theology of baptism. Central to baptism is its connection with worship. Each group of texts associates the various effects of water—life, death, redemption, purity—with the worship of God. Through this entrance into worship, the baptized will receive true life, a life grounded in communion with God but a life that comes about through death. It is only by putting to death the "old human being" with his or her arrogance and pride that a person can enter God's presence. This entry into God's presence is true freedom, a freedom marked by purity from the sins that defile and exclude a person from that presence. In its baptismal references, the New Testament attests to these themes but interprets them in light of the passion, death, and resurrection of Christ.

PART 2

The Substance Belongs *to* Christ

Baptism in the New Testament

5

Christ, the Model of Baptism

> The LORD said to me, "You are my Son;
> today I have begotten you."
>
> —Psalm 2:7b ESV

Although the theology of baptism has deep roots in the Old Testament, the actual practice of baptism finds its origin in the ministry of John the Baptist. His nickname points to the newness of the rite he administered in the river Jordan. While ancient Jews regularly performed a variety of bathing rituals, what set John apart was that he plunged *other people* into the waters of the river. John's baptism is the most important immediate predecessor of the Christian sacrament of baptism, as can be seen in two aspects of the New Testament. Even after the gospel had begun to spread throughout the Mediterranean, there were still disciples who knew only of John's baptism (see Acts 19:1–6). More important, Jesus himself submitted to John's baptism, thus implicitly endorsing John's ministry and connecting it to his own. The washing in the Jordan is not the only narrative in the Gospels that uses baptismal language, however. In Mark and Luke, Jesus speaks of his own impending suffering and death as a kind of "baptism." In this chapter we will consider John's ministry of baptism as the context for the beginning of

Jesus's ministry as well as the connection between Jesus's baptism by John and Jesus's death. As we will see, the baptismal language in Matthew, Mark, and Luke shares important affinities with other discussions of baptism in the New Testament.

The Baptism of John

In one of the controversies with the Jewish leaders during Jesus's last days in Jerusalem, they ask him where he gets his authority. Rather than answer the question directly, Jesus asks them about the authority of John's baptism (Mark 11:27–33 and parallels). Jesus's answer (or nonanswer) implicitly affirms the authority of John. Unfortunately, the New Testament gives us only the briefest of accounts of John's baptism. Despite this scarcity of information, the symbolism of John's rite and the little material we do have in the Gospels is invaluable for understanding the early Christian movement. Three aspects of John's baptism bring out its theological significance: its location in the wilderness and the Jordan, its interpretation in light of the promises of Isaiah, and its connection with the forgiveness of sins.[1]

As we saw in chapter 3, the crossing of the Jordan served as the culmination of the exodus, as the people finally entered the land God had promised to their fathers. Several features of Joshua's account allude to the events of the exodus. Some of the Psalms bring the two events together (see, e.g., Pss. 66:6; 114:3–6). The Jordan also gained symbolic significance through the various activities of the prophets Elijah and Elisha as described in the books of Kings.[2] While these latter traditions may have played some role in John's choice of the Jordan for his activity, as well as in the evangelists' accounts of Jesus's baptism, it seems more likely that the entry of the people into the land was the most important aspect of the Jordan's symbolism with respect to John's baptism.

The Gospels describe John going out into the wilderness to call the people to repentance. The geographical symbolism of this choice would not have been lost on his audience. Those who went out to receive the baptism of

1. For a recent discussion of John's activity and its relation to Isa. 40, see Tucker S. Ferda, "John the Baptist, Isaiah 40, and the Ingathering of the Exiles," *JSHJ* 10 (2012): 154–88.

2. For a survey of patristic traditions relating to Elijah, Elisha, and the Jordan as types of baptism, see Jean Daniélou, *The Bible and the Liturgy* (Notre Dame, IN: University of Notre Dame Press, 1956), 99–113.

John entered the river from the wilderness and so symbolically reentered the land after being immersed in the water by John.[3] In other words, John's baptism replicated an important foundational event for the people of Israel. Such a gesture would have tapped into lively Jewish hopes of the first century.

All four Gospels interpret John's activity in light of the words of the prophet Isaiah, "In the wilderness prepare the way of the Lord" (Isa. 40:3b; see Matt. 3:3; Mark 1:3; Luke 3:4–6; John 1:23). These words from Isaiah, as well as their larger context, formed part of a profound hope among many first-century Jews.[4] In Isaiah 40–55, originally addressed to the Jews in their Babylonian exile, God promises that he will act once again to redeem his people. Although from the perspective of the first century the Jews had returned from Babylon some five hundred years earlier, at least some Jews of that time saw the fulfillment of Isaiah's words as incomplete. Stirred up by promises made in the writings of the prophets (not just Isaiah), many first-century Jews were hoping for a new exodus. The wilderness setting of Isaiah's promises would evoke Israel's wandering in the wilderness. Moreover, as we saw in chapter 3, the prophet frequently alludes to the crossing of the Red Sea in describing God's plans for Israel's future (see, e.g., Isa. 43:16–21; 51:9–11). By presenting John's baptism through the lens of these words of Isaiah, then, the evangelists suggest that his activity marks the beginning of the true fulfillment of these promises. John's emphasis on the forgiveness of sins further underscores the first-century Jewish hope for God's redeeming activity.

In the modern age, people see the forgiveness of sins predominantly in terms of the individual. Especially for Catholics, who (mercifully) practice the sacrament of confession in private, sins are treated primarily as a personal affair. The Old Testament certainly attests to this individual understanding of sin—one need think only of David's condemnation in 2 Samuel 12 or of Psalm 51, which came to be associated with David's misdeeds. Nevertheless, for ancient Jews sin also had an important corporate dimension. The Old Testament is filled with prayers acknowledging communal guilt, such as

3. See John Dominic Crossan, *The Historical Jesus: The Life of a Mediterranean Peasant* (San Francisco: HarperCollins, 1991), 231.

4. Several of the Dead Sea Scrolls draw on the imagery of Isa. 40, as do other Second Temple Jewish texts such as Baruch and the Psalms of Solomon. For a concise discussion of this tradition, see Ferda, "John the Baptist, Isaiah 40, and the Ingathering of the Exiles," 174–86.

Daniel's plea on behalf of Israel (Dan. 9:4–19) or Ezra's prayer in Nehemiah 9:6–37.[5]

It seems likely that, based on its connection with Isaiah and other prophetic oracles regarding Israel's sins, John's baptism addressed this corporate dimension of sin at least as much as the personal dimension. In the verse immediately before the words about preparing the way of the Lord, Isaiah writes,

> Speak tenderly to Jerusalem,
> and cry to her
> that she has served her term,
> *that her penalty is paid,*
> *that she has received from the* Lord*'s hand*
> *double for all her sins.* (Isa. 40:2)

The prophet speaks of the collective sins of Israel, not just of individual sins. Similarly, in one of the most famous oracles of Jeremiah, God says about Israel, "For I will forgive their iniquity, and remember their sin no more" (Jer. 31:34c). Both these verses appear in the context of God promising to redeem Israel after their exile.

Jesus's acceptance of John's baptism suggests that an important part of his mission was to fulfill these Jewish hopes. His baptism in the Jordan served as the public beginning of this mission.

The Baptism of Jesus

The connection between Jesus and John pervades all four Gospels, although each evangelist portrays this relationship in different ways. John, for example, particularly emphasizes the rivalry between the Baptist's disciples and Jesus's disciples, though this tension appears in some form in all four Gospels.[6] Despite these variations, all four refer to Jesus's baptism by John, and the synoptic Gospels share several important features in their account of the event.[7] Before examining each account, then, let us first consider the elements common to the three synoptic accounts of Jesus's baptism.

5. For a helpful discussion of this phenomenon, see John P. Meier, *A Marginal Jew: Rethinking the Historical Jesus*, 5 vols., AYBRL (New Haven: Yale University Press, 1991–2016), 2:113–15.
6. For John's account of this rivalry, see John 3:22–36; in the synoptic Gospels, see Mark 2:19–20 and parallels as well as Matt. 11:2–6 and Luke 7:18–23.
7. The Gospel of John alludes to Jesus's baptism by John most obliquely. See John 1:29–34.

Jesus's Royal Anointing and the Beginning of a New Creation

The three accounts of Jesus's baptism in Matthew, Mark, and Luke share the following features: (1) after Jesus is baptized, the heavens are opened; (2) the Spirit descends upon Jesus in the form of a dove; and (3) a voice comes from heaven, identifying Jesus as God's beloved Son. Each of these three elements has resonances with different parts of the Old Testament.[8]

The image of the heavens being opened evokes a passage discussed in chapter 3 above, one of the many Old Testament texts that appeal to the exodus as a model of Israel's hopes. The lengthy communal lament of Isaiah 63:7–64:11 draws on numerous features of the exodus in an appeal to God to save his people. At the heart of this appeal, the prophet pleads with the Lord: "O that you would tear open the heavens and come down, so that the mountains would quake at your presence" (Isa. 64:1). The opening of the heavens is not the only point of contact between Jesus's baptism and this passage from Isaiah. Earlier in the prayer the prophet appeals to Israel's crossing of the Red Sea, suggesting that the Lord had put his Spirit within them at that time (Isa. 63:11–12). Seen in this light, the evangelists present Jesus's baptism as the initial fulfillment of this hope. Jesus passes through the Jordan, a river closely associated with the Red Sea. Not only does he pass through it but he immerses himself in it and comes back out (cf. Isa. 63:11b: "Where is the one who brought them up out of the sea?"). After Jesus emerges from the water, God sends his Spirit upon him.

The descent of the Spirit would evoke not only this passage from Isaiah but also a few other texts from the Old Testament. On one level, the descent of the Spirit could allude to creation, thus characterizing Jesus's baptism as a new creation. In Genesis 1:2 the Spirit of God hovers over the chaotic waters that precede God's act of creation.[9] The first creation account, however, is not the only place in Genesis with bird imagery. At the end of the flood, as Noah awaits God's command to leave the ark, three times he sends out a dove that flies over the earth, newly emerged from the waters of the flood. The juxtaposition of the Spirit and the dove thus suggests that Jesus's baptism in some way resembles God's act of (new) creation.

In addition to the cosmic dimension of the descent of the Spirit, this aspect of Jesus's baptism also has messianic connotations. In at least two places

8. For an excellent exposition of the biblical and theological significance of Jesus's baptism, see Meier, *A Marginal Jew*, 2:106–7.

9. The Hebrew word used to describe the Spirit "hovering" also appears in contexts that describe the activity of a bird. For the use of this imagery among the Fathers, see Daniélou, *The Bible and the Liturgy*, 72–73.

in the Old Testament, the gift of the Spirit is associated with kings. When Samuel anoints David the son of Jesse as king, the Spirit of the Lord comes upon him (1 Kings 16:13). Isaiah, perhaps alluding to this tradition, likewise expresses hope for a new descendant of Jesse to usher in an era of justice and peace (Isa. 11:1–9). Just as the Spirit came upon David at the time of his anointing, so the Spirit will descend and rest upon the new king (11:1–3). Jesus's baptism, then, can also be seen as his royal anointing.[10]

This messianic interpretation of the Spirit's descent finds further confirmation in the words of the voice from heaven, which address Jesus as the "beloved Son." Many Christians tend to jump quickly to the conclusion that this title means everything that the name "Son" has come to mean for the Christian faith when applied to Jesus. While there are places in the New Testament where the title "Son" contains this fuller meaning, not every text that calls Jesus "Son" necessarily refers to his identity as the Second Person of the Trinity.[11] At times the Old Testament refers to Israel as God's "son" (Exod. 4:22–23; Hosea 11:1). Perhaps more importantly with reference to Jesus's baptism, the Old Testament also ascribes the title "son" to the king (2 Sam. 7:14; Ps. 2:7). In light of the messianic connotation of the Spirit's descent on Jesus, it seems likely that this is the primary meaning of the title at the baptism.

Jesus's baptism, then, is simultaneously an act of new creation and a fulfillment of God's promises to Israel to send them a new king in David's line. Fittingly, the event takes place at a location (the river Jordan) with profound symbolic value, connecting Jesus's baptism with the culmination of Israel's foundational saving event, the exodus. In addition to these common themes, each of the synoptic Gospels also brings out other dimensions of Jesus's baptism.

Matthew: Fulfilling All Righteousness as the Beloved Son

The most distinctive aspect of Matthew's account of Jesus's baptism is the dialogue between John and Jesus that precedes the actual baptism. When Jesus approaches to be baptized, John expresses reluctance, acknowledging his own need to be cleansed by Jesus (Matt. 3:13–14). In reply Jesus tells John, "Let it be so now; for it is proper for us in this way to fulfill all righteousness"

10. This seems to be the way that Luke interprets the event. See Jesus's synagogue sermon in Luke 4:16–21 as well as Peter's speech to Cornelius in Acts 10:37–38.

11. For a lucid discussion of the development of the understanding of Jesus as the "Son," see Joseph Ratzinger, *Introduction to Christianity*, trans. J. R. Foster and Michael J. Miller (San Francisco: Ignatius, 2004), 216–28.

The Iconography of Christ's Baptism

The classical icon of the Baptism of the Lord, also known as the Epiphany, integrates several scriptural images with later trinitarian theology. Reflecting all four Gospels, the image includes a dove coming forth from heaven and descending upon Jesus. As the name "Epiphany" implies, the imagery depicts the baptism as the first revelation of God's trinitarian life. In addition to understanding the dove as a symbol of the Holy Spirit, some early Christians interpreted it in light of the story of Noah. The dove in Genesis symbolizes a return of peace; the dove in the baptismal icon signifies God's mercy.[a] Jesus is frequently depicted as either wearing a loincloth or completely naked, reflecting both the ancient practice of baptism in the nude and the connection between his baptism and his crucifixion. In this regard, it is significant that the waters typically engulf his whole body, thus resembling a tomb.[b] Christ's submission to John's action indicates his self-humbling. Many icons also allude to the Old Testament by their inclusion of two figures riding sea creatures toward the bottom of the icon. These symbolize either the flight of the Jordan and the Red Sea referred to in Psalm 114:3 or Christ's victory over the sea creatures Rahab and Leviathan.

a. Leonid Ouspensky and Vladimir Lossky, *The Meaning of Icons*, 2nd ed. (Crestwood, NY: St. Vladimir's Seminary Press, 1982), 164–67.

b. Benedict XVI, *Jesus of Nazareth: From the Baptism in the Jordan to the Transfiguration*, trans. Adrian J. Walker (New York: Doubleday, 2007), 19.

(3:15b). The conversation between John and Jesus reflects the Christian belief in Jesus's sinlessness. Since John's baptism calls for repentance, the question naturally arises: Why did Jesus choose to be baptized? We will return to this question later in the chapter. For now, let us focus on the import of Jesus's words as well as another aspect of Matthew's telling of the event.

Jesus's reply is cryptic and has puzzled interpreters for some time. Part of the difficulty stems from the language of "fulfillment," which features prominently in Matthew's Gospel. The evangelist repeatedly presents the events of Jesus's life as "fulfilling" various prophecies from the Old Testament. Seven times in the first four chapters alone, Matthew uses a refrain to the effect of "This took place to fulfill what had been spoken through the prophet" (Matt. 1:22; 2:5, 15, 17, 23; 3:3; 4:14). Because of this repeated emphasis on fulfillment, some interpreters have taken Jesus's words in a similar vein, pointing to some aspect of the Old Testament that the baptism fulfills.[12]

Recently, Nathan Eubank has suggested a different interpretation of Jesus's words.[13] Although Matthew certainly uses the language of fulfillment to connect Jesus's life to the Old Testament, in Matthew 3:15 the word also seems to have other connotations.[14] This same word can mean to "fill up," either literally or metaphorically. Later in the Gospel, Matthew uses the word in just such a metaphorical way, as he upbraids the scribes and Pharisees for their misdeeds: "Fill up, then, the measure of your ancestors" (Matt. 23:32). Similar imagery appears in 2 Maccabees, as the author notes that in some cases the Lord does not punish certain nations until "the full measure of their sins" is completed (2 Macc. 6:14). Eubank suggests that Jesus's words point to a corresponding measure of righteousness. Through his mission, Jesus accrues the righteousness necessary to save his people (cf. Matt. 1:21). In this regard, it is significant that Jesus describes his death as a "ransom payment" for the many (Matt. 20:28). Jesus's submission to baptism is the beginning of this process of filling up all righteousness, which he accomplishes through acts of humility and obedience, especially through the cross. As he notes later in the Gospel, his ministry is one of service and of self-gift for the many: "The Son of Man came not to be served but to serve, and to give his life [as] a ransom for many" (20:28). This first act of submission to baptism, then, points forward to his self-gift on the cross. Jesus's kingship is oriented toward self-sacrifice.

Another feature of Matthew's account suggests this connection between Jesus's baptism and the cross—namely, his identification by the voice from heaven as the "beloved Son."[15] For many first-century Jews, the phrase would

12. For a survey of the possible ways to interpret the phrase "fulfill all righteousness," see W. D. Davies and Dale C. Allison Jr., *A Critical and Exegetical Commentary on the Gospel according to St. Matthew*, 3 vols., ICC (Edinburgh: T&T Clark, 1988–97), 1:325–27. Davies and Allison describe the reading of the phrase as referring to the fulfillment of prophecy as "the most convincing approach" (326).

13. Nathan Eubank, *Wages of Cross-Bearing and Debt of Sin: The Economy of Heaven in Matthew's Gospel*, BZNW 196 (Berlin: de Gruyter, 2013), 121–32. I have relied on Eubank for most of what follows regarding the phrase "fill up all righteousness."

14. Matthew most frequently uses the word *plēroō* with the sense of "fulfillment" of the Old Testament. Of the sixteen occurrences of the word in Matthew, thirteen have the connotation of fulfilling Scripture in some way (1:22; 2:15, 17, 23; 4:14; 5:17; 8:17; 12:17; 13:35; 21:4; 26:54, 56; 27:9). However, he can also use the word with the meaning of "filling up," either literally (13:48) or figuratively (23:32). On Eubank's reading, the use in 3:15 matches that in 23:32.

15. While it is true that all three synoptic Gospels use this title, Matthew develops the title more fully in other ways. For what follows, I have relied on Leroy Andrew Huizenga, *The New Isaac: Tradition and Intertextuality in the Gospel of Matthew*, NovTSup 131 (Leiden: Brill, 2009).

have evoked one of the most haunting stories in the Bible: the Binding of Isaac (Gen. 22:1–19), as the story came to be known. In the Hebrew text, God refers to Isaac three times as Abraham's "only" son (22:2, 12, 16). Later Greek translations, however, rendered the phrase as "your beloved son," and the expression was closely associated with Isaac.[16]

Other elements of the baptism connect the event with Abraham's (near) sacrifice of Isaac. The voice from heaven at Jesus's baptism resembles the voice of the angel of the Lord who twice calls out to Abraham "from heaven" in order to prevent the sacrifice (Gen. 22:11–12, 15–16). Matthew in particular draws other subtle connections between Jesus and Isaac elsewhere in the Gospel, which famously begins, "The book of the genesis of Jesus the Christ, the son of David, the son of Abraham" (Matt. 1:1, my translation).[17] Most translations render the second word of Matthew's Gospel as "genealogy." While in general this is a fine translation, the Greek word literally is *genesis*, which would evoke not just Jesus's ancestry but also the story of Israel's origins. In this light, it is significant that Matthew begins the genealogy by highlighting two of Jesus's ancestors, David the king and Abraham. The son of Abraham, the son of the promise, is Isaac.[18] Moreover, just as Isaac was conceived under unusual circumstances by an elderly woman well past childbearing years, so Jesus was conceived under unusual circumstances, from a Virgin by the power of the Holy Spirit.[19] These allusions to Isaac's life thus prepare the reader for the connection to the baptism.

But what does all this have to do with Jesus's humility and obedience, much less the cross? According to Jewish interpretations of the Isaac story current at the time of the New Testament, Abraham's son was already a full-grown man when his father took him to Moriah.[20] Because Abraham was an elderly man, Isaac could have easily overpowered him and escaped. Instead, according to these traditions, Isaac willingly offered himself up on the mountain. One representative of this tradition can be found in 4 Maccabees, a philosophical treatise that draws on examples from the Jewish revolt against Antiochus IV

16. In Hebrew, the expression is *et-binka et-yehidka*; in Greek, *ton huion sou ton agapēton*.

17. On the translation of Matt. 1:1, see Dale C. Allison Jr., *Studies in Matthew: Interpretation Past and Present* (Grand Rapids: Baker Academic, 2005), 157–62.

18. Paul highlights this aspect of Isaac's identity in Gal. 4:21–5:1.

19. For more details on the connections between these two conceptions, see Huizenga, *The New Isaac*, 144–51.

20. For an excellent discussion of the development of this tradition, see Jon D. Levenson, *The Death and Resurrection of the Beloved Son* (New Haven: Yale University Press, 1993), esp. 173–99.

in the second century BC. Perhaps the most famous of these examples is the story of the seven brothers and their mother who suffered death rather than transgress the law of Moses. Toward the end of the account, the author narrates the way the brothers exhorted one another:

> "Let us not be cowardly in the demonstration of our piety." While one said, "Courage, brother," another said, "Bear up nobly," and another reminded them, "Remember whence you came, and the father *by whose hand Isaac would have submitted to being slain for the sake of religion*." (4 Macc. 13:10–12)

The text speaks of Isaac willingly going to his death in a much more explicit way than the account of Genesis suggests. The first-century Jewish historian Flavius Josephus also reflects this tradition in his telling of the Binding of Isaac:

> The son of such a father could not but be brave-hearted, and Isaac received these words with joy. He exclaimed that he deserved never to have been born at all, were he to reject the decision of God and of his father and not readily resign himself to what was the will of both, seeing that, were this the resolution of his father alone, it would have been impious to disobey; and with that he rushed to the altar and his doom. (Josephus, *Antiquities of the Jews* 1.232 [trans. Thackeray, LCL])

On Josephus's telling, Isaac not only accepts the will of God—he accepts it with joy and rushes to offer himself on the altar, only to be thwarted by God's intervention. Many early Christians saw Isaac's obedience as a prefiguration of Christ's (see, e.g., *1 Clement* 31:3).

The parallels between Jesus and Isaac, then, foreshadow Jesus's self-gift on the cross. Like Isaac, Jesus obeys his Father and carries the wood for the sacrifice up the mountain. The allusions to Isaac at the baptism scene thus point forward to the cross and interpret Jesus's reception of this water immersion as an anticipation of his complete gift of self, by which he "fulfills all righteousness."[21]

21. Some works on baptism question whether Jesus himself interpreted his baptism in this way. See G. R. Beasley-Murray, *Baptism in the New Testament* (Grand Rapids: Eerdmans, 1962), 52–53. Beasley-Murray is responding to Oscar Cullmann, who argues the opposite point (*Baptism in the New Testament*, trans. J. K. S. Reid [London: SCM, 1964], 15–20). While the question is an interesting one, the present work is more concerned with the way the evangelists present and interpret the event than with Jesus's own intentions in receiving baptism. As we will see in the next part of the chapter, Mark also connects the baptism with Jesus's gift of self on the cross. Given these connections, as well as the way Jesus later uses baptismal language

Mark: "Truly This Man Was the Son of God"

Mark also weaves images from the crucifixion into his account of Jesus's baptism by John, thus connecting the two events. In particular, the phrasing of the message addressed to Jesus from heaven and the way in which Mark describes the opening of the heavens subtly prefigure the circumstances of Jesus's death. For Mark that death is not the unfortunate and unjust death of a righteous man but rather the key to understanding Jesus's identity as the Son of God.

One of the most prominent features of Mark's Gospel is a theme that scholars since the early twentieth century have referred to as the "Messianic Secret."[22] This phrase, coined by the German scholar William Wrede, points to some important characteristics of Mark, though it is actually a misnomer. Secrecy certainly abounds in Mark's Gospel: people frequently wonder aloud who Jesus is, and he, in turn, regularly enjoins people to keep quiet about the healings and miracles he performs.[23] But the primary secret in Mark is not so much that Jesus is the Messiah—Peter himself recognizes and confesses this by the midpoint of the Gospel (Mark 8:29). Instead, the secret concerns what it means for Jesus to be the "Son of God." Throughout Mark's Gospel, the demons seem to be the only ones who see this, and Jesus commands silence whenever they try to make him known (e.g., 1:25, 34). In contrast to Matthew, not a single human being openly calls Jesus the "Son of God" until nearly the end of Mark, when the centurion confesses Jesus's identity at the moment of his death on the cross (15:39). This confession serves as a bookend to the scene of Jesus's baptism in Mark 1.

Comparing Matthew's version of the baptism with Mark's reveals an important difference in the words from heaven. Whereas in Matthew the voice says, "This is my beloved Son" (Matt. 3:17 [NRSV marginal note]), in Mark the voice says, "*You* are my beloved Son" (Mark 1:11 [NRSV marginal note]). Matthew's version, with the demonstrative pronoun, could be interpreted as an announcement to the world. By contrast, in Mark the words from heaven seem to be a personal address directed only to Jesus. The rest of the Gospel bears this out, as no human being calls Jesus the Son of God until the centurion at the crucifixion. One can see this contrast between Matthew and

---

to describe his impending death (Mark 10:38 and Luke 12:50), it seems plausible, at the very least, that Jesus understood his baptism as an anticipation of the cross.

22. William Wrede, *The Messianic Secret*, trans. J. C. G. Greig (London: James Clarke, 1971). The original German edition appeared in 1901. For some criticisms of Wrede's thesis, see, among others, Jack Dean Kingsbury, *The Christology of Mark's Gospel* (Philadelphia: Fortress, 1983).

23. For speculation about Jesus's identity, see Mark 1:27; 4:41; 6:3; for injunctions to silence, see 1:44; 5:43; 9:9.

Mark in a number of other places. For example, in Matthew's version of Jesus walking on the water, when Jesus gets into the boat, the disciples confess, "Truly you are the Son of God" (Matt. 14:33b). Mark, on the other hand, has no such confession (Mark 6:45–52). Mark's version of Peter's confession likewise reflects this secrecy motif. Whereas in Matthew Peter tells Jesus, "You are the Messiah, *the Son of the living God*" (Matt. 16:16), in Mark Peter simply says, "You are the Messiah," full stop (Mark 8:29).

Many interpreters have suggested with good reason that the suppression of the title "Son of God" on the lips of human beings throughout much of the Gospel is deliberate on Mark's part. He does so to heighten the tension and the mystery surrounding Jesus's identity, but also to direct his audience to a proper understanding of what it means for Jesus to be the Son of God. At the heart of that identity lies not the many mighty deeds he performs but rather his complete gift of self as a ransom for the many (Mark 10:45). It is worth noting that at one other point in Mark's Gospel, at the transfiguration (9:2–8), God identifies Jesus as his Son. Significantly, this event follows immediately after Peter's confession, Jesus's first passion prediction, and the call to take up one's cross and follow Christ (8:27–9:1). At the transfiguration the Father, in addition to identifying Jesus as his Son, tells the disciples, "Listen to him!" (9:7). At the beginning, at the middle, and at the end of Mark's Gospel, then, Jesus's sonship and his crucifixion go hand in hand. This suggests that Mark closely associates Jesus's baptism with his death on the cross.

Another element of the baptism scene connects it to the crucifixion. Mark offers a much more vivid description of the opening of the heavens than Matthew and Luke do. Rather than writing simply that the heavens were "opened," Mark writes, "And just as he was coming up out of the water, he saw *the heavens torn apart* and the Spirit descending like a dove on him" (Mark 1:10). The imagery of the heavens being "torn apart" points both backward and forward. Looking backward, Mark evokes the passage from Isaiah 64 (discussed above) more clearly than Matthew and Luke do. Looking forward, Mark's language of "tearing" reappears at Jesus's death, when the temple veil is "torn in two, from top to bottom" (Mark 15:38). The ordering of the events surrounding Jesus's death is significant: Jesus dies (15:37), the temple veil is torn in two (15:38), and the centurion identifies Jesus as the "Son of God" (15:39 [NRSV marginal note]). In the baptism we have a similar sequence: Jesus is baptized (Mark 1:9), the heavens are torn open (1:10), and the voice from heaven acknowledges Jesus as God's Son (1:11). In this way, Mark's account of the baptism subtly anticipates the events of Jesus's death and presents the two events as crucial for understanding Jesus's identity as the Son of God.

Luke: Anointing, Prayer, Solidarity

Luke offers a succinct account of Jesus's baptism, spanning only two verses. Despite its brevity, Luke adds important elements to the New Testament understanding of the baptism. Specifically, he underscores the nature of the event as Jesus's anointing, highlights his prayer at the time of his baptism, and presents him in solidarity with the people.

As noted above, the descent of the Spirit upon Jesus at his baptism signifies, among other things, his messianic anointing. Luke makes this aspect of the baptism even clearer by the material that surrounds his account of the event.[24] Shortly before Jesus's baptism, in Luke's description of John's preaching, he notes, "All were questioning in their hearts concerning John, *whether he might be the Messiah*" (Luke 3:15). John implicitly denies the status of messiahship by pointing forward to another who will baptize with the Holy Spirit and bring judgment (Luke 3:16–17). Both the people's questioning and John's response set up an expectation that Luke answers in Jesus's baptism and his sermon at Nazareth. Indeed, the sermon confirms explicitly what the description of the baptism implicitly suggests: that it was Jesus's messianic anointing. In the synagogue at Nazareth Jesus reads from the prophet Isaiah,

> The Spirit of the Lord is upon me,
> because he has anointed me
> to bring good news to the poor. (Luke 4:18, citing Isa. 61:1)

The selection of this passage from Isaiah is significant because it suggests that Jesus's anointing marks him out not only as a king but also as a prophet.[25]

In keeping with one of his favorite themes, Luke also portrays Jesus as praying at the time of the baptism. Jesus is a model of prayer, conversing with his Father at many of the most significant points in his ministry. In addition to the baptism, Jesus prays before choosing the Twelve (Luke 6:12), at the

24. See Mark Strauss, *The Davidic Messiah in Luke-Acts: The Promise and Its Fulfillment in Lukan Christology* (Sheffield, UK: Sheffield Academic, 1995), 200–203.

25. This multifaceted understanding of messiahship seems to be a consistent aspect of Luke's portrayal of Jesus. In Peter's first speech in the Acts of the Apostles, he refers to King David as a prophet (Acts 2:29–30). See again Strauss, *The Davidic Messiah in Luke-Acts*, 131–47.

time of Peter's confession (9:18), and at the transfiguration (9:29). For Luke, Jesus's baptism combines a ritual washing with prayer, a beautiful illustration of the close bond between word and sacrament.

Finally, Luke also emphasizes Jesus's solidarity with the people in receiving baptism. He introduces the revelation of Jesus's identity as the Son of God by presenting him together with the people: "Now when all the people were baptized, and when Jesus also had been baptized and was praying, the heaven was opened" (Luke 3:21). Although Jesus's identity is certainly unique, he nevertheless stands with the people. This solidarity helps to address the question of whether Jesus receives John's baptism because he has any sins of which to repent. In the ancient Jewish tradition, prayers of repentance need not imply personal sin.[26] Both Ezra the priest and the prophet Daniel offer prayers of repentance on behalf of the people (Neh. 9:6–37; Dan. 9:4–19). Neither of these men would be considered a "sinner" in ancient Israel, yet both identify with the communal guilt of the people. In the same way, by accepting John's baptism Jesus places himself squarely in the midst of the people, joining with them in their plea for forgiveness.

Jesus's Death as a Baptism

In addition to using baptismal language literally with respect to the ritual John introduced, the New Testament also depicts Jesus speaking on at least one occasion of a metaphorical baptism that he is to undergo (Mark 10:35–45; cf. Luke 12:50). In light of the connections Mark draws between Jesus's baptism and his death on the cross, it should come as no surprise that Jesus uses baptismal imagery to signify his impending fate at Jerusalem.

The context of this saying is Jesus's third and final passion prediction in Mark, shortly before he and his disciples arrive at Jerusalem. Three times in Mark Jesus predicts his passion, death, and resurrection, only to be met with the disciples' lack of understanding, which he subsequently corrects (Mark 8:31–9:1; 9:30–37; 10:32–45).[27] Following his third prediction, James and John approach Jesus and ask that they might sit at his right and at his left in his glory (10:35–37). Rather than answer their request directly, Jesus

26. See again Meier, *A Marginal Jew*, 2:113–15.

27. Richard B. Hays, *The Moral Vision of the New Testament: Community, Cross, New Creation; A Contemporary Introduction to New Testament Ethics* (San Francisco: HarperSanFrancisco, 1996), 80–82.

Anointed to Bring Good News to the Poor

One of the prayers for the Church's celebration of the feast of the Baptism of the Lord has a particularly Lukan ring to it, as it brings together Jesus's anointing with his mission to preach good news to the poor:

> For in the waters of the Jordan you revealed with signs and wonders a new Baptism, so that . . . by the Spirit's descending in the likeness of a dove we might know that Christ your Servant has been anointed with the oil of gladness and sent to bring the good news to the poor.[a]

a. *The Roman Missal* (Totowa, NJ: Catholic Book Publishing, 2011), 67.

poses a question: "You do not know what you are asking. Are you able to drink the cup that I drink, *or be baptized with the baptism that I am baptized with*?" (10:38). When the two brothers reply with more than a touch of self-confidence that they can, Jesus, rather than granting their request, informs them that they will in fact undergo such a fate but that it is not for him to give the seats that they request (10:39–40).

Most interpreters rightly take the language of "baptism" and "cup" as pointing to Jesus's crucifixion. At least two features of the text support such a reading. First, the imagery of baptism, which originally meant immersion or submersion in water, fits with the tradition of the psalm texts discussed in chapter 2, where the overwhelming power of water frequently appears as a threat of death (see, e.g., Pss. 69:14–15; 88:6–7). Second, the language of the "cup" appears at another crucial moment in Mark: Jesus's prayer in Gethsemane. There, on the cusp of his arrest and crucifixion, Jesus prays, "Abba, Father, for you all things are possible; remove *this cup* from me; yet, not what I want, but what you want" (Mark 14:36). In light of Jesus's three passion predictions, as well as his words to the disciples at the Last Supper (14:18, 27), the cup must refer to the death he is about to undergo.

Mark's account of the institution of the Eucharist further confirms this interpretation, as Jesus identifies a cup with the shedding of his blood. In between his conversation with James and John and his prayer in Gethsemane, Jesus anticipates his crucifixion and institutes a ritual to commemorate it. As

Mark writes, "Then he took *a cup*, and after giving thanks he gave it to them, and all of them drank from it. He said to them, 'This is my blood of the covenant, which is poured out for many'" (Mark 14:23–24). These three occurrences of the word "cup"—in the third passion prediction, at the Last Supper, and in Gethsemane—establish a close connection between the rite of the Eucharist and Jesus's death. In light of this connection and of the widespread early Christian practice of baptism, it seems likely that Mark sees a similar symbolism behind the latter. The two most foundational rites of the early Christians both interpret and draw their power from Christ's death and resurrection. It is hardly surprising, then, that other early Christian writers also associate baptism with Jesus's death and resurrection (see, e.g., Rom. 6:2–11). Indeed, Jesus's response to James and John is an implicit invitation to participate in his gift of self on the cross. Regardless of whether Jesus himself intended to draw a connection between the metaphorical baptism he was about to undergo and the actual rite of baptism, the baptismal language of his response to James and John seems to have influenced early Christian interpretation of the sacrament.

Christ, the Model of Baptism

None of the passages we have considered in this chapter explicitly describes the Christian sacrament of baptism. On an important level, Christ's baptism by John is unique. Jesus alone is the messianic Son of God, the Father's beloved in whom he is well pleased. Jesus alone has the unique mission of giving his life as a ransom for many. Jesus alone is the beginning of the new creation. This uniqueness notwithstanding, the baptismal language and imagery of the synoptic Gospels nevertheless also informs Christian baptismal theology in at least three ways. First, Jesus's baptism and use of baptismal language in one of the passion predictions underscores the connection between baptism and the cross. Second, the Father's acknowledgment of Jesus's unique sonship at the baptism points forward to the adoptive sonship that Christians receive through their baptism (see Gal. 3:26–29). Finally, the close thematic links between baptismal language, Jesus's death, and the Last Supper suggest that Christian baptism is oriented toward the central Christian act of worship, the Holy Eucharist.

6

Christ, the Source of Baptism

Then he brought me back to the door of the temple; there, water was flowing from below the threshold of the temple toward the east.

—Ezekiel 47:1a

Toward the end of John's Gospel, in a moment charged with symbolic significance, one of the Roman soldiers pierces Jesus's side with a lance, and immediately blood and water flow out (John 19:34). This outpouring of water evokes several Old Testament passages that describe a river flowing out from the temple, one of the primary images John uses to interpret Jesus's body (see, e.g., John 2:21).[1] The final reference to water in this Gospel serves as the culmination of a prominent motif. John repeatedly appeals to the symbolic value of water to interpret various aspects of Jesus's ministry and teaching. Just as the water symbolism of the Old Testament sheds light on the Christian theology of baptism, so too John's water symbolism can illuminate the meaning of the sacrament. The Johannine water motif makes at least four contributions to a theology of baptism: baptism brings about new birth,

1. Many studies have explored the temple imagery in John. See, e.g., Mary L. Coloe, *God Dwells with Us: Temple Symbolism in the Fourth Gospel* (Collegeville, MN: Liturgical Press, 2001); Mark Kinzer, "Temple Christology in the Gospel of John," in *Society of Biblical Literature Seminar Papers* 27, ed. David Lull (Missoula, MT: Scholars Press, 1988), 447–64.

baptism is closely associated with the Spirit, baptism effects healing, and baptism serves as a call to imitate Christ through the complete gift of self in service to others. Moreover, in a manner analogous to the synoptic accounts of Jesus's baptism, the Johannine water symbolism subtly draws a close connection between baptism and the Eucharist.

"You Must Be Born from Above"

John does not explicitly describe Jesus's baptism in the Jordan but simply alludes to it in the words of John the Baptist (John 1:30). Nevertheless, the early chapters of this Gospel are saturated with baptismal imagery. Like Matthew, Mark, and Luke, the body of the Fourth Gospel begins with the baptizing activity of John. When leaders from Jerusalem come to question John regarding his ministry, he indicates that the primary purpose of his activity is to reveal the one who is to come after him (John 1:26–27). The next day, when Jesus approaches, John testifies to his identity, indirectly alluding to Jesus's reception of this baptism. John notes that he himself came baptizing "that he [i.e., Jesus] might be revealed to Israel" (1:31). Moreover, he describes what happened at the baptism: "I saw the Spirit descending from heaven like a dove, and it remained on him" (1:32).[2] From the first chapter of the Gospel, then, baptism is closely associated with the gift of the Spirit.

A little later in the Gospel, the evangelist once again refers to baptism, noting that at some point Jesus and John had a parallel ministry, with Jesus and his disciples baptizing in the Judean countryside and John continuing to baptize at Aenon near Salim (John 3:22–23). This parallel activity causes some concern among John's disciples, and they point out to him that Jesus's baptism is taking followers away from him (3:26). In keeping with his vocation to testify to the light (1:7), John reminds his disciples of his identity as a witness and a revealer, not as the Christ (3:27–29). In words that every Christian should appropriate, John says of Christ, "He must increase, but I must decrease" (3:30). This leads into a brief meditation on Jesus's identity as the one sent from heaven (3:31–36).[3]

2. On the messianic significance of this imagery, see Joshua W. Jipp, *The Messianic Theology of the New Testament* (Grand Rapids: Eerdmans, 2020), 119–27.

3. As is often the case in John's Gospel, it is difficult to determine whether this meditation continues John the Baptist's words to his disciples or whether it is the evangelist's own commentary on the events. Thankfully, the answer to that question does not affect the present point.

It is worth highlighting one aspect of this meditation—namely, its emphasis once again on the Spirit: "He whom God has sent speaks the words of God, for he gives the Spirit without measure. The Father loves the Son and has placed all things in his hands" (John 3:34–35). Interpreters disagree about who "gives the Spirit without measure," the Father or the Son.[4] The Gospel speaks elsewhere of both the Father and the Son imparting the Spirit (14:26; 15:26). Whatever the case may be, it is significant that this reference to the gift of the Spirit appears in the context of a discussion of baptism. In fact, it is immediately followed by one more reference to Jesus's baptismal activity, though the evangelist quickly offers the correction that it was only Jesus's disciples who were baptizing and not Jesus himself (4:1–2).[5]

Situated as it is between these two references to the Baptist's ministry and shortly before the reference to Jesus's baptismal activity, the conversation between Jesus and Nicodemus must be interpreted in light of these episodes.[6] This dialogue is filled with important symbols: water, new birth, the Spirit, and the lifting up of the serpent in the wilderness. At the time of the Passover, and moved by the signs Jesus has performed, Nicodemus comes to him by night for instruction (John 3:1–2).[7] An important point of the conversation turns on one of John's favorite literary techniques, double meaning and misunderstanding. Jesus tells Nicodemus, "No one can see the kingdom of God without being born *anōthen*" (3:3). The Greek word *anōthen* has two meanings, "again" and "from above." Nicodemus, mistakenly interpreting the word only in the first sense, takes Jesus's statement as absurd: "How can anyone be born after having grown old? Can one enter a second time into the mother's womb and be born?" (3:4). Jesus then clarifies his meaning, speaking of a birth of water and the Spirit: "Very truly, I tell you, no one can enter the kingdom of God without being born of water and Spirit" (3:5).[8]

We have already seen connections between water and the Spirit, once (indirectly) in John's description of the Spirit's descent upon Jesus (John 1:32–33)

4. See Raymond E. Brown, *The Gospel according to John*, 2 vols., AB 29–29A (New York: Doubleday, 1966, 1970), 1:161–62.

5. The reason for this correction has to do with the Gospel's later statement that the Spirit was not given until after Jesus's death (John 7:37–39).

6. See the helpful discussion in G. R. Beasley-Murray, *Baptism in the New Testament* (Grand Rapids: Eerdmans, 1962), 227–30.

7. The last reference to time before the conversation with Nicodemus indicates that it was Passover (John 2:23), and John gives no indication of a change of setting. See Brown, *John*, 1:129.

8. It is perhaps worth noting here that in 1 Cor. 6 Paul closely associates the kingdom of God with baptism (1 Cor. 6:9–11). See the discussion of this text in chaps. 7 and 11 below.

and then, toward the end of John 3, in the description of the baptismal activity of Jesus and his disciples. Moreover, with the exception of the water turned into wine at the wedding feast at Cana (2:1–11), every use of the word "water" to this point has referred to baptism. Given this context, the new birth Jesus proposes to Nicodemus must refer to baptism.[9] Seen in this light, the double meaning of the Greek word *anōthen* serves not only to further the dialogue between Jesus and Nicodemus but also to point to the reality of baptism, which is simultaneously a new, spiritual birth and a birth from above, a birth from the Spirit (3:8). This birth from above resembles Jesus's own experience at his baptism, when the Spirit descended and remained upon him (1:32).

Toward the end of the dialogue between Jesus and Nicodemus, Jesus adds two important and closely related elements: the cross and faith. Nicodemus has asked for clarification about this new birth (John 3:9), and in response Jesus appeals to his descent from heaven. He then points forward to the fate he will meet at another Passover in Jerusalem: "And just as Moses lifted up the serpent in the wilderness, so must the Son of Man be lifted up, that whoever believes in him may have eternal life" (3:14–15).[10] Although the accent of Jesus's baptismal teaching in John 3 falls primarily on new birth and the Spirit, John also links baptism to the cross, though in a more subtle way.[11] Moreover, this last element of Jesus's conversation with Nicodemus underscores the importance of faith. Indeed, the meditation that follows (3:16–21) emphasizes the importance of faith for coming to eternal life.[12] Furthermore, this passage draws on another of John's favorite images—namely, light. The close connection between baptism or water and light is common throughout the New Testament, and it explains the popularity of the name "illumination" for baptism in the early Church.[13] Baptism is not simply a new birth but also the enlightening of the mind to know God and so to come to eternal life.

9. So also Lars Hartman, *"Into the Name of the Lord Jesus": Baptism in the Early Church*, SNTW (Edinburgh: T&T Clark, 1997), 156–57.

10. In John, the "lifting up" of Jesus may also refer to his ascension (8:28; 12:32). So Hartman, *"Into the Name,"* 157.

11. Oscar Cullmann puts it well: "Baptism is the Christ event become present." See Cullmann, *Early Christian Worship*, trans. A. Stewart Todd and James B. Torrance, SBT 10 (London: SCM, 1953), 77.

12. As with John 3:31–36, it is unclear whether 3:16–21 should be interpreted as a continuation of Jesus's speech to Nicodemus or as the evangelist's meditation on the conversation. Again, the answer to this question does not make much difference to the present discussion.

13. See Gregory of Nazianzus, *Oration* 40; Clement of Alexandria, *The Instructor* 1.6.

Water and the Spirit

The intimate association between water and the Spirit, first indicated by the Gospel's allusion to Jesus's baptism (John 1:32) and made more explicit in Jesus's late-night conversation with Nicodemus (3:1–8), reappears numerous times throughout the Fourth Gospel. Indeed, the very next chapter returns to this theme in the famous encounter between Jesus and the Samaritan woman at the well. Water and the Spirit serve as the central images of their conversation, prompted by their location at Jacob's well.

As is often the case in John's Gospel, double meaning and misunderstanding drive the story, with Jesus speaking on a higher level and the woman at first seeing things only on an earthly level. The dialogue begins, however, with Jesus making a simple earthly request: "Give me a drink" (John 4:7). When the woman objects to his request based on the long-standing animosity between the Samaritans and the Jews (4:9), Jesus quickly shifts to speaking of things in the spiritual realm, referring to living water (4:10). The woman, missing the shift in Jesus's meaning, asks him how he expects to get water without anything to draw with and (with a hint of Johannine irony) asks further if he is greater than their father Jacob (4:11–12). In response, Jesus gives another subtle indication that he is speaking not of ordinary, earthly water but rather of a higher reality: "Everyone who drinks of this water [i.e., the water from Jacob's well] will be thirsty again, but those who drink of the water that I will give them will never be thirsty. The water that I will give will become in them a spring of water *gushing up to eternal life*" (4:13–14). Despite Jesus's hints, the woman nevertheless remains on the earthly level, thinking that if she can have the water Jesus offers, she will no longer have to go to the well (4:15).

At this point, Jesus takes a different tack, demonstrating his prophetic knowledge of the woman's past. This leads to another shift in the conversation, turning to the question of authentic worship. The thread that holds the conversation together is Jesus's reference to the Spirit, which the water in the story symbolizes. In response to the woman's question about the proper place of worship, Jesus replies by speaking of worshiping the Father "in the Spirit and in truth" (John 4:23–24, modified). The shift from water to Spirit language suggests that the two are closely related. Moreover, it suggests that the water Jesus offers—the water that wells up to eternal life—is oriented to true worship of the Father.

Even though Jesus in this passage speaks not of ordinary, earthly water but rather of a spiritual reality, his words also have implications for a theology of baptism. The story follows shortly after the conversation with Nicodemus and the description of John's and Jesus's baptismal activity.[14] Moreover, the smooth transition from the discussion of living water to worship in the Spirit and in

Robin Margaret Jensen

Figure 2. Johannine water scenes in the Baptistery of Santa Restituta, Naples

14. On the connection between Jesus's conversation with the Samaritan woman and his conversation with Nicodemus, see Cullmann, *Early Christian Worship*, 81–82.

Johannine Water Themes in Ancient Baptisteries and Homilies

Ancient baptisteries confirm that many early Christians interpreted baptism through the lens of the water imagery in John's Gospel. Among the motifs that appear in some of these churches are Jesus's meeting with the Samaritan woman at the well and the jars of the wedding feast at Cana (see figure 2). The latter scene was taken by some to symbolize "the transformation of ordinary water into a spiritual substance, thus prefiguring the eucharist that the newly baptized receive for the first time."[a] Similarly, in order to interpret the sacrament, early homilies drew on episodes from John's Gospel that do not explicitly refer to baptism.

a. Robin Margaret Jensen, *Living Water: Images, Symbols, and Settings of Early Christian Baptism*, Supplements to Vigiliae Christianae 105 (Leiden: Brill, 2011), 279.

truth also reflects the meeting with Nicodemus, in which water and the Spirit are closely connected. Seen in this light, the encounter with the Samaritan woman suggests that baptism is closely bound up with worship.

The imagery of thirst and of living water reappears in John 7. Here the identification of this water with the Spirit becomes explicit. On the last day of the Feast of Tabernacles, Jesus makes an offer similar to the one he had made to the Samaritan woman: "Let anyone who is thirsty come to me, and let the one who believes in me drink. As the scripture has said, 'Out of his heart shall flow rivers of living water'" (7:37–38, modified). This brief statement contains an ambiguity as well as some important allusions to the Old Testament.

Interpreters disagree about the referent of the pronoun "his" in the phrase "out of his heart shall flow rivers of living water."[15] On the one hand, some argue that the most natural way to read the Greek is to take the pronoun to refer back to "the one who believes in me." In other words, on this interpretation Jesus promises that rivers of living water will flow from *the believer*.[16]

15. For a concise discussion of the issues involved, with references to scholars on both sides of the issue, see Coloe, *God Dwells with Us*, 125–28.

16. This is how the NRSV interprets the verse.

While this might seem like an unusual promise, recall that in his conversation with the Samaritan woman Jesus tells her, "The water that I will give will become *in them* a spring of water gushing up to eternal life" (John 4:14b). Reading John 7:38 as referring to the believer thus has precedent and would continue a theme begun earlier in the Gospel.

On the other hand, at least two aspects of the text might suggest that the one out of whose "heart" (literally, "belly") the living water will flow is Jesus himself. First, toward the end of John, water literally flows out of Jesus's side after his death on the cross (John 19:34). It would be fitting, then, for this earlier verse also to refer to Jesus. Second, Jesus's brief statement also alludes to several of the Old Testament texts considered above in chapter 1. His invitation to come and drink evokes the offer of water and food in Isaiah 55. Perhaps more importantly, the rivers of living water would bring to mind the final vision of Ezekiel—in which just such a river streams forth from the temple, giving life to all the surrounding land—as well as the other prophetic texts that witness to such a tradition.[17] Particularly given John's identification of Jesus's body with the new temple (John 2:21), it would make more sense for the rivers of water to stream from the heart of Christ than from the believer.

It is possible that the ambiguity is intentional. After all, John does draw a close connection between Jesus and believers. In John 15 Jesus describes himself as the vine and his disciples as the branches, suggesting that they participate in his own life. Perhaps in the statement of John 7:38 there is a subtle indication of how believers become a part of the temple of Jesus's body. Regardless of the solution to the question, Jesus offers living water, and here John explicitly clarifies that the water refers to the Spirit: "Now he said this about the Spirit, which believers in him were to receive; for as yet there was no Spirit, because Jesus was not yet glorified" (7:39). Once again, as in the conversation with the Samaritan woman, John closely binds water and the Spirit together.

A brief comment is in order here regarding the piercing of Christ's side after his death, where the images of water and the Spirit once again appear in close proximity to one another. At the moment of Jesus's death, the evangelist tells us that "[Jesus] bowed his head and gave up his spirit" (John 19:30b). Although this is a perfectly legitimate way of rendering the Greek, it seems likely, as many interpreters have suggested, that John is using his characteristic

17. See the discussion of Ezekiel and other texts in chap. 1 above.

double meaning. Another way to translate the last phrase of the verse is that Jesus "handed over *the Spirit*." [18] At the hour of Jesus's death, now that he has been glorified (12:23), he can hand over the Spirit (7:39).[19] The connection with the promise of John 7:37–39 becomes even clearer in light of the blood and water that flow from the side of Christ when the soldier pierces it with a lance (19:34).

Water and Healing

Water features in two important healing stories in John's Gospel, but in remarkably different ways. The first healing takes place during one of Jesus's visits to Jerusalem at an unnamed feast (John 5:1). The setting is the pool of Bethesda, located near one of the gates of the city (5:2). The water of this pool was thought to have healing properties at certain times.[20] There Jesus encounters a man who has been crippled for thirty-eight years and asks him, "Do you want to be made well?" (5:6). Rather than take Jesus up on the offer, the man replies, "Sir, I have no one to put me into the pool when the water is stirred up; and while I am making my way, someone else steps down ahead of me" (5:7). The man has narrow vision, thinking that only the water of the pool can heal him.

Perhaps for this reason Jesus does not use the water in this healing. Particularly in light of the references to the life-giving power of water in the chapters that precede this encounter, it is significant that Jesus does not use the water of the pool to heal the man. This story underscores the point that Jesus is the source of the true water that heals. It is by his word that the man's legs are strengthened and he takes up his mat and walks. Rather than express gratitude for his healing, the man reports Jesus to the Jewish leaders, who are angry that Jesus performed this healing on a sabbath (John 5:9–17). Despite the healing of his legs, the man remains spiritually blind.

By contrast, the second healing involving water features a man who is physically blind but who gradually comes to see who Jesus is and worships

18. In favor of such a reading, see Brown, *John*, 2:910.

19. In support of the connection between John 19 and John 7, see Francis J. Moloney, *The Gospel of John*, SP (Collegeville, MN: Liturgical Press, 1998), 504–5, 508–9.

20. The earliest copies of John do not specify where these healing powers came from, but later manuscripts offer an explanation: "For an angel of the Lord went down at certain seasons into the pool, and stirred the water; whoever stepped in first after the stirring of the water was made well from whatever disease that person had" (John 5:4 [NRSV marginal note]).

him (John 9:1–41). In this story Jesus uses water as an instrument of healing rather than simply healing the man by a word. Additionally—and not surprisingly, in light of the man's physical ailment—the healing of the blind man continues the theme of Jesus as the light of the world that serves as one of the central images of John 8.

The story begins as Jesus and his disciples pass by a man born blind. When the disciples ask Jesus whose sin caused the man's blindness, his own or that of his parents, Jesus replies that the ailment is not a punishment for sin. Rather, the man's blindness offers another occasion for Jesus to perform the works of God (John 9:3). Having identified himself once more as the light of the world (9:5; see also 8:12), Jesus makes a paste of saliva and dirt, rubs it on the man's eyes, and tells him, "'Go, wash in the pool of Siloam' (which means Sent)" (9:7). The man obeys Jesus's command and receives his sight. There follows a controversy between the man and the Pharisees, because Jesus had once again performed the healing on a sabbath, but the details of the controversy are not essential for our purposes. Rather, we will focus on four details of the story as a whole: the use of water, the name of the pool in which the man washes, Jesus's self-identification as the "light of the world" in the broader context of John 7–9, and the man's response to Jesus when he encounters him once more after the controversy.

The first important aspect of the healing is Jesus's use of water. If John's Gospel only included the healing of the paralytic in John 5, one might get the impression that Jesus shunned the use of physical matter to convey healing. In a setting in which people expected to be healed by the water of a pool, Jesus heals the paralytic with a mere word. The healing of the blind man, however, suggests that the purpose of the earlier story is primarily to emphasize that the power of healing comes not from any intrinsic property of the water but rather from Jesus himself. In a similar way, the waters of baptism receive their power from Jesus's word.

Second, the name of the pool to which Jesus sends the man to wash himself has a highly symbolic value, particularly in light of the way Jesus speaks about his own mission in John. As the evangelist tells us, the name of the pool, "Siloam," means "Sent" (John 9:7). Some interpreters have seen in this name an allusion to Jesus himself.[21] At several points in the Fourth Gospel,

21. As is common in Scripture, the connection depends more on a popular etymology than on the actual meaning of the name of the pool. See Moloney, *John*, 297.

Baptized into the Sent One

St. Thomas Aquinas, drawing out the significance of the name of the pool of Siloam, both acknowledges the fittingness of this water as a place for the healing of the blind man and underscores the fact that the healing power of the baptismal waters comes from Christ:

> So he sends him to the pool of Siloam to wash and receive his sight, i.e., to be baptized, and in baptism to receive full enlightenment. Thus, according to Dionysius, baptism is an enlightenment: "I will sprinkle clean water upon you, and you will be clean from all your uncleanness" (Ezek. 36:25). And so this Gospel is appropriately read in Lent, on Holy Saturday, when those about to be baptized are examined. Nor is it without reason that the Evangelist adds the meaning of the pool, saying, "which means sent," because whoever is baptized must be baptized in Christ, who was sent by the Father: "as many of you as were baptized in Christ have put on Christ" (Gal. 3:27). For if Christ had not been sent, none of us would have been freed from sin.[a]

a. Thomas Aquinas, *Commentary on John* c. 9 lect. 1 (1311, formatting modified), in Thomas Aquinas, *Commentary on the Gospel according to John Chapters 9–21*, ed. The Aquinas Institute, trans. Fabian R. Larcher, vol. 36, Latin/English edition of the works of St. Thomas Aquinas (Lander, WY: Aquinas Institute for the Study of Sacred Doctrine, 2013), 8.

the evangelist speaks of the Father "sending" the Son into the world.[22] Symbolically, the blind man washes not just in water but in Christ himself. The significance of this name would not have been lost on a Christian community that in all likelihood practiced baptism as the rite of initiation. Indeed, this healing would have informed their baptismal practice, reminding them that through the waters of baptism they not only received cleansing—they were, in a very real sense, immersed in Christ himself and so united to him.

The man's condition and Jesus's self-identification as the "light of the world" bring out another important aspect of baptism. As already noted, one of the most popular names for baptism in the early Church was "illumination." The healing of the blind man is one of many New Testament passages that contributed to this understanding, and it serves as the culmination of

22. See, e.g., John 3:17, 34; 5:36; 6:29, 57; 7:29; 8:42; 10:36; 11:42; 17:3.

the preceding chapters. The entire sequence of John 7:1–10:21 is set during the Feast of Tabernacles, one of the major Jewish feasts in antiquity. In his teaching, Jesus appropriates the major symbols of the feast, suggesting that they find their fulfillment in him.[23] The Feast of Tabernacles lasted seven days, and it involved two main symbols, water and light. Every day the priests would draw water from the pool of Siloam and pour the water, together with wine, into bowls with holes in them on the altar of the temple. The water would thus spill over the altar and out the drainage of the temple. During the feast, the temple was also lit up by four large menorahs, meant to evoke the pillar of fire that accompanied the Israelites in the wilderness. Jesus's teaching in John 7–8 draws on these symbols. His offer of "rivers of living water" reflects both the symbolism of the feast and one of the Old Testament passages that underlie this symbolism and later served as one of the readings for the feast, Zechariah 14.[24] Likewise, by his statement "I am the light of the world" (John 8:12), Jesus points to himself as the true source of the light symbolized by the menorahs.

The light that Jesus gives appears most clearly in the healing of the man born blind, which brings together both symbols. Through his washing in the water of Siloam (the "Sent One"), the man no longer walks in darkness but sees the light. Most importantly, the light that he sees is Jesus himself. According to early Jewish texts, another important rite of the Feast of Tabernacles was an expression of faith in God meant to contrast with the faithlessness of earlier generations.[25] In the Gospel of John, faith is now directed to Jesus, the incarnate Lord. After the Jewish leaders throw the man born blind out of the synagogue, he encounters Jesus, who asks him, "Do you believe in the Son of Man?" (John 9:35b). When Jesus makes himself known, the man expresses his faith by worshiping him (9:38). This act complements and completes Jesus's appropriation of the other symbols of the Feast of Tabernacles.[26]

Read together, the two healings involving water, that of the crippled man and that of the man born blind, shed considerable light on the meaning of baptism. The first healing emphasizes the power of Jesus's word, which lies

23. For a brief discussion of the rituals of the feast, see Coloe, *God Dwells with Us*, 119–22, as well as the literature she cites there.

24. Coloe, *God Dwells with Us*, 121.

25. Coloe, *God Dwells with Us*, 122, citing the early Jewish tractate Mishnah Sukkoth 5.4.

26. Coloe (*God Dwells with Us*, 122) suggests that the three aspects of the feast are completed in John 7–8, but the man's expression of faith in John 9 seems a more fitting completion of that element of the feast, particularly in light of John's Christology.

at the root of baptism's efficacy. Water does not of itself have the capacity to heal people of illnesses. The healing of the man born blind, however, brings out other important aspects of baptism. First, it illustrates the instrumental power of water to heal when combined with Jesus's word. Second, the symbolism of the pool of Siloam suggests that baptism is, most fundamentally, an immersion in and a joining to the "Sent One," Jesus himself. Third, the healing of the blind man shows the illuminating role of baptism. The sacrament brings people out of darkness into the light of Christ. Finally, the man's response to Jesus once again shows that baptism is oriented ultimately to worship.

Water and the Gift of Self

Few instances of water imagery in John's Gospel have the power to move us as much as Jesus's act of washing his disciples' feet. The humility with which Jesus performs a task ordinarily reserved for a menial servant encapsulates the tenor of his whole life. Indeed, some have interpreted the foot washing as a symbolic enactment and anticipation of his death.[27] The language of setting aside his garments and taking them up again also evokes the Good Shepherd discourse, where Jesus, using the same language, says that the Good Shepherd sets aside his life and takes it up again (John 10:11–18).[28]

John closely links the washing of the disciples' feet with Jesus's death in at least three other ways. First, he notes once more the Passover setting of the act, introducing the action by speaking of Jesus's love for his disciples to the end: "Now before the festival of the Passover, Jesus knew that his hour had come to depart from this world and go to the Father. Having loved his own who were in the world, he loved them to the end" (John 13:1).[29] Second, he refers to Judas's act of betrayal (13:2). Third, the evangelist describes Jesus's motivation in washing the disciples' feet—namely, that he knew "that the Father had given all things into his hands, and that he had come from God and was going to God" (13:3). Much like baptism, this symbolic act draws its significance from and points toward Jesus's gift of self on the cross.

27. See Brown, *John*, 2:565–68.

28. See Moloney, *John*, 378. The Greek words connecting the two passages are *tithēmi* (to "lay aside") and *lambanō* (to "take up").

29. On the twofold meaning of the phrase *eis telos*, here translated "to the end," see Brown, *John*, 2:550.

There is another, looser connection between Jesus's foot washing and the cross. In Mark's Gospel, after Jesus predicts his passion for the first time, Peter takes him aside and tries to dissuade him from such a fate (Mark 8:31–33). Prior to receiving the gift of the Spirit at Pentecost, he cannot accept that Jesus should meet such a gruesome death. In a similar way, in John's account of the Last Supper, Peter at first refuses to allow Jesus to wash his feet, scandalized at the thought of his master serving him in such a lowly way. As in Mark, Jesus corrects Peter and persuades him to receive the foot washing. Moreover, Jesus makes it clear that, much like his death on the cross (see Mark 8:34–9:1), his act is an example that the disciples are to follow: "So if I, your Lord and Teacher, have washed your feet, you also ought to wash one another's feet. For I have set you an example, that you also should do as I have done to you" (John 13:14–15). Jesus's posture of service, most clearly seen in his death on the cross (cf. Mark 10:45), is the model for Christian discipleship.

The final occurrence of the word "water" in John's Gospel appears, significantly, at the time of Jesus's death in a passage that we have already discussed and to which we will return once more (John 19:34). At the cross, when a soldier pierces Christ's side with a lance to make sure that he has died, blood and water flow out. These two instances of water, the foot washing and the water flowing from Christ's side, both occur within the same celebration of Passover. Moreover, both witness to Christ's profound humility. If, as I will argue in the next section, the water flowing from Christ's side symbolizes baptism, then these texts suggest that baptism calls those who receive the sacrament to give of themselves as Christ does on the cross.

Baptism, Passover, and Eucharist

To this point, we have passed over one of the most famous instances of water imagery in John's Gospel, the wedding feast at Cana. A brief consideration of some details of that story, together with an analysis of Christ's teaching at the various Passovers in John, suggests that for John baptism is ordered to the Eucharist.

The story is a familiar one. Jesus attends a wedding feast with his disciples and his mother. The newlyweds run out of wine, and his mother intervenes. After a reply that seems like a refusal, Jesus acts. The details of this miracle are significant. Jesus performs the act using "six stone water jars for the Jewish rites of purification" (John 2:6). He then orders that the servants fill the jars

From the Side of Christ

The interpretation of the blood and water flowing from Christ's side as symbolizing the sacraments of baptism and the Eucharist is an ancient one. St. John Chrysostom writes of the event:

> "There flowed from his side water and blood." Beloved, do not pass this mystery by without a thought. For I have still another mystical explanation to give. I said that there was a symbol of baptism and the mysteries in that blood and water. It is from both of these that the Church is sprung "through the bath of regeneration and renewal by the Holy Spirit," through baptism and the mysteries [i.e., the Eucharist]. But the symbols of baptism and the mysteries come from the side of Christ. It is from his side, therefore, that Christ formed His Church, just as He formed Eve from the side of Adam.[a]

a. John Chrysostom, *Baptismal Instructions* 3.17 (modified), trans. Paul W. Harkins, ACW 31 (London: Longmans, Green, 1963), 62.

with water, which turns into wine (2:7, 9). For early Christians, the combination of water and purification would likely evoke baptism.[30] Similarly, the reference to wine in the context of a banquet subtly suggests an image of the Eucharist. Seen in this way, one could interpret the changing of the water into wine as an indication that baptism leads to the Eucharist, the Christian act of worship. Although such an interpretation may seem strained, other aspects of this Gospel suggest a close relationship between baptism and the Eucharist—namely, the events that surround each of the Passovers to which John refers.

At the first Passover in John, which immediately follows the wedding feast at Cana, Jesus alludes to his coming death and resurrection (John 2:19–21). Shortly after this passage, Jesus has the encounter with Nicodemus in the night, in which he speaks cryptically to the teacher of Israel about baptism. Particularly significant is Jesus's reference to "water and Spirit" (3:5), which points forward to Jesus's gift of the Spirit and the flow of water from his side on the cross. At the second Passover (6:4), Jesus first multiplies loaves and

30. For a similar reading of the connections between Cana, the Bread of Life discourse, and the crucifixion, though without a baptismal interpretation, see Cullmann, *Early Christian Worship*, 68–70.

then, on the next day, delivers the famous Bread of Life discourse (6:35–58). In that teaching Jesus twice speaks of the resurrection on the last day, promising to raise up those who believe in him (6:39–40, 54). As at the first Passover in this Gospel, Jesus alludes to his impending death: "And the bread that I will give for the life of the world is my flesh" (6:51c). This reference to his death, however, specifically introduces the sacramental element of the Bread of Life discourse: "Very truly, I tell you, unless you eat the flesh of the Son of Man and drink his blood, you have no life in you" (6:53). As others have noted, this is the first of two instances in which John refers to Jesus's blood. The other, significantly, also takes place at Passover, the final Passover of Jesus's earthly life. There, in an image that has been discussed many times in this chapter, blood and water flow from Christ's side (19:34). Given the Passover connections between Jesus's discussion of baptism with Nicodemus and the Bread of Life discourse, it seems likely, as others have suggested, that on at least one level the blood and water flowing from the side of Christ symbolize the gifts of baptism and Eucharist, the two sacraments most clearly associated with Jesus's death on the cross.[31]

Christ, the Source of Baptism

The imagery of water flowing from Christ's side serves as a symbol for an important truth about baptism: Christ himself is its source. John makes this point in a number of ways. In the first chapter of the Gospel, John the Baptist refers to Christ as the one who will baptize with the Holy Spirit (John 1:33), and Jesus both implicitly (3:1–8) and explicitly (4:10–14) identifies himself as the source of the Spirit. Jesus is the source of healing, with or without water (9:1–41; 5:1–17). Jesus exemplifies the meaning of baptism through his humble washing of the disciples' feet and through the gift of his life on the cross (13:1–20; 19:34). Jesus gives his Church the sacraments as a pledge of future resurrected glory. Baptism is the gateway to this eternal life, and all are invited to enter it by invoking the name of the Lord. We now turn to the significance of that name in connection to baptism.

31. Moloney, *John*, 505–6; Brown, *John*, 2:951–52. Brown is less sanguine than I am about the sacramental symbolism of the flow of blood and water for reasons that are unclear to me. In light of the Passover connections with baptism and the Eucharist earlier in John, I find the sacramental symbolism likely.

7

Baptism "in the Name"

> But you shall seek the place that the Lord your God will choose out of all your tribes as his habitation to put his name there. You shall go there, bringing there your burnt offerings and your sacrifices, your tithes and your donations, your votive gifts, your freewill offerings, and the firstlings of your herds and flocks.
>
> —Deuteronomy 12:5–6

Toward the end of the Acts of the Apostles, as Paul relates his encounter with Christ on the road to Damascus to his fellow Jews in Jerusalem, he describes the instructions Ananias gave to him when he welcomed him: "Get up, be baptized, and have your sins washed away, calling on his name" (Acts 22:16).[1] The association between baptism and the name—whether the name of Jesus or the name of the Trinity—appears with some frequency in the New Testament.[2] But what exactly does it mean to be baptized "in the name" of someone? Scholars have proposed various interpretations, ranging from an economic image of the transfer of money to a bank account to a simple demarcation of Christian baptism in contradistinction to the baptism of John.[3]

1. Luke relates Paul's encounter with Christ three times in Acts, once as the narrator (Acts 9:1–9) and twice in speeches on the lips of Paul (Acts 22:6–21; 26:12–18).

2. In addition to the texts in Acts, see Matt. 28:19; 1 Cor. 1:13–15; 6:11.

3. For a useful recent discussion of the issues involved, see Lars Hartman, "Usages—Some Notes on the Baptismal Name-Formulae," in *Ablution, Initiation, and Baptism: Late Antiquity,*

For the most part, these interpretations tend to minimize the significance of the name in the various formulae.[4] The evidence of the Acts of the Apostles, however, suggests that the name may play a much more important role than is commonly recognized. Both in Peter's opening speech in Acts (the first call to Christian baptism) and in Paul's account of his conversion (the last occurrence of the verb "to baptize" in Acts), baptism and calling on the name of the Lord are closely associated. The name of the Lord has a rich and profound significance in the Old Testament, with implications for a theology of baptism. In particular, two closely related ideas concerning the name relate to the worship of God: calling upon the name of the Lord and the designation of a place where the name of the Lord will dwell. These associations between the name and worship, on the one hand, and between the name and baptism, on the other, once again point to worship as an important aspect of baptism. More specifically, the invocation of the name in baptism suggests a temple typology. Before we consider the various texts that speak of baptism "in the name," whether of Jesus or of the Father and of the Son and of the Holy Spirit, we will examine the association between the name and worship in the Old Testament.

Calling Upon the Name of the Lord

The expression "to call upon the name of the Lord" appears with some frequency in the Old Testament, and it often accompanies acts of sacrifice, whether on Mount Zion or at some other location.[5] The first occurrence of the phrase in the Pentateuch is brief and allusive, offering little by way of context to indicate its exact meaning. Toward the end of Genesis 4 the narrator writes, "At that time people began to call upon the name of the Lord" (Gen. 4:26b ESV). Placed between the story of Cain and his descendants and the genealogy of the line of Seth, the verse remains vague. The next use of the phrase, however, provides a little more context and indicates that calling upon the name of the

Early Judaism, and Early Christianity, ed. David Hellholm et al., 3 vols., BZNW 176 (Berlin: de Gruyter, 2011), 1:397–413.

4. English translations tend to obscure that the New Testament actually has three different "formulae" used in conjunction with baptism, reflecting the three Greek prepositions *en*, *epi*, and *eis*.

5. For a similar discussion of the expression "to call upon the name of the Lord," focusing primarily on the Septuagint, see Joel D. Estes, "Calling On the Name of the Lord: The Meaning and Significance of ἐπικαλέω in Romans 10:13," *Themelios* 41 (2016): 20–36, esp. 26–30.

Lord can have sacrificial connotations. During Abraham's early wanderings in response to the Lord's call, the patriarch comes to the hill country between Bethel and Ai, "and there," the narrator tells us, "[Abraham] built an altar to the LORD and called upon the name of the LORD" (Gen. 12:8b ESV). Here calling upon the name of the Lord and sacrifice go hand in hand, and the rest of the patriarchal narratives underscore this close connection. Abraham again calls "on the name of the LORD" in the same spot in Genesis 13:4, which refers to the altar he had built earlier. Later, shortly before God calls Abraham to offer up Isaac on Mount Moriah, Abraham once again calls on the name of the Lord, though this time without building an altar (Gen. 21:33).

Like Abraham, both Isaac and Jacob also build altars. In Genesis 26 we read that in response to God's renewal of the promises he had made to Abraham, Isaac "built an altar there, called on the name of the LORD, and pitched his tent there" (Gen. 26:25a). Although Genesis nowhere tells us that Jacob calls upon the name of the Lord, he, too, builds an altar, twice (33:20; 35:1–7). Throughout Genesis altars play an essential role in the relationship between human beings and God.[6]

Elsewhere in the Old Testament, the expression to "call upon the name of the Lord" often relates to sacrificial worship.[7] Examples of this usage appear in the historical books, in the Prophets, and in the Psalms.

One of the most well-known stories of the Old Testament, the contest between Elijah and the prophets of Baal (1 Kings 18:20–40), illustrates the sacrificial sense of this expression. On Mount Carmel, Elijah confronts the prophets of Baal who have led the people of Israel to stray after other gods. Challenging them to a contest, Elijah proposes that he and the prophets of Baal each prepare a bull for sacrifice, but without igniting the fire for the offering. Instead, the prophets are to call upon the name of their god—Elijah on the name of the Lord, and the other prophets on the name of Baal—in order to see which deity kindles the offering. There is no need to review the details of the story, entertaining though they may be. For our purposes it suffices to note that calling upon the name of a god in general, and of the Lord in the case of Israel, relates to sacrificial worship.[8]

6. In addition to the texts just cited, see also Gen. 8:20; 13:18; 22:9.

7. This is a major oversight in J. Gary Millar, *Calling On the Name of the Lord: A Biblical Theology of Prayer*, New Studies in Biblical Theology 38 (Downers Grove, IL: InterVarsity, 2016), 19–27.

8. On the patristic interpretation of the rain following Elijah's sacrifice as a type of baptism, see Jean Daniélou, *The Bible and the Liturgy* (Notre Dame, IN: University of Notre Dame Press, 1956), 106–7.

A similar use of the expression appears in 1 Chronicles 16, which describes David's act of bringing the ark of the Lord to Jerusalem. References to sacrifice permeate the account, as David brings the ark into a tent and offers numerous offerings to the Lord (16:1). In this context, David appoints Levites to offer regular sacrifices before the ark, and he offers a prayer of thanksgiving, which begins, "O give thanks to the LORD, call on his name, make known his deeds among the peoples" (16:8). Once again, the phrase has a sacrificial connotation.

Several texts in the prophetic writings associate calling on the name of the Lord with sacrificial worship, either explicitly or implicitly. An implicit connection appears in an important passage from the book of Joel. In a text made famous by Peter's first public speech in the Acts of the Apostles, the prophet writes, "Then everyone who calls on the name of the LORD shall be saved; for in Mount Zion and in Jerusalem there shall be those who escape, as the LORD has said, and among the survivors shall be those whom the LORD calls" (Joel 2:32). One could take the references to Zion and Jerusalem as mere geographical indicators, but toward the end of the book Joel closely identifies these places with the house of the Lord (3:17–18), the liturgical center of ancient Israel. Implicitly, then, for Joel, calling upon the name of the Lord has sacrificial connotations.

The prophet Zephaniah also speaks of people calling upon the name of the Lord, but he more explicitly connects the idea with sacrificial worship. Moreover, Zephaniah describes a time when not only the Israelites but also the nations will worship the Lord:

> For at that time I will change the speech of the peoples
> to a pure speech,
> that all of them may *call upon the name of the* LORD
> and serve him with one accord.
> From beyond the rivers of Cush
> *my worshipers*, the daughter of my dispersed ones,
> shall bring *my offering*. (Zeph. 3:9–10 ESV)

The whole context of the oracle emphasizes the sacrificial dimension of this event. In addition to the reference to calling upon the name of the Lord, the word for "serve" (*ʿābad*) that follows this phrase is related to the word used in the Pentateuch to speak of the priestly activity in the tabernacle (see Num.

3:7–8; 8:25; 18:5–6). Moreover, the references to the Lord's "worshipers" and "offering" unmistakably give the oracle a cultic connotation.

The book of Psalms also attests to the sacrificial connotation that calling upon the Lord's name often has. The clearest example appears in Psalm 116, which uses the expression three times. The first instance of the phrase does not seem to have a sacrificial dimension; rather, it serves as a simple cry for help in a time of distress. In the face of a deadly threat (116:3), the psalmist notes, "Then I called on the name of the Lord: 'O Lord, I pray, save my life!'" (116:4). Later in the psalm, however, the phrase takes on a more technical sense, as the psalmist speaks of how he will respond to the Lord's favor:

> What shall I return to the Lord
>   for all his bounty to me?
> I will lift up the cup of salvation
>   and call on the name of the Lord,
> I will pay my vows to the Lord
>   in the presence of all his people. (Ps. 116:12–14)

The psalmist repays the Lord with a public act, raising the "cup of salvation."[9] A few verses later the sacrificial imagery becomes even more explicit:

> I will offer to you a thanksgiving sacrifice
>   and call on the name of the Lord.
> I will pay my vows to the Lord
>   in the presence of all his people,
> in the courts of the house of the Lord,
>   in your midst, O Jerusalem.
> Praise the Lord! (Ps. 116:17–19)

The thanksgiving sacrifice in ancient Israel was an actual sacrifice that included a grain offering in fulfillment of a vow asking for the Lord's protection.[10] Once again, calling upon the name of the Lord has a sacrificial dimension. This connection between the name and sacrifice should come as no surprise in light of another aspect of the Old Testament understanding of the name of the Lord: the name represented the manner of God's presence among his people in the temple.

9. This cup refers to part of the thanksgiving sacrifice. See Leslie C. Allen, *Psalms 101–150*, WBC 21 (Waco: Word, 1983), 113.

10. See Lev. 7:11–15.

A House for the Name of the Lord

As we have seen, the patriarchal narratives draw an implicit link between the name of the Lord and offering a sacrifice on an altar. Elsewhere in the Pentateuch, this connection becomes explicit, and the association between the name of the Lord and a particular place shapes the Old Testament understanding of the temple.

In the book of Exodus, the first law that the Lord gives to Moses after the Decalogue concerns the building of altars. Reiterating the prohibition against idolatry and the worship of false gods, the Lord says to Moses, "You need make for me only an altar of earth and sacrifice on it your burnt offerings and your offerings of well-being, your sheep and your oxen; *in every place where I cause my name to be remembered* I will come to you and bless you" (Exod. 20:24). Sacrificial worship plays an essential role in Israel's relationship with the Lord. But whereas the law for altars in Exodus leaves the details of such worship vague, speaking of "every place," the book of Deuteronomy prescribes one centralized place for the worship of the Lord.

Deuteronomy 12 lays out the decrees for the building of a place to offer sacrifice. At the heart of Deuteronomy's description of this place is the name of the Lord. Having stipulated the destruction of the foreign altars in the land, Moses writes:

> But you shall seek the place that the Lord your God will choose out of all your tribes as his habitation to put his name there. You shall go there, bringing there your burnt offerings and your sacrifices, your tithes and your donations, your votive gifts, your freewill offerings, and the firstlings of your herds and flocks. (Deut. 12:5–6)

The name serves as a way of describing God's presence in Israel's midst. Twice more the passage uses some variation of the phrase "the place that the Lord your God will choose out of all your tribes as his habitation to put his name there" (Deut. 12:11, 21), and throughout the rest of Deuteronomy the name of the Lord designates the centralized place of Israel's worship (14:23; 16:2, 6, 11; 26:2).

This association between the name of the Lord and the sanctuary features prominently in the accounts of the dedication of Solomon's temple in both 1 Kings and 2 Chronicles. Indeed, the "name" is one of the most prominent features of Solomon's dedication speeches, building on the promise God had

The High Priesthood and the Divine Name

For the ancient Israelites, in addition to the notion that the name of the Lord dwelt in the temple, there was a close association between the divine name and the high priest. While ministering in the temple, the high priest would wear on his forehead, as part of his vestments, a plate of gold with the phrase "Holy to the LORD" engraved on it (Exod. 28:36). This connection between the priesthood and the divine name helps explain why the New Testament speaks of believers as both a temple and a holy priesthood; both images underscore the fact that the baptized now bear the name of the Lord. The book of Revelation attests to the importance of bearing the name (Rev. 3:12; 14:1; 22:4), almost certainly reflecting the imagery of the vestments of the high priest. Combining this priestly tradition with a passage from Ezekiel 9, one scholar has suggested that the name imagery in Revelation reflects the early Christian baptismal theology of being sealed with the divine name in baptism.[a]

a. Charles A. Gieschen, "Sacramental Theology in the Book of Revelation," *CTQ* 67 (2003): 149–74.

made to David that his son would "build a house for my name" (2 Sam. 7:13). In his opening speech (1 Kings 8:15–21), Solomon refers to the "name" of the Lord five times, and he repeatedly appeals to the name in his extensive prayer (8:29, 33, 35, 41–44, 47–48). The books of Chronicles make the association between the temple and the name even clearer. Solomon's speech (2 Chron. 6) includes many of the same references to the name as 1 Kings, and when David charges Solomon to build the temple he speaks of it repeatedly as a house for the name of the Lord (1 Chron. 22:6–19).[11]

This close association between temple, sacrifice, and the name of the Lord has significant implications for understanding what it means for baptism to be administered "in the name" of Christ or of the Trinity.

11. This association between the name of the Lord, the temple, and sacrifice also appears in the writings of the prophets. Isaiah, for example, refers to "Mount Zion, the place of the name of the LORD of hosts" (18:7) and speaks of those who come "to love the name of the LORD" (56:6). The Lord goes on to say through the prophet, "These I will bring to my holy mountain, and make them joyful in my house of prayer; their burnt offerings and their sacrifices will be accepted on my altar" (Isa. 56:7).

"Repent and Be Baptized"

The Acts of the Apostles opens with a reference to two kinds of baptism, John's baptism with water and a baptism with the Holy Spirit, which the disciples are to receive on Pentecost (Acts 1:5). This distinction recalls John's own message, attested to in all four Gospels, that the one who is to come after him will baptize with the Spirit (Matt. 3:11; Mark 1:8; Luke 3:16; John 1:33). Some interpreters, especially those with Pentecostal leanings, argue that John's saying, echoed by Jesus in Acts, implies a devaluation of water baptism.[12] While it is certainly true that the gift of the Spirit, as depicted in Acts, is not strictly limited to water baptism, the text nevertheless repeatedly shows that water baptism is the normative rite of entry into the Christian community and is in some way associated with the gift of the Spirit.[13] The events of Pentecost fundamentally shape the meaning of baptism in Acts.

Jesus's words prior to his ascension (Acts 1:5, 8) interpret the first Christian Pentecost as the disciples' "baptism" in the Holy Spirit. Toward the end of Peter's Pentecost speech, he exhorts his audience to be baptized, promising that they will receive "the gift of the Holy Spirit" (2:38). In other words, the experience of the disciples serves as a model for what people will receive in baptism.[14] Let us consider, then, Luke's description of this event:

> When the day of Pentecost had come, they were all together in one place. And suddenly from heaven there came a sound like the rush of a violent wind, and it filled the entire house where they were sitting. Divided tongues, as of fire, appeared among them, and a tongue rested on each of them. All of them were

12. See, e.g., James D. G. Dunn, "Baptism as Metaphor," in *Baptism, the New Testament and the Church: Historical and Contemporary Studies in Honour of* R. E. O. *White*, ed. Stanley E. Porter and Anthony R. Cross, JSNTSup 171 (Sheffield, UK: Sheffield Academic, 1999), 294–310.

13. Two different episodes in Acts point to the fluidity in the relationship between baptism and the Spirit. In the case of Cornelius, the Gentile centurion and his companions receive the Spirit while listening to Peter speak, which prompts the apostle to receive them through baptism (Acts 10:44–48). By contrast, the disciples in Ephesus who have received only John's baptism receive the Holy Spirit *after* they receive water baptism "in the name of the Lord Jesus" (19:1–7). See also the events at Samaria (8:9–17), where the baptized receive the Holy Spirit only after Peter and John lay their hands upon them. Despite the reference to baptism in the Spirit at the beginning of Acts, the vast majority of the occurrences of the verb "to baptize" in Acts refer to physical baptism (see Acts 2:38, 41; 8:12–13, 16, 36, 38; 9:18; 10:47–48; 16:15, 33; 18:8; 19:3–5; 22:16).

14. Alan Streett puts it well: "For Peter, water baptism 'in the name' and Spirit baptism were two sides of the same coin, constituting a single baptism." See Streett, *Caesar and the Sacrament: Baptism—a Rite of Resistance* (Eugene, OR: Cascade Books, 2018), 99.

> filled with the Holy Spirit and began to speak in other languages, as the Spirit gave them ability. (Acts 2:1–4)

Much could be said about these events, but we will focus on three features of this passage. (1) The image of a "rush of a violent wind" is an apt one for the movement of the Spirit, because in both Greek and Hebrew the word for "spirit" can also mean "wind" or "breath."[15] (2) The phrase "tongues, as of fire" seems to draw on the association between fire and the presence of God. Several times in the Old Testament, God makes his presence manifest by fire, such as when he appears on Mount Sinai (Exod. 19:18) and when he takes up his dwelling in the tabernacle (40:38). (3) The symbolism of fire, then, suggests that God has taken up his residence in his disciples as in a new temple. This explains why, as Acts notes, "all of them were filled with the Holy Spirit" (Acts 2:4), fulfilling Jesus's promise at the beginning of the book (1:8).

In his speech, Peter both implicitly and explicitly makes a similar promise. In interpreting the events of Pentecost, he appeals to a passage from Joel, which promises the outpouring of God's Spirit upon the people in the last days (Acts 2:17–21, quoting Joel 2:28–32). Peter's citation of the text culminates with the saying considered earlier in this chapter: "Then everyone who calls on the name of the Lord shall be saved" (Acts 2:21). This is the first instance of the phrase "the name of the Lord" in Acts, some variation of which appears in connection with baptism several times. We will return to this point in a moment. First, it is worth recalling that in the Old Testament the phrase "to call upon the name of the Lord" frequently has a sacrificial connotation, evoking worship in the temple. In light of the phenomenon of the Spirit descending on the disciples with the appearance of the tongues as of fire, the connection with the temple at the very least lies in the background. Moreover, Peter's exhortation and promise to his listeners suggests that baptism, too, has this temple connection. When those listening to Peter ask him what they should do, he replies, "Repent, and be baptized every one of you in the name of Jesus Christ so that your sins may be forgiven; and you will receive the gift of the Holy Spirit" (Acts 2:38). There is a connection between this exhortation and the use of the catchword "name" at the beginning of Peter's speech. In light of this connection, two conclusions seem to follow. First, Peter interprets the "Lord" of Joel's prophecy as Jesus Christ. Second,

15. Luke here uses a different word for the wind, but the fittingness of the image remains. Jesus plays on this double meaning in his conversation with Nicodemus (John 3:8).

baptism is one important way in which people "call upon the name of the Lord." Given the cultic connotations of this phrase as well as the promise of the reception of the Holy Spirit, Acts implicitly portrays baptism in terms of a temple theology. Like those who received the Holy Spirit at Pentecost, all those who are baptized and receive the Spirit become temples of God's presence within them.

Before we briefly consider the other references to baptism in Acts, let us return to Paul's narration of his encounter with Christ on the road to Damascus and the events that followed. As noted, this speech includes the last reference to baptism in Acts, forming a bookend with the first exhortation to baptism at Pentecost. Paul recounts Ananias's exhortation, "And now why do you delay? Get up, be baptized, and have your sins washed away, *calling on his name*" (Acts 22:16). The final phrase closely resembles Peter's quotation of Joel in Acts 2, substituting the personal pronoun "his" for "the Lord." In the context of Paul's speech, it is clear that Ananias is encouraging Paul to call on the name of the "Righteous One," one of Luke's titles for Jesus (cf. Acts 7:52). This should come as no surprise, given the prominence of the name of Jesus throughout Acts, both with respect to baptism and in other contexts. The allusion to Joel and to Peter's speech once again suggests a temple theology.

During the first mission to Samaria, Philip preaches the gospel "about the kingdom of God and the name of Jesus Christ," and those listening receive baptism (Acts 8:12). A few verses later Luke describes this as a baptism "in the name of the Lord Jesus" (8:16). In the next chapter, the first description of Paul's conversion, Ananias describes the Christian community as "all who call on your name" (9:14 ESV). A few verses later, Ananias addresses Paul: "Brother Saul, the Lord Jesus, who appeared to you on your way here, has sent me so that you may regain your sight *and be filled with the Holy Spirit*" (9:17b). The following verse describes how Ananias's promise comes true. Significantly, it involves two steps: "And immediately something like scales fell from his eyes, and his sight was restored. Then he got up and was baptized" (9:18). The parallelism between Ananias's words and Paul's experience suggests a close connection between his baptism and his reception of the Holy Spirit. The experience of the centurion Cornelius and his companions, by contrast, suggests that the Spirit is not bound to the sacrament but can manifest himself even before baptism (10:44–48). However, the example of Cornelius seems to be exceptional and to have a particular purpose—namely, to show the inclusion of the Gentiles. Cornelius and his companions receive the gift that ordinarily goes with baptism, so Peter draws the logical conclusion that they should be baptized (10:48). In a few other places, Luke describes the baptism of new believers with no commentary (16:15, 33; 18:8). He clearly presumes the rite to be the normative initiation into the Christian community, regardless of the fluidity in the relationship between the gift of the Spirit and baptism.

To return to our consideration of the temple as the dwelling place for the name of the Lord, it seems that for Luke, baptism incorporates the believer into the new temple. She calls upon the name of the Lord Jesus, and, whether before or after baptism, the Spirit comes to dwell in her as in a temple. The association between the name and baptism thus points to this sacrificial dimension of the identity of the baptized. A similar understanding of baptism appears in 1 Corinthians.

"Were You Baptized in the Name of Paul?"

Temple imagery pervades 1 Corinthians. Paul repeatedly appeals to the Corinthians' status as God's temple and draws on language associated with Israel's feasts in order to ground his instruction.[16] In a subtle way Paul also draws on the significance of the name of the Lord, particularly as it relates to the temple and to baptism.

Paul addresses the letter "to the church of God that is in Corinth" and reminds the Corinthians that they are "called to be saints, together with all those *who in every place call on the name of our Lord Jesus Christ*, both their Lord and ours" (1 Cor. 1:2). As we have seen, in the Old Testament the idea of calling upon the name of the Lord often connotes liturgical worship. It is possible, moreover, that Paul has a particular reference in mind with this expression. The prophet Malachi, critiquing the corruption of Israel's priesthood, prophesies, "For from the rising of the sun to its setting *my name is great* among the nations, and *in every place* incense is offered *to my name*, and a pure offering; *for my name is great among the nations*, says the LORD of hosts" (Mal. 1:11).[17] Three times the prophet emphasizes the

16. See Rodrigo J. Morales, "A Liturgical Conversion of the Imagination: Worship and Ethics in 1 Corinthians," *Letter and Spirit* 5 (2009): 103–24.

17. See Roy E. Ciampa and Brian S. Rosner, *The First Letter to the Corinthians*, PNTC (Grand Rapids: Eerdmans, 2010), 57–58. I owe this reference, as well as the broader point about the emphasis on worship in Paul's letter opening, to Michael P. Barber and John A. Kincaid, "Cultic Theosis in Paul and Second Temple Judaism," *JSPHL* 5, no. 2 (2015): 237–56.

glory given to God's name, and, even more importantly, he affirms that this worship will occur "in every place," the same phrase Paul uses to describe Christians.

The importance of the name reappears not long after the letter opening, in the context of a reference to baptism. One of the major problems that prompt Paul to write 1 Corinthians is the factionalism plaguing the church at Corinth. At least twice in the letter Paul appeals to baptism to remind the Corinthians of their unity.[18] The first such appeal takes place in the opening chapter, where he reminds them of the connection between crucifixion and baptism and of the name in which they were baptized. Castigating them for their allegiance to certain Christian leaders to the exclusion of others, Paul poses a set of rhetorical questions: "Has Christ been divided? Was Paul crucified for you? Or *were you baptized in the name of Paul*?" (1 Cor. 1:13). These questions serve as a reminder that baptism joined the Corinthians first to Christ and then by extension to other Christians (see 1 Cor. 12). In case they miss the point the first time, Paul goes on to state, "I thank God that I baptized none of you except Crispus and Gaius, *so that no one can say that you were baptized in my name*" (1:14–15). Because this statement comes so soon after the introduction with its reference to calling upon the name of the Lord Jesus Christ, it seems likely that Paul understands baptism in close relation to worship. Another allusion to baptism later in the letter makes this connection clearer.

Toward the middle of 1 Corinthians 6, Paul appeals positively to the Corinthians' baptism as the rite that changed their status: "And this is what some of you used to be. But *you were washed*, you were sanctified, you were justified *in the name of the Lord Jesus Christ* and in the Spirit of our God" (1 Cor. 6:11). Given the common early Christian association of baptism with washing (Acts 22:16; Eph. 5:26; Titus 3:5), in a letter that frequently appeals to baptism (1 Cor. 1:13; 10:2; 12:13; 15:29), the language of being "washed" almost certainly refers to the Corinthians' baptism. The appeal to "the name of the Lord Jesus Christ," so frequently linked to baptism (see Acts 2:38; 8:16; 10:48), further strengthens this baptismal reading. Moreover, the surrounding context, both before and after the appeal to washing, contains numerous

18. For a brief discussion of baptism in 1 Corinthians, see Isaac Augustine Morales, "Baptism and Union with Christ," in *"In Christ" in Paul: Explorations in Paul's Theology of Union and Participation*, ed. Michael J. Thate, Kevin J. Vanhoozer, and Constantine R. Campbell, WUNT 2/384 (Tübingen: Mohr Siebeck, 2014), 156–79, here 164–71.

images associated with baptism.[19] We will return to this text again in later chapters. For our present purposes, it will suffice to consider the temple imagery to which Paul appeals.

Immediately after his allusion to baptism, Paul addresses the problem of sexual immorality among the Corinthians, criticizing them for their loose morals. Toward the end of this instruction, Paul appeals to the presence of the Spirit dwelling within the Corinthians: "Or do you not know that your body is a temple of the Holy Spirit within you, which you have from God, and that you are not your own? For you were bought with a price; therefore glorify God in your body" (1 Cor. 6:19–20). The Corinthians—and all Christians—are to treat their bodies as temples of the Holy Spirit and to offer acceptable worship to God in those temples ("therefore glorify God in your body"; cf. Rom. 12:1). The close conjunction of an appeal to baptism in the name of Jesus and the notion that believers are now temples of the Holy Spirit makes sense in light of the Old Testament understanding of the Jerusalem temple as a place for the name of the Lord. Through baptism and the invocation of the name of the Lord, believers become temples of the Spirit dwelling within them. By their upright conduct, they offer God spiritual worship and in this way fulfill Malachi's prophecy that "in every place incense is offered to my name."[20]

"Go Therefore and Make Disciples of All Nations"

The most famous invocation of the name with reference to baptism appears in a passage commonly known as "the Great Commission" (Matt. 28:16–20). Though brief, the passage is dense with allusions to the Old Testament, among them Daniel 7, the common Old Testament type of the mountain as the place of encounter with God, and a subtle allusion to Isaiah 7, which serves as a bookend around the Gospel (cf. Matt. 1:23). Rather than elaborate on each

19. For a more detailed argument in favor of a baptismal interpretation of this passage, see Isaac Augustine Morales, "Washed, Sanctified, Justified: 1 Corinthians 6 and Baptismal Participation in Christ," in *A Scribe Trained for the Kingdom of Heaven: Essays on Christology and Ethics in Honor of Richard B. Hays*, ed. David M. Moffitt and Isaac Augustine Morales (Lanham, MD: Fortress Academic, 2021), 91–108. For more on 1 Cor. 6 and on the purificatory nature of baptism, see chap. 11 below.

20. For the connection between 1 Cor. 1:2, Malachi, and 1 Cor. 6:20, see Ciampa and Rosner, *First Letter to the Corinthians*, 58. Paul frequently uses temple and sacrificial imagery to describe Christian behavior. For a recent study of this aspect of Paul's thought, see Nijay K. Gupta, *Worship That Makes Sense to Paul: A New Approach to the Theology and Ethics of Paul's Cultic Metaphors*, BZNW 175 (Berlin: de Gruyter, 2010).

of these allusions, let us focus on a few features of the passage, particularly as they relate to the importance of the name.

As just noted, the mountain serves as a prominent motif throughout the Old Testament, representing the place where the Israelites meet God. Two particular mountains dominate the history of Israel: Sinai and Zion.[21] The former serves as the setting of the establishment of the Mosaic covenant (Exod. 19–24). The latter is the goal and culmination of the Davidic covenant (2 Sam. 7:5–17). What both mountains have in common, in addition to being the place of encounter with God, is that they also serve as the setting for sacrificial worship (Exod. 24; 1 Kings 8). It should come as no surprise, then, that when the disciples see Jesus on the mountain, they worship (Matt. 28:17). In this context of worship on the mountain, Jesus sends the disciples out on a mission: "Go therefore and make disciples of all nations, baptizing them in the name of the Father and of the Son and of the Holy Spirit, and teaching them to obey everything that I have commanded you. And remember, I am with you always, to the end of the age" (Matt. 28:19–20). The mountain setting, combined with the risen Lord's promise of his continued presence with the disciples, has intriguing implications for understanding baptism "in the name." As we saw above, the "name" is one of the most common ways to describe God's presence in the temple in the Old Testament.[22] Seen in this light, baptism serves for Matthew as the rite by which God comes to take up his dwelling in believers. Being baptized "into" the name (as the Greek more literally says) results in the name coming to dwell in the baptized.

One final element of the Great Commission may support this reading of the command to baptize. The close conjunction of references to "all nations" and the "name" may subtly allude to Malachi. Recall the latter's prophecy: "For from the rising of the sun to its setting *my name is great among the nations*, and in every place incense is offered to my name, and a pure offering; for *my name is great among the nations*, says the LORD of hosts" (Mal. 1:11). The spreading of the name to the nations, resulting in acceptable worship to God, comes about through the disciples' preaching of the gospel and, importantly, baptizing people "into the name."

21. See Jon D. Levenson, *Sinai and Zion: An Entry into the Jewish Bible* (San Francisco: Harper & Row, 1987).

22. For a fascinating argument that the "name" in the baptismal formula refers to the divine name in the Old Testament, see Charles A. Gieschen, "The Divine Name in Holy Baptism," in *All Theology Is Christology: Essays in Honor of David P. Scaer*, ed. Dean O. Wenthe et al. (Fort Wayne: Concordia Theological Seminary Press, 2000), 67–77.

The divine indwelling, which fulfills the promise of Isaiah 7:14 as well as Malachi's promise of universal worship of the Lord, has implications for how disciples are to lead their lives. Jesus commands the disciples not only to baptize but also to teach the nations "to obey everything that I have commanded you" (Matt. 28:20). As in Paul's Letters, an important aspect of the worship that disciples are to offer to God is their obedience to Jesus. In this way the Lord's name will be great among the nations (cf. Ezek. 36:22–28).

The Name of the Crucified One

One of the most important commands Jesus gives the disciples is the call to take up the cross. It is the first teaching that Jesus gives immediately after Peter's confession (Matt. 16:13–28). At the transfiguration, which follows the call to take up the cross, the voice of the Father from the cloud says, "This is my Son, the Beloved; with him I am well pleased; *listen to him!*" (17:5). As Jesus and his disciples descend the Mount of Transfiguration, he underscores the necessity of his suffering once again (17:12). In light of the centrality of this

Baptized in the Name of the Ineffable God

There is evidence that early Christians retained the Jewish sense of reverence for the name of God, understood now in a trinitarian way. Speaking of baptism, St. Justin Martyr writes,

> There is pronounced over him who chooses to be born again, and has repented of his sins, the name of God the Father and Lord of the universe; he who leads to the laver the person that is to be washed calling him by this name alone. For no one can utter the name of the ineffable God; and if any one dare to say that there is a name, he raves with a hopeless madness. And this washing is called illumination, because they who learn these things are illuminated in their understandings. And in the name of Jesus Christ, who was crucified under Pontius Pilate, and in the name of the Holy Spirit, who through the prophets foretold all things about Jesus, he who is illuminated is washed.[a]

a. Justin Martyr, *First Apology* 61 (*ANF* 1:183, modified).

teaching, as well as the subtle connections between Jesus's baptism and his death, one can see why some early Christians interpreted Christian baptism in light of the cross. In 1 Corinthians Paul implicitly speaks of baptism in this way, as he asks the Corinthians rhetorically, "Has Christ been divided? Was Paul crucified for you? Or were you baptized in the name of Paul?" (1 Cor. 1:13). In other passages, Paul much more clearly draws out the cruciform shape of baptism. To those passages we now turn.

8

Dying and Rising with Christ

> You have put me in the depths of the Pit,
> in the regions dark and deep.
> Your wrath lies heavy upon me,
> and you overwhelm me with all your waves.
>
> —Psalm 88:6–7

At the heart of Paul's understanding of the Christian life lies the notion of union with Christ, particularly in his death and resurrection.[1] Few verses express this vision of the Christian life better than a famous text from the Letter to the Galatians: "I have been crucified with Christ; and it is no longer I who live, but it is Christ who lives in me. And the life I now live in the flesh I live by faith in the Son of God, who loved me and gave himself for me" (Gal. 2:19b–20). This idea of co-crucifixion pervades Paul's Letters, and it plays a fundamental role in his teaching on baptism.[2] The link between baptism and

1. See the essays in Michael J. Thate, Kevin J. Vanhoozer, and Constantine R. Campbell, eds., *"In Christ" in Paul: Explorations in Paul's Theology of Union and Participation*, WUNT 2/384 (Tübingen: Mohr Siebeck, 2014).

2. See Isaac Augustine Morales, "Baptism and Union with Christ," in Vanhoozer and Campbell, *"In Christ" in Paul*, 156–79; on the broader question of the cruciform shape of Paul's spirituality, see Michael J. Gorman, *Cruciformity: Paul's Narrative Spirituality of the Cross* (Grand Rapids: Eerdmans, 2001).

crucifixion appears implicitly toward the beginning of 1 Corinthians (1 Cor. 1:13), but its fullest explication appears in later letters, especially Romans and Colossians. In addition, a few instances of crucifixion language in Galatians may also allude to baptism.

Divorced from the resurrection, the cross would make no sense. For this reason, Paul's understanding of union with Christ, and especially of baptism, draws on the resurrection as much as it does on the crucifixion. To be baptized into Christ is to enter into the mystery of salvation, Christ's complete gift of self and his consequent return from the dead, glorious and immortal. This baptismal entry into Christ's death serves as a foretaste of the future glory believers hope for, and it carries with it consequences for how Christians are to conduct themselves in the world. Our manner of life draws its strength from the resurrection and should reflect that future hope.

"You Were Buried with Him in Baptism"

Early Christians performed baptism by full immersion. That is, the baptized would be fully submerged under the water, which is, in fact, one of the original meanings of the Greek verb "to baptize"—namely, to "immerse" someone or something. Such a practice readily lent itself to a symbolic interpretation: the submersion under the water represented being buried with Christ in the tomb, while the reemergence from the water signified rising with Christ.

Paul's emphasis on baptism as death and burial fits into a larger argument regarding the relationship between sin and grace. Toward the end of Romans 5 Paul writes, "Where sin increased, grace abounded all the more" (Rom. 5:20b). This verse points to the superabundance of God's generosity in Christ's self-gift. Such a statement, however, could also easily be misinterpreted, and Paul anticipates such a misconstrual at the beginning of the next chapter: "What then are we to say? Should we continue in sin in order that grace may abound? By no means! How can we who died to sin go on living in it?" (6:1–2). Paul locates this death to sin at the moment of baptism, which he describes as a burial with Christ, and the imagery of baptism shapes much of the subsequent argument.[3] In the course of that argument two aspects of baptism emerge: baptism liberates believers from sin, empowering them to lead a life of righ-

3. For a good discussion, see G. R. Beasley-Murray, *Baptism in the New Testament* (Grand Rapids: Eerdmans, 1962), 130–35.

A Watery Tomb

The themes of death and new life appear frequently in early Christian discussions of baptism. St. Basil the Great explicitly compares the water to a tomb:

> The image of death is fulfilled in the water, and the Spirit gives us the pledge of life. Therefore it is clear why water is associated with the Spirit: because of baptism's dual purpose. On the one hand, the body of sin is destroyed, that it may never bear fruit for death. On the other hand, we are made to live by the Spirit, and bear fruit in holiness. *The water receives our body as a tomb, and so becomes the image of death*, while the Spirit pours in life-giving power, renewing in souls which were dead in sin the life they first possessed. This is what it means to be born again of water and Spirit: the water accomplishes our death, while the Spirit raises us to life.[a]

a. Basil the Great, *On the Holy Spirit* 15.35, trans. David Anderson (Crestwood, NY: St. Vladimir's Seminary Press, 1980), 58–59 (emphasis added).

teousness in the present; and baptism serves as a down payment on the future hope of the resurrection. The two aspects are intimately related.[4]

Although Paul initially speaks of baptism simply as a baptism "into [Christ's] death" (Rom. 6:3), the subsequent verses repeatedly affirm both death and resurrection as consequences of the rite. The death of which Paul speaks is not the cessation of biological life but rather a symbolic—though nevertheless real—death to the power of sin. By contrast, Paul's resurrection language points to two realities: the present reality of the power to live well and the future hope of resurrection to a glorified body. The structure of Romans 6:5–10 reflects this twofold resurrection. Paul exhorts his audience to live in a manner worthy of the future for which they hope.

In his first explication of the death that takes place in baptism, Paul writes, "Therefore we have been buried with him by baptism into his death, so that, just as Christ was raised from the dead by the glory of the Father, so we too might walk in newness of life" (Rom. 6:4, modified). Paul's description of

4. I have made this argument briefly in Morales, "Baptism and Union with Christ," 160–64, and at greater length and in more detail in Isaac Augustine Morales, "Baptism, Holiness, and Resurrection Hope in Romans 6," *CBQ* 83 (2021): 466–81.

being "buried with him" is the first of a series of compound words in the passage, words that imply a joining with another.[5] The dominant theme throughout the passage is union with Christ and its effects. The first effect Paul highlights is moral transformation. This should come as no surprise, since the passage begins with the question of whether believers ought to sin in order to receive more grace. In response, Paul notes that baptism gives us the power to "walk in newness of life." "Walking" is a common image for conduct before God that goes back to the Old Testament.[6] The ongoing nature of this "walking" suggests that the "newness of life" refers to present upright behavior, freed from sin. In the next few verses Paul develops the idea, introducing the imagery of slavery.

Many interpreters take Romans 6:5 as pointing forward to the future resurrection. Paul writes, "For if we have been united with him in a death like his, we will certainly be united with him in a resurrection like his." On the surface, a reading of the text as referring to future resurrection is understandable, as the future tense of the verb would seem naturally to anticipate a participation in Christ's glorious resurrection. If we consider the passage more closely, however, a better reading would take Romans 6:5–7 as continuing to speak of present behavior rather than future hope. On this reading, the future-tense verb of verse 5 should be understood as a logical future rather than a temporal future.[7] The emphasis in these three verses remains on sin, with the added imagery of slavery to and liberation from sin (6:6–7). In verse 6 Paul writes, "We know that our old self was crucified with him so that the body of sin might be destroyed, *and we might no longer be enslaved to sin.*" Paul thus focuses on the immediate consequence of liberation from sin rather than on the future resurrection. Moreover, he connects the baptismal death with justification in verse 7, where he writes, "For whoever has died is freed from sin." The Greek verb translated "freed" comes from the word group relating to justification or righteousness, a major theme throughout Romans. Justification has been the source of much debate since the time of the Reformation, and it would be impossible to do the question justice in such a short

5. In Greek this is expressed by words that include the preposition *syn*, which typically means "together with." These *syn*- compounds appear in Rom. 6:4, 5, 6, and 8. The preposition also appears in v. 8.

6. A classic example appears in Micah: "He has told you, O mortal, what is good; and what does the LORD require of you but to do justice, and to love kindness, and *to walk humbly with your God*?" (Mic. 6:8).

7. The technical name for this is the "gnomic" future.

space.[8] Suffice it to say that, on a Catholic understanding, justification entails, among other things, conversion to God and liberation from sin.[9] The root of this teaching can be found here in Paul's words to the Romans.

With Romans 6:8, Paul shifts his focus from the present life to the future resurrection. A subtle but important difference between verse 5 and verse 8 signals this transition. Whereas in verse 5 Paul says, "We will certainly be united with him in a resurrection like his," in verse 8 he writes, "But if we have died with Christ, *we believe* that we will also live with him."[10] The use of the verb "believe" in the latter verse suggests that Paul is now speaking about something for which Christians hope, and the verses that follow bear this out. In verse 9 Paul speaks of the indestructibility of Christ's resurrected body: "We know that Christ, being raised from the dead, will never die again; death no longer has dominion over him." Paul continues this emphasis on a resurrection to immortality, referring first to the death Christ died and then to the life he (currently) lives (6:10). In contrast to Romans 6:6–7, which focuses on liberation from sin, verses 9–10 present a future-oriented hope. Paul rounds out this part of his exhortation by reminding the Romans, "So you also must consider yourselves dead to sin and alive to God in Christ Jesus" (6:11). The baptized ought to think of themselves as presently alive to God, though not in the same way that Christ is alive through the glorification of his body.

It is important to note that these two understandings of resurrection—a present life of upright conduct and a future glorious resurrection—are related. This hope for the future undergirds and motivates proper behavior in the present. In fact, walking "in newness of life" anticipates the future glory for which believers hope and prepares them for it. Toward the end of Romans 6, Paul makes the connection explicit: "But now that you have been freed from sin and enslaved to God, the advantage you get is sanctification. The end is eternal life. For the wages of sin is death, but the free gift of God is eternal life in Christ Jesus our Lord" (Rom. 6:22–23). A life of sanctification, which begins with baptism, leads ultimately to eternal life.

In light of the connection between baptism and liberation from sin in Romans 6:6–7, it seems likely that Paul's comments later in the chapter continue

8. For an ecumenical approach to the question, see David E. Aune, ed., *Rereading Paul Together: Protestant and Catholic Perspectives on Justification* (Grand Rapids: Baker Academic, 2006).

9. See the discussion in CCC 1987–95.

10. The Greek of v. 5 is actually more compressed, but the NRSV translation essentially gets the meaning of the phrase.

to explicate some of the consequences of baptism, even though the rite is no longer the central focus of his argument. Through baptism, believers have been transferred from the reign of sin to obedience to God. Paul thus exhorts them to lead their lives in light of the implications of their baptism (6:12–14). For Paul, as for many ancient and medieval thinkers, freedom does not mean complete autonomy. Rather, paradoxically, freedom comes about through obedience, and this obedience is made possible by the transfer from death to life that baptism brings about.

Paul develops this notion of slavery, contrasting his audience's former slavery to sin with a new kind of slavery. He describes this new slavery in three different but related ways. Whereas previously the baptized were enslaved to sin, now they have become slaves to obedience (Rom. 6:16), to righteousness (6:18–19), and, ultimately, to God (6:22). Through this "slavery" they will attain to sanctification and, through sanctification, eternal life (6:22–23). As I have suggested in chapter 3 above, this contrast between two kinds of slavery may subtly allude to the exodus story, which repeatedly contrasts the service of Pharaoh with the service of God. The Israelites passed through the waters of the Red Sea from slavery into freedom, but it was a freedom characterized by serving (that is, worshiping) the Lord. Similarly, the baptized pass through the waters of baptism, liberated from the power of sin and enslaved to God.

"Your Life Is Hidden with Christ in God"

With respect to Romans 6, interpreters disagree as to whether Paul speaks of believers rising with Christ through baptism. Although he describes one of the consequences of baptism as walking "in newness of life," he does not explicitly refer to a present resurrection with Christ. By contrast, Colossians does speak of a present resurrection in which the baptized participate. The reference to baptism in Colossians resembles Romans 6, but it takes the imagery of dying and rising with Christ in new directions. Moreover, Paul draws on the imagery of dying with Christ in baptism throughout his exhortation.[11]

11. Modern scholars disagree as to whether Colossians came directly from Paul or not, with a majority holding the latter position. I lean toward the minority position in favor of Pauline authorship, but the answer to this question does not affect the contribution of Colossians to a theology of baptism. I will refer to the author as "Paul" simply for the sake of convenience. For a judicious discussion of the issues involved, see John M. G. Barclay, *Colossians and Philemon*, T&T Clark Study Guides (Edinburgh: T&T Clark, 2004), 18–36.

"Baptism Is the Cross"

Some interpreters have expressed the connection between baptism and the cross in stark terms. St. John Chrysostom, for example, says,

> What does being "baptized into His Death" mean? That it is with a view to our dying as He did. For Baptism is the Cross. What the Cross then, and Burial, is to Christ, that Baptism has been to us, even if not in the same respects. For He died Himself and was buried in the Flesh, but we have done both to sin.[a]

a. John Chrysostom, *Homilies on Romans* 10 (*NPNF*[1] 11:405).

The baptismal reference appears in the midst of a lengthy exhortation that begins at Colossians 2:6. Having described his ministry to the church, Paul turns to offer them instructions on some of the issues facing their community. Before diving into the details, he begins with a general exhortation (2:6–7). Twice in this opening exhortation Paul draws on the imagery of being "in Christ," exhorting them to "walk in him" (NRSV marginal note) and reminding them that they are "rooted and built up in him." The phrase indicates the closeness of the relationship between the believer and Christ. As Romans 6 shows, this relationship is established through baptism. It is hardly surprising, then, that a few verses later in Colossians Paul appeals to baptism.

Paul's major concern is that the Colossians should not abandon Christ for any way of life antithetical to him (Col. 2:8), because in him they have received everything they could hope for. Building on Colossians 1:15–20, where he speaks eloquently about the priority of Christ above all things, Paul tells his audience, "For in him the whole fullness of deity dwells bodily, and you have come to fullness in him, who is the head of every ruler and authority" (2:9–10). Here again we see a variation of the phrase "in him," pointing to the close relationship between the believer and Christ. By their union with Christ, the baptized receive a share in his fullness, which no merely human philosophy or tradition can impart.

Against this backdrop Paul continues to develop the notion of receiving things "in Christ," shifting to a discussion of spiritual circumcision and baptism, which are closely related. Some aspects of the imagery in these verses resemble language found in Romans 6. Paul writes, "In him also you were circumcised with a circumcision made without hands, by putting off the body of the flesh in the circumcision of Christ" (Col. 2:11, modified). The phrase "made without hands" suggests a spiritual rather than a physical circumcision, an idea that goes back to Deuteronomy (Deut. 10:16; 30:6). As the context makes clear, the circumcision of which Paul speaks is a kind of death that takes place through baptism. This circumcision entails a "putting off" of "the body of the flesh." As we have seen above, in Romans 6 Paul uses a similar expression, writing of the destruction of the "body of sin" (6:6). In both verses, the apostle is speaking not of the cessation of biological life but rather of a liberation from sin, the source of spiritual death (cf. Rom. 5:12–21). The "circumcision of Christ" seems, then, to refer not to Christ's actual circumcision as a baby but rather to his death on the cross, to which believers are joined.

This union with Christ, which includes not just death but also (spiritual) resurrection, comes about through baptism: "When you were buried with him in baptism, you were also raised with him through faith in the power of God, who raised him from the dead" (Col. 2:12). The similarity with Romans 6 is obvious. Both texts speak of baptism as a burial with Christ, thus making death one of the primary images and effects of baptism. Colossians, however, goes further than Romans in explicitly speaking of the new life of the baptized as a participation in Christ's resurrection ("you were also raised with him").[12] In this way the letter draws the connection between baptism and resurrection even more closely, though it still maintains a distinction between the present and the future (see Col. 3:3–4).

There is another difference between Colossians and Romans. In Romans, Paul speaks primarily of "sin" in the singular (some interpreters even render the word "Sin," suggesting that, for Paul, sin is a personified or cosmic power), but in Colossians he speaks of the forgiveness of plural "trespasses" (Col. 2:13).[13] Once again, however, Paul describes the forgiveness of trespasses in terms of union with Christ, particularly as a participation

12. We should not overstate the difference, however. Paul's reference to "newness of life" in Rom. 6:4 and the way he uses the language of "life" more generally in Rom. 6:1–11 is not far from Col. 2:12–13. Moreover, in speaking of being "raised with Christ," Col. 2:12 refers to a present (spiritual) resurrection manifested in the way the baptized conduct themselves.

13. Again, it is important not to overstate the difference. Romans does speak occasionally about personal sins (e.g., Rom. 3:23).

in Christ's death and resurrection. Through this forgiveness the baptized receive a new life that, paradoxically, comes about through Christ's death on the cross (2:14).

Paul continues to draw on the imagery of dying and rising with Christ throughout the rest of his exhortation in Colossians 2–3. Toward the end of Colossians 2 Paul asks, "If with Christ you died to the elemental spirits of the universe, why do you live as if you still belonged to the world? Why do you submit to regulations, 'Do not handle, Do not taste, Do not touch'?" (2:20–21). This question and the exhortation that follows advance Paul's earlier warning about mere human philosophies (2:8). Ascetical practices carried out without reference to Christ, to whom believers are joined in baptism, have no value in restraining our sinful inclinations (2:23). The only effective way to overcome these kinds of temptations is to live out the meaning of baptism, which has both positive and negative dimensions.

At the beginning of Colossians 3, Paul shifts to the positive dimension, drawing out the implications of being raised from the dead through baptism: "So if you have been raised with Christ, seek the things that are above, where Christ is, seated at the right hand of God" (Col. 3:1). Baptism ought to bring about a change in perspective and attitude. Rather than keep our minds on earthly things, Paul argues, we must direct our gaze toward Christ's victory. Pursuing heavenly things in the present serves as preparation for full participation in Christ's glory when he returns (3:2–4). The life of the baptized is characterized by a paradox: we are both dead to this world and alive in Christ—but not yet fully alive. Paul maintains what scholars sometimes refer to as an "eschatological reserve." Even though he teaches that through baptism we are raised with Christ, this resurrection is not the fullness of glory for which we hope. The task of the baptized is to live in the present in a manner that anticipates the glory that is to come.

An important part of that life in the present involves putting to death old ways of life. Again, we see the paradox of the current condition of the baptized. The death experienced in baptism is not a once-for-all event that accomplishes everything God has in store for us. Rather, this baptismal death empowers us to bring that death to bear on our lives each day. So, following his expression of hope for the glory to be revealed in Christ, Paul exhorts the Colossians to put to death various vices (Col. 3:5–6). This part of the exhortation clarifies what Paul means by seeking "the things that are above" (3:1), contrasting them with "whatever in you is earthly" (3:5). The earthly things Paul has in mind are the vices that characterized the Colossians' former way of life (3:7). Most of the vices in the first list of this paragraph seem to be what are traditionally called "sins of the flesh," but Paul follows up with an additional list of sins that must be put to death (3:8–9).[14] Baptism demands a new way of life, one that puts to death the vices that belong to the earthly mindset.

Because these exhortations appear somewhat removed from Paul's reference to baptism earlier in the letter (Col. 2:11–12), some might wonder whether one should interpret them as an explication of the significance of baptism. In answer to this question, we should first note that Paul introduces the imagery of dying and rising with Christ in his reference to baptism.[15] Only after this reference does the image become programmatic for his exhortation. In addition to the predominant death and resurrection imagery, Paul's exhortation draws on other baptismal themes, which we will discuss in later chapters. Thus, he writes to the Colossians:

> Do not lie to one another, seeing that you have stripped off the old self with its practices and have clothed yourselves with the new self, which is being renewed in knowledge according to the image of its creator. In that renewal there is no longer Greek and Jew, circumcised and uncircumcised, barbarian, Scythian, slave and free; but Christ is all and in all! (Col. 3:9–11)

Clothing imagery similar to what Paul uses here appears in a baptismal context in Galatians 3:26–29. Paul's reference to the insignificance of ethnic and social distinctions also suggests a baptismal context, since in at least two other places in the Pauline Epistles he roots the unity of people from disparate ethnic groups and classes in their common baptism (1 Cor. 12:13; Gal. 3:28). We will consider these texts more closely in chapter 12.

More can and will be said about the contribution of Colossians to a theology of baptism. The letter brings together many of the central themes associated with baptism in the New Testament. For now, however, we move on to one more letter that speaks of dying with Christ and its implications for an understanding of baptism.

14. The traditional phrase "sins of the flesh" is in some ways an unfortunate one, since for Paul the "flesh" means much more than simply sexual sins. In Gal. 5:19–21, for example, sexual sins do not represent the majority of the "works of the flesh."

15. Technically, Paul speaks of burial and resurrection, but burial necessarily implies death.

"Those Who Belong to Christ Jesus Have Crucified the Flesh"

The most well-known and personal expression of Paul's spirituality of union with Christ appears in the Letter to the Galatians. In a text that has played a crucial role in the theology of Pope Benedict XVI, Paul writes, "I have been crucified with Christ; and it is no longer I who live, but it is Christ who lives in me. And the life I now live in the flesh I live by faith in the Son of God, who loved me and gave himself for me" (Gal. 2:19b–20). Here we see once again the great paradox of Christian existence. On the one hand, Paul speaks of having died with Christ and of no longer living himself. On the other hand, he refers to "the life I now live in the flesh." The Christian life is characterized by both death and life in a constant tension this side of eternity.

Paul's famous statement does not explicitly mention baptism, but that has not stopped interpreters from seeing in these verses a reference to baptism.[16] As early as the late fourth century, St. John Chrysostom saw in this text an allusion to baptism. His explication of these verses encapsulates some important aspects of Paul's baptismal theology:

> In these words, "I am crucified with Christ," he alludes to Baptism and in the words "nevertheless I live, yet not I," our subsequent manner of life whereby our members are mortified. By saying "Christ lives in me," he means nothing is done by me, which Christ disapproves; for as by death he signifies not what is commonly understood, but a death to sin; so by life, he signifies a delivery from sin.[17]

Chrysostom bases this interpretation of the verses in part on some of the themes they share with other baptismal texts in the Pauline corpus, particularly Romans 6:6 and Colossians 3:5. As we have seen, both verses speak of putting to death either the "old self" (Romans) or specific sins (Colossians). Chrysostom explicitly says that the crucifixion of the "old self" took place "in the bath."[18] One could also point to the context of Paul's baptismal reference in Colossians, which speaks of "putting off the body of the flesh" (Col. 2:11).

16. For a slightly fuller discussion of baptism in Galatians, see Rodrigo J. Morales, "Baptism, Unity, and Crucifying the Flesh," in *A Man of the Church: Honoring the Theology, Life, and Witness of Ralph del Colle*, ed. Michel René Barnes (Eugene, OR: Wipf & Stock, 2012), 249–62.

17. John Chrysostom, *Homilies on Galatians* 2 (*NPNF*[1] 13:22, modified).

18. Chrysostom, *Homilies on Galatians* 2.

Despite these similarities, some modern interpreters reject the baptismal interpretation of Galatians 2:19–20, arguing that the connection between baptism and crucifixion with Christ is only a later development, first appearing in Romans 6. One commentator asserts that those who see a baptismal allusion in Galatians 2:20 are reading the text from Romans into Galatians.[19] A more careful consideration of Paul's Letters, however, suggests otherwise. As early as 1 Corinthians, Paul seems to draw at least an implicit connection between baptism and crucifixion. In his initial appeal to the Corinthians regarding the divisions plaguing their church, he asks them rhetorically, "Has Christ been divided? Was Paul crucified for you? Or were you baptized in the name of Paul?" (1 Cor. 1:13). In this brief verse Paul brings together two themes closely related to baptism—namely, unity and crucifixion. Although he elaborates on the former theme later in the letter (1 Cor. 12), he offers no explication of the connection between baptism and crucifixion. Nevertheless, the implicit connection is significant.

Other aspects of Galatians 2:19–20 also resonate with baptismal images or themes.[20] Paul's statement about being crucified with Christ serves as the culmination of his first discussion of justification in the letter, a theme that features prominently throughout Galatians 3. As we saw above, in Romans 6 Paul briefly alludes to justification in the context of baptism (6:7). In another passage from 1 Corinthians that we considered in the previous chapter and to which we will return, Paul also brings together justification and baptism. Exhorting the Corinthians to mend their ways, he reminds them, "But you were washed, you were sanctified, you were *justified* in the name of the Lord Jesus Christ and in the Spirit of our God" (1 Cor. 6:11b). The connection between justification and baptism in this letter is all the more significant because justification is not one of the main issues Paul addresses in the Corinthian correspondence.

By contrast, justification does feature prominently in Galatians 3, toward the end of which Paul explicitly appeals to baptism (Gal. 3:26–29). We will discuss this text at greater length in later chapters. For now, it suffices to note that even within Galatians Paul links justification with baptism. Although he does not explicitly interpret baptism as a co-crucifixion with Christ, the

19. Hans Dieter Betz, *Galatians: A Commentary on Paul's Letter to the Churches in Galatia*, Hermeneia (Philadelphia: Fortress, 1979), 123.

20. For many of the points in this and the following paragraphs, see Morales, "Baptism, Unity, and Crucifying the Flesh," 251–54.

connection between the two would be a natural one. The way Paul speaks of his experience in Galatians 2:20—as well as the crucifixion language in 5:24, which we will consider shortly—seems to point to a onetime event. Some scholars suggest that Paul's co-crucifixion took place on the road to Damascus.[21] Because Paul speaks of this co-crucifixion in a way that applies both to himself and to the Galatians, however, it would seem more natural to see baptism as the event in which co-crucifixion takes place, especially in light of the evidence of Romans 6.

Before we turn to Galatians 5:24, it is worth making one more point in connection with Galatians 2:20. As noted above, the whole structure of the passage reflects the pattern and the paradox we have seen in Romans and Colossians. The death Paul experiences through baptism leads to a new life, a life lived with Christ and for God (Gal. 2:19–20; cf. Rom. 6:10–11; Col. 2:12–13).[22] These parallels further support a baptismal reading of the passage. For a fuller explication of what this new baptismal life looks like, we turn to another of Paul's references to crucifixion in Galatians.

Toward the end of Galatians 5 Paul draws on crucifixion imagery once again, this time in the context of an exhortation. Following a contrast between the "works of the flesh" and the "fruit of the Spirit," Paul writes, "And those who belong to Christ Jesus have crucified the flesh with its passions and desires" (Gal. 5:24). Much like Galatians 2:20, on its surface this verse seems to have little to do with baptism. If we look closer, however, we can see a number of connections with other baptismal texts both in Galatians and in other Pauline Letters. The first hint of a baptismal allusion lies in Paul's phrase "those who belong to Christ Jesus." One could render the phrase a bit more literally (and clunkily) as "those who are Christ Jesus's." The same imagery appears toward the end of Paul's only explicit reference to baptism in Galatians, where he writes, "And if you belong to Christ, then you are Abraham's offspring, heirs according to the promise" (Gal. 3:29). The earlier discussion suggests that the Galatians came to belong to Christ through baptism. In Galatians 5:24, Paul expands on the implications that this new state has for their lives.

The imagery of crucifying the flesh resembles the two main baptismal texts we have considered in this chapter. In Romans, Paul writes, "We know that our old self was crucified with him so that the body of sin might be destroyed, and

21. F. F. Bruce, *The Epistle to the Galatians: A Commentary on the Greek Text*, NIGTC (Grand Rapids: Eerdmans, 1982), 144.

22. See Morales, "Baptism, Unity, and Crucifying the Flesh," 251.

we might no longer be enslaved to sin" (Rom. 6:6). The language of Colossians is even closer to that of Galatians: "In him also you were circumcised with a circumcision made without hands, by putting off *the body of the flesh* in the circumcision of Christ, when you were buried with him in baptism" (Col. 2:11–12a, modified). In both Romans and Colossians, this imagery of destroying the body refers to a death to sin, the same idea behind Galatians 5:24 ("And those who belong to Christ Jesus have crucified the flesh *with its passions and desires*"). The whole build-up to Paul's reference to crucifying the flesh concerns the works of the flesh, which Paul enumerates in a list of vices that stem from obedience to the flesh (Gal. 5:19–21). This is not uncommon in baptismal texts; Paul elsewhere appeals to baptism in order to remind his churches about the kind of life to which they are called.

A few of the themes in Galatians 5 also resemble Paul's exhortation in 1 Corinthians 6. At the end of the vice list of Galatians 5, Paul writes, "I am warning you, as I warned you before: those who do such things will not inherit the kingdom of God" (Gal. 5:21b). Compared to the Gospels, Paul's Letters rarely mention the kingdom of God. For this reason, it is significant that a similar constellation of images—the kingdom of God, a vice list, and an allusion to baptism—also appears in 1 Corinthians. In the midst of criticizing the Corinthians for their practice of taking their fellow believers to court and their engagement in sexual immorality, Paul writes, "Do you not know that wrongdoers will not inherit the kingdom of God?" (1 Cor. 6:9a). Immediately there follows a vice list similar to the one in Galatians 5, ending with a second warning that those who practice these vices will not "inherit the kingdom of God" (1 Cor. 6:9b–10). He then appeals to the change that took place at the Corinthians' baptism to motivate them to put away these vices: "And this is what some of you used to be. But you were washed, you were sanctified, you were justified in the name of the Lord Jesus Christ and in the Spirit of our God" (6:11). Here we see the same cluster of ideas that appears in Galatians 5: a list of vices, a warning about not entering the kingdom of God, and an appeal to a change that has taken place for Paul's audience. Moreover, the text in 1 Corinthians associates baptism with justification, one of the central themes of Galatians.

In light of the many similarities between Galatians 5:24 and these various baptismal texts both within and outside of Galatians, it seems likely that this verse also alludes to the rite. Baptism is the event in which believers first put to death the reality that Paul describes by a variety of terms—the "body of sin" (Rom. 6:6), the "body of the flesh" (Col. 2:11), or "the flesh with its passions and desires" (Gal. 5:24). Through the sacrament, we are joined to Christ's crucifixion, the source of our redemption, and thus liberated from the enslaving power of sin and of our disordered desires.

"Putting Off the Old Human Being"

Dying and rising with Christ is one of the most common—and most powerful—images for Paul's spirituality of union with Christ. It underscores the radical break that this union brings about in the believer. Moreover, it suggests that Christ's death on the cross, the source of our salvation, is not only a death for our sake but also a reality we are called to enter into and embody in our own lives. Baptism initiates us into this paradoxical pattern of death and life and offers us the hope that one day we will enter fully into the reality of Christ's glorious resurrection.

But dying and rising with Christ is not the only image Paul uses to describe a life lived in union with Christ. In Colossians, as he introduces the notion of a baptismal dying and rising with Christ, Paul also speaks of the "putting off" of the body of the flesh (Col. 2:11), an image echoed later when he speaks of "putting off the old human being" (3:9, my translation). On one level, this imagery complements the notion of dying with Christ. On another level, though, this is the language of taking off and putting on clothing, and Paul also draws on this imagery in connection with baptism. To this theme of "putting on the new human being" we now turn.

9

Being Clothed with Christ

> I will greatly rejoice in the LORD,
>   my whole being shall exult in my God;
> for he has clothed me with the garments of salvation,
>   he has covered me with the robe of righteousness,
> as a bridegroom decks himself with a garland,
>   and as a bride adorns herself with her jewels.
>
> —Isaiah 61:10

In Shakespeare's *Hamlet*, as Polonius gives his son Laertes a bit of long-winded advice before setting off for France, the father tells the son, "Apparel oft proclaims the man."[1] The bard's line is just one variation of an idea that goes back to antiquity, the notion that people often judge others by what they wear. As with many sayings, the most amusing version of this adage is attributed to Mark Twain, who is said to have quipped, "Clothes make the man. Naked people have little or no influence on society." The clothes we wear make a first impression on people and influence the way that others perceive us—in some ways with good reason. Clothes can be seen as an extension of our interior life, a reflection of the things we value.

Whether or not Paul was aware of this understanding of clothing, in a few of his letters he draws on clothing imagery to discuss two related topics:

1. William Shakespeare, *Hamlet*, act 1, scene 3.

baptism and the Christian life. Paul's use of this imagery broadly reflects a theme that pervades the writings of the New Testament, though the apostle brings out his own emphases.[2] Among other things, clothing imagery contributes to his depiction of union with Christ and overlaps in important ways with the notion of dying and rising with Christ. Particularly in the Letter to the Colossians, Paul combines death and resurrection language with clothing imagery to ground his exhortation to a new way of life. Other instances of clothing imagery in Paul's writings, such as that found in Romans 13, most likely stem from this baptismal theme. Before we turn to those texts, however, we should begin with Paul's earliest use of this imagery, in his Letter to the Galatians.

"For in Christ Jesus You Are All Sons of God through Faith"

One of the central themes of Galatians is the question of justification, a topic that has been the subject of controversy since the time of the Reformation. We need not get into the details of this long-standing debate. For our purposes, it will suffice to note the significance and basic contours of the topic in Galatians. In a section that many interpreters take as programmatic for the letter (Gal. 2:15–21), Paul introduces the theme, insisting that justification comes by faith and not by works of the law.[3] By the phrase "works of the law," Paul does not mean good works, which he encourages among his congregations. In fact, later in the very same letter, Paul writes, "For in Christ Jesus neither circumcision nor uncircumcision counts for anything; the only thing that counts is *faith working through love*" (5:6). The "works" to which Paul refers throughout much of Galatians are the works of the law of Moses, which include, among other things, circumcision. In fact, circumcision is one of the crucial points of controversy in the letter (see Gal. 2:3, 12; 5:2–3, 6, 11–12; 6:12–15). According to many interpreters' reconstruction of the situation, after Paul had founded the church in Galatia, some missionaries, whom Paul refers to as "agitators" or "troublers" (e.g., 1:7; 5:10), came and told the church that the men among them needed to be circumcised in order to become full

2. Martin Connell notes that the significance of clothing in the New Testament, although quite pervasive, has been largely neglected by modern scholarship. See Connell, "Clothing the Body of Christ: An Inquiry about the Letters of Paul," *Worship* 85 (2011): 128–46, esp. 129–30.

3. See Hans Dieter Betz, *Galatians: A Commentary on Paul's Letter to the Churches in Galatia*, Hermeneia (Philadelphia: Fortress, 1979), 113–14.

members of the Christian movement.[4] It seems likely that these "agitators" appealed to the covenant God made with Abraham, the sign of which was circumcision (Gen. 17:10–14). This would help explain why Paul devotes so much of his argument in Galatians 3 to interpreting the story of Abraham.

This emphasis on circumcision also sheds light on an important aspect of justification. For Paul, justification is not simply about what many modern Christians understand by individual salvation. Rather, an essential part of the question of justification concerns how one becomes a member of Abraham's family and thus an heir to the promise God made to the great patriarch (Gal. 3:29). As Michael Gorman puts it, central to Paul's argument is the idea that the cross and the Spirit suffice.[5] Indeed, at the beginning of Galatians 3 Paul bases his argument on the Galatians' reception of the Spirit: "The only thing I want to learn from you is this: Did you receive the Spirit by doing the works of the law or by believing what you heard?" (3:2).[6] For Paul, the Spirit is the fundamental sign of belonging to Abraham's family, and the Galatians received the Spirit not because they had themselves been circumcised but because they heard and accepted the gospel in faith.

While it is true, as Gorman suggests, that the cross and the Spirit suffice, for Paul these realities are mediated through baptism. Toward the end of Galatians 3, as he draws an important part of the letter's argument to a close, Paul appeals to baptism in a way that pulls together many of the central themes of Galatians: being in Christ, faith, the unity of Jews and Gentiles, and being Abraham's descendants (3:26–29). Here Paul draws on a different symbol than he does in Romans to explicate the significance of baptism: that of putting on a garment.[7] The clothing imagery—indeed, the whole description of the effects of baptism—closely relates to Paul's depiction of Christ as both the Son of God and the crucified one.[8]

4. For a careful reconstruction of the situation that prompted the letter, see John M. G. Barclay, "Mirror-Reading a Polemical Letter: Galatians as a Test Case," *JSNT* 10 (1987): 73–93.

5. Michael J. Gorman, *Apostle of the Crucified Lord: A Theological Introduction to Paul and His Letters*, 2nd ed. (Grand Rapids: Eerdmans, 2017), 235.

6. For a detailed study of the significance of this verse for the letter, see Rodrigo J. Morales, *The Spirit and the Restoration of Israel: New Exodus and New Creation Motifs in Galatians*, WUNT 2/282 (Tübingen: Mohr Siebeck, 2010).

7. This is what the Greek verb *enduō* in Gal. 3:27 means.

8. The section that follows depends and builds upon Rodrigo J. Morales, "Baptism, Unity, and Crucifying the Flesh," in *A Man of the Church: Honoring the Theology, Life, and Witness of Ralph del Colle*, ed. Michel René Barnes (Eugene, OR: Wipf & Stock, 2012), 249–62, esp. 255–57.

Galatians 3:26–29 functions as the climax of Paul's argument against taking up the law of Moses, which he describes as a "disciplinarian" (3:24–25) whose task came to an end with the appearance of Christ. With the arrival of Christ and their acceptance of him by faith, the Galatians' situation has changed dramatically. They are now "in Christ Jesus," and because of that new location they are "sons of God" (3:26).[9] This change in status dominates Galatians 3:23–4:7, as does the notion of being under "guardians." In Galatians 4:1–7, Paul speaks of this change as a movement from being slaves "under guardians and trustees" to being sons.[10] As a result of this adoption, the Galatians have become sons and thereby heirs (4:7; cf. 3:29).

The language of being "in Christ" is one of Paul's favorite ways to refer to the notion of participation in or union with Christ, and it is significant that Paul introduces his reference to baptism with this imagery as well as with a reference to faith.[11] For Paul, faith and baptism are inseparable, and it is through them that believers become sons of God in Christ Jesus. But what does it mean to be a "son of God"? In order to answer this question, let us consider some of the ways Paul uses the language of sonship, first in Galatians and then in Romans.

As already noted, Paul uses the phrase "Son of God" in Galatians 2:20, a crucial verse for the letter and for Paul's thought more generally. There he writes, "I have been crucified with Christ; and it is no longer I who live, but it is Christ who lives in me. And the life I now live in the flesh I live by faith in the Son of God, who loved me and gave himself for me" (2:19b–20). Christ's identity as the "Son of God" is closely bound up with his crucifixion. Paul introduces the phrase in the context of his own crucifixion with Christ. Moreover, he explicates the phrase in light of Christ's gift of self. As in the Gospel according to Mark, for Paul, Christ's identity as the "Son of God" is bound up with this gift.[12]

This emphasis on self-gift has implications for what it means for believers to be "sons of God."[13] Paul associates the status of believers as God's sons with

9. I have modified the NRSV from "children" to "sons." See n. 13 below for my reasoning. This idea of being "in Christ Jesus" relates back to Paul's description of his union with Christ in Gal. 2:19–20, a passage in which Paul also uses the phrase "Son of God" with reference to Christ.

10. The Greek word for "guardians" in Gal. 4:2 is different from the word in 3:25, but the basic idea is the same.

11. On the pervasiveness of "in Christ" language in Paul's Letters, see James D. G. Dunn, *The Theology of Paul the Apostle* (Grand Rapids: Eerdmans, 1998), 390–400.

12. See the discussion of Mark in chap. 5 above.

13. For Paul, the term "sons" includes both men and women (Gal. 3:28). One of the reasons he uses the term is to make clear the connection between the sonship of the baptized and that of Christ.

the gift of the Spirit and with the early Christian exclamatory prayer "Abba! Father!" (Gal. 4:6). Elsewhere in the New Testament, including in Paul's own writings, this cry is associated with suffering. The phrase appears again in the Letter to the Romans in connection with the question of inheritance, as in Galatians. In Romans 8 Paul appeals to his audience's status as sons of God in the context of the conflict between the Spirit and the flesh. "For all who are led by the Spirit of God," Paul writes, "are sons of God" (Rom. 8:14 ESV). It is by that same Spirit that believers cry out, "Abba! Father!" and are shown to be children and heirs (8:15–16). This inheritance, however, depends on the willing acceptance of suffering with Christ (8:17). God's sons are called to "put to death the deeds of the body" (8:13). This close connection between the "Abba" prayer and suffering should come as no surprise. The other context in which the phrase "Abba, Father" appears in the New Testament is in Mark's account of Jesus's prayer in Gethsemane (Mark 14:32–42). To be a son of God means to accept the will of the heavenly Father, even if it includes terrible suffering.

This is the new status of those who are "in Christ," and they receive it through baptism. Paul's use of the conjunction "for" links his statement about being sons of God in Galatians 3:26 with the rite of baptism in verse 27. One could rearrange and paraphrase those verses to say, "Since by your baptism into Christ you have been clothed with Christ, in Christ you are sons of God through faith." The imagery of clothing should not be seen merely as an exterior garment. Rather, "wearing" Christ transforms a person's status. This new status has numerous implications for the life of the Church, including interactions between people of different ethnicities and social status. We will return to this question in a later chapter. Skipping over Galatians 3:28 for now, in the last verse of Galatians 3 we see that baptism brings about three additional and interrelated changes for those who receive the sacrament.

First, Paul implicitly describes baptism as a transfer of ownership. Those who are baptized now belong to Christ—Galatians 3:29 begins with the phrase "And if you are Christ's." As I argued in the preceding chapter, belonging to Christ necessarily implies co-crucifixion with him and putting to death the desires of the flesh. Paul says precisely this in a later chapter: "And *those who belong to Christ Jesus* have crucified the flesh with its passions and desires" (Gal. 5:24). This further confirms that putting on Christ as a garment in baptism is no mere external act but rather a transformative one.

Second, because the baptized belong to Christ, they are also Abraham's "offspring" (Gal. 3:29). This conclusion follows from an earlier point in Paul's argument concerning the promises to Abraham. Discussing the nature of these promises, Paul notes that Genesis speaks of Abraham's "offspring" (singular), not "offsprings" (Gal. 3:16).[14] Paul takes this "offspring" as referring to Christ. All those who through faith and baptism have come to be in Christ, then, are included in Abraham's offspring.

Finally, belonging to Christ and being Abraham's "offspring" make the baptized "heirs according to the promise" (Gal. 3:29b). "Promise" has a number of connotations in Galatians. In several places it refers simply to the promise God spoke to Abraham (e.g., Gal. 3:15–18; 4:23, 28). At an important point in the letter, however, Paul also closely identifies the promise with the Spirit and with the blessing of Abraham. Describing Christ's act of redemption, Paul writes, "Christ redeemed us from the curse of the law by becoming a curse for us . . . in order that in Christ Jesus the blessing of Abraham might come to the Gentiles, so that we might receive the promise of the Spirit through faith" (3:13–14). It is by the reception of the Spirit that the baptized are sons in the Son. As I suggested above, Paul makes a similar point in the subsequent chapter (4:6–7). The reception of the Spirit through the act of putting on Christ makes the baptized believer a son and an heir.

"Having Put On the New Human Being"

The clothing imagery of Galatians is brief, and it is only by relating it to other parts of the letter that one can get a better sense of what Paul means by it. In the Letter to the Colossians, Paul develops the idea at greater length, fleshing out the significance of this symbolism. As in Galatians, the imagery of donning Christ like a garment overlaps with the notion of dying with Christ and putting to death the deeds of the body.[15]

The first appearance of clothing language occurs in a passage that brings together three images found also in Galatians: circumcision, the body of flesh, and baptism (Col. 2:11–12). Paul speaks here of the Colossians having under-

14. One might be tempted to say that Paul is playing a little fast and loose with the text. While it is true that Genesis speaks of a singular "offspring" or "seed" (Hebrew *zera'*, Greek *sperma*), the noun in Gen. 15 and 17 is meant as a collective. On the other hand, Gal. 3:29 shows that for Paul, Abraham's seed is also collective, including all those who are in Christ.

15. It is worth noting that the actual phrase "put on Christ" does not appear in Colossians. Rather, Paul speaks here of putting on the "new human being [*anthrōpos*]." Nevertheless, this idea, which he links with the language of "image" (Col. 3:10), relates back to the poem in Col. 1:15–20, which begins by referring to Christ as "the image of the invisible God."

gone a "putting off [of] the body of the flesh." As in Galatians 5—indeed, as is often the case in Paul's Letters—here the "flesh" refers not to muscle and tissue but rather to the weakened human condition dominated by sin.[16] In Colossians the connection between clothing imagery and dying and rising with Christ, mediated by the symbol of Christ's "circumcision," is even clearer than in Galatians. As I suggested in chapter 8, the "circumcision" of which Paul speaks here is not the Jewish rite of initiation but rather a symbolic way of speaking of Christ's death. Through baptism believers are joined to Christ's death, being buried with him in the rite and rising with him in an anticipatory sense (Col. 2:12). For much of the rest of this section of the letter, Paul focuses on the imagery of dying with Christ, applying it to the Colossians' spiritual life (2:20; 3:5). In chapter 3, however, he shifts back to the imagery of taking off and putting on clothing.

This shift once again highlights the close connection between the imagery of dying and of taking off clothing. Following an expression of hope for future glory and life with Christ (Col. 3:3–4), Paul exhorts the Colossians to put to death various vices (3:5–7). In 3:8, however, the imagery takes a new direction. Paul speaks first of getting rid of other vices, and in the next verse he returns to clothing imagery, grounding his exhortation in the reminder "You have stripped off the old human being [*anthrōpos*] with its practices" (3:9, modified). Providing a contrast to the stripping off of the "body of flesh" and the "old human being," Paul also reminds his audience that they "have clothed themselves with the new human being [*anthrōpos*], which is being renewed in knowledge according to the image of its creator" (3:10, modified).

Although this language of stripping off the old human being and putting on the new human being is considerably removed from Paul's reference to baptism in Colossians 2:12, at least three factors suggest a baptismal interpretation of the imagery. First, there is the evidence of Galatians, where Paul describes baptism as an act of putting on Christ (Gal. 3:27). Second, and closely related to the first point, in Colossians 3 Paul uses the clothing imagery in connection with the notion of unity across ethnic and social differences. Immediately after his reference to putting on the new human being, Paul writes, "In that renewal there is no longer Greek and Jew, circumcised and uncircumcised, barbarian, Scythian, slave and free; but Christ is all and in all!" (Col. 3:11). Similar lists of such pairings appear in baptismal contexts elsewhere in Paul's Letters. As

16. See Morales, *The Spirit and the Restoration of Israel*, 141–43.

we saw above, in Galatians Paul moves immediately from the imagery of putting on Christ to an affirmation of unity in Christ across the various divisions among believers (Gal. 3:27–28). A similar list appears in one of Paul's appeals to baptism in 1 Corinthians: "For in the one Spirit we were all baptized into one body—Jews or Greeks, slaves or free—and we were all made to drink of one Spirit" (1 Cor. 12:13). Unity is one of the primary effects of baptism, a point to which we will return in chapter 12. For now, it suffices to note the association of baptism with unity. Finally, there is the close connection between the idea of disrobing and donning new clothes and the imagery of death and life. The latter imagery clearly relates to baptism (Col. 2:12), and the former makes its first appearance in the context of a baptismal reference, as noted above. The way Paul shifts seamlessly from speaking of death to putting off and putting on the new human being suggests an affinity between the two images as ways of speaking about the significance of baptism.

The language of Colossians 3:9–10 differs slightly from that of Galatians 3:27. Whereas in Galatians Paul speaks of putting on "Christ," in Colossians he speaks of donning the "new human being." The letter, however, offers a clue suggesting that these are simply two different ways of referring to the same reality. With respect to the new human being, Paul notes that it is "being renewed in knowledge according to the image of its creator" (Col. 3:10). One could take the reference to the "image" as an allusion to the opening chapter of Genesis, which describes how God made human beings in the "image of God" (Gen. 1:27). On one level, the creation of human beings in Genesis certainly lies in the background of the notion of "being renewed." On a more important level, however, the image language refers to Christ. The word "image" appears only one other time in Colossians, in one of the most well-known and important passages of the letter. The poetic section that describes Christ's preeminence in both creation and redemption begins by calling Christ "the image of the invisible God, the firstborn of all creation" (Col. 1:15). Putting on the "new human being," then, means putting on Christ, the true "image of the invisible God."

One other aspect of the reference to putting on the "new human being" deserves further consideration. As already noted, when Paul reminds the Colossians that they have put on the new human being, he writes that this new human being "is being renewed in knowledge according to the image of its creator" (Col. 3:10). This statement suggests that being clothed with a new human being involves a onetime event in the past with ongoing implications. For the reasons discussed above, the moment at which believers put on the new human being is baptism. But baptism is just the beginning of a lifelong transformation, a continual donning of Christ, the new human being. It seems likely, then, that when Paul uses this imagery in other contexts, its roots remain in baptism. The Christian life, therefore, is a matter of growing into the reality begun at baptism. The way Paul phrases this renewal, however, underscores the priority of grace. Growth in the Christian life comes not from our own natural efforts but rather from the work of God within us. The apostle describes this renewal using the passive voice ("which is being renewed"), suggesting that God acts as the primary agent in the ongoing transformation of the Christian.

The primacy of God's grace does not mean, however, that believers have nothing to do. Paul expounds on this aspect of baptism in the following paragraph of Colossians, shifting to the mode of exhortation but continuing to use clothing imagery: "As God's chosen ones, holy and beloved, clothe yourselves with compassion, kindness, humility, meekness, and patience" (Col. 3:12). Once again, Paul leads with the primacy of God's action: the Colossians have been chosen by God. In light of this election, they are called to put on various virtues. Paul emphasizes virtues that contribute to unity, which should come as no surprise given the close connection between baptism

Stripping Off the Passions

In the ancient Church, catechumens approaching the waters of baptism literally stripped themselves, seeing in this act a profound and multilayered symbolism. St. Cyril of Jerusalem writes,

> Immediately, then, upon entering, you removed your tunics. This was a figure of the "stripping off of the old man with his deeds." Having stripped, you were naked, in this also imitating Christ, who was naked on the cross, by His nakedness "throwing off the cosmic powers and authorities like a garment and publicly upon the cross leading them in triumphal procession." For as the forces of the enemy made their lair in our members, you may no longer wear the old garment. I do not, of course, refer to this visible garment, but to "the old man which, deluded by its lusts, is sinking towards death."[a]

a. Cyril of Jerusalem, *Second Lecture on the Mysteries* 2, in *The Works of St. Cyril of Jerusalem*, vol. 2, trans. Leo P. McCauley and Anthony A. Stephenson, FC 64 (Washington, DC: Catholic University of America Press, 2000), 161–62.

and unity.[17] In the verses that follow, he urges the Colossians to bear with and forgive one another, finally appealing to the highest of Christian virtues, love: "Above all, clothe yourselves with love, which binds everything together in perfect harmony" (Col. 3:14).

Paul follows this appeal with an allusion to the image of Christians making up one body, which elsewhere is associated with baptism: "And let the peace of Christ rule in your hearts, to which indeed you were called in the one body" (Col. 3:15). In 1 Corinthians Paul speaks of being baptized "into one body" (1 Cor. 12:13). This reference to "one body" appears in a context similar to that of Colossians 3:11, a relativizing of the divisions of ethnicity and social status. In a brief encomium on unity in Ephesians, Paul refers to both "one body" and "one baptism" (Eph. 4:4–6), though the two phrases do not appear as closely together as they do in 1 Corinthians. Baptism into the body of Christ brings about—and therefore demands of the baptized—behavior that contributes to unity, as the heart of Paul's exhortation in Colossians 3:12–15 shows. We will return to these texts from 1 Corinthians and Ephesians in chapter 12.

In addition to behavior that fosters unity, Paul encourages the Colossians to take up or continue three further practices. First, he exhorts them, "Let the word of Christ dwell in you richly" (Col. 3:16a). Baptism and faith go hand in hand, and faith draws its nourishment from the word of God. Familiarity with the Scriptures, whether through personal reading or through regular attendance at the liturgy, constitutes a crucial aspect of the Christian life.[18] Paul then urges the Colossians, "And whatever you do, in word or deed, do everything in the name of the Lord Jesus, giving thanks to God the Father through him" (3:17). Rather than describe separate practices, then, this exhortation sums up two attitudes essential to the Christian life. The first is to do everything in the name of the Lord, keeping him ever in mind in all that we do. The second is one that pervades the Letter to the Colossians: a posture of gratitude to God for his many abundant gifts.[19]

17. For more on this point, see chap. 12 below.

18. Access to the Scriptures has varied by historical period as well as cultural context. It is important to remember that the high rates of literacy in the modern West are the exception rather than the rule. Nevertheless, the ordinary believer in the Middle Ages could heed Paul's exhortation through attentive participation in the Church's liturgy, as can modern believers who by reason of circumstance are unable to read the Scriptures for themselves, whether because of lack of access or because of illiteracy.

19. In addition to the reference to thanksgiving in Col. 3:17, Paul emphasizes the importance of gratitude in Col. 1:12; 2:7; 3:15; 4:2.

An Interior Clothing

The imagery of clothing might lend itself to a superficial interpretation of the effects of baptism, as if the sacrament only provides a covering. The fourteenth-century Byzantine theologian Nicholas Cabasilas makes it abundantly clear that being clothed with Christ is as much an interior reality as an exterior one:

> He does not merely bestow a crown or give them some share in His glory, He gives them Himself, the Victor who is crowned with glory. When we come up from the water we bear the Saviour upon our souls, on our heads, on our eyes, in our very inward parts, on all our members—Him who is pure from sin, free from all corruption, just as He was when He rose again and appeared to His disciples, as He was taken up, as He will come again to demand the return of His treasure.[a]

a. Nicholas Cabasilas, *The Life in Christ* 1.11, trans. Carmino J. DeCatanzaro (Crestwood, NY: St. Vladimir's Seminary Press, 1974), 62.

Putting on the new human being and being renewed in the image of the Creator is not simply an external act. Rather, donning Christ as a garment brings about a transformation of life, empowering the baptized to live in unity and put on the virtues that Christ exemplifies. Little wonder, then, that Paul also uses this imagery in his moral exhortation elsewhere in his letters.

"Put On the Armor of Light"

Sitting alone in a garden in Milan, wrestling violently with his addiction to sin and beseeching the Lord to liberate him, St. Augustine heard a little child saying in a singsong voice, "Take and read, take and read!" Interpreting the phrase as a divine command, Augustine returned to the place where he had left his copy of the Letters of Paul and read the first lines that caught his eye: "Not in reveling and drunkenness, not in debauchery and licentiousness, not in quarreling and jealousy. Instead, put on the Lord Jesus Christ, and make no provision for the flesh, to gratify its desires" (Rom. 13:13–14).[20] The rest,

20. I have quoted the NRSV rather than a translation of the Latin version Augustine would have read. The scene is beautifully recounted, as only Augustine could tell it, in book 8 of the *Confessions*.

as the cliché goes, is history. This was the moment of his definitive conversion and decision to receive baptism, but not before a period of retirement and study. Heeding the exhortation to put on Christ, Augustine approached the waters of baptism, knowing full well that receiving the sacrament would be just the beginning of his transformation. Indeed, few people have understood the ongoing struggle of the Christian life as well as the great bishop of Hippo.

In light of the lifelong nature of discipleship, it makes sense that, in addition to referring to baptism as a onetime event in which the baptized are clothed with Christ, Paul would also use this imagery to exhort Christians to live out their baptismal vocation. Given the baptismal context of the imagery, it is important not to treat these two different applications of clothing as completely unrelated to one another. Rather, it seems more likely that Paul's exhortations to put on Christ flow naturally from the significance of baptism, even if he does not always make the connection explicit.

Toward the end of Romans, Paul urges his audience to "put on the Lord Jesus Christ" (Rom. 13:14). This appeal serves as a summation of what has gone before it, at least as far back as Romans 13:8. There Paul calls on the Romans to love one another because love is the fulfillment of the law. Reflecting a tradition that pervades the New Testament, Paul affirms that all of the commandments (or at least those concerning our fellow human beings) are encapsulated in the command "Love your neighbor as yourself" (13:9b).[21]

Paul follows this summary of the law by shifting to the imagery of light and darkness, a common theme throughout much of early Christianity. Twice in this section the apostle uses the language of putting on a garment of some sort: the exhortation to put on Christ (Rom. 13:14) and an exhortation to put on armor. Reminding the Romans that their salvation is fast approaching, he urges them, "Let us then lay aside the works of darkness and *put on* the armor of light" (13:12b). The imagery of armor is a common one in Paul's Letters, with roots in a few texts from the Old Testament. In 1 Thessalonians, which many scholars consider to be his earliest letter, Paul appeals again to the contrast between night and day, reminding the Thessalonians that they have "put on the breastplate of faith and love, and for a helmet the hope of salvation" (1 Thess. 5:8b). A similar use of this image occurs in Ephesians 6, where Paul exhorts his audience to arm themselves for spiritual battle (6:11, 14–17). Both these texts, as well as Romans 13, draw upon Isaiah 59, which

21. This commandment, which first appears in Lev. 19:18, features prominently in Jesus's last days in Jerusalem (Matt. 22:39; Mark 12:31) and is also found in Gal. 5:14 and James 2:8.

describes the Lord as a warrior who dons metaphorical armor and clothing (59:17). The Wisdom of Solomon, a text from shortly before the time of the New Testament, likewise develops this motif (Wis. 5:17–20). Paul's application of the divine warrior imagery to his congregations suggests that a close union with the Lord is essential to living out the Christian life well.

Continuing his exhortation, Paul specifies the "works of darkness" that the Romans are to cast off, which include sins of the body such as drunkenness and disordered sexual acts as well as sins of division (Rom. 13:13). Although a bit shorter, the brief vice list of Romans 13:13 resembles the list in Galatians 5:19–21 in terms of substance. As I argued in chapter 8, the list in Galatians precedes an allusion to baptism as a crucifixion of the flesh (Gal. 5:24). It also follows the only explicit baptismal reference in Galatians, a reference that speaks of baptism as donning Christ like a garment (3:27). It is easy to see, then, why Paul in Romans appeals again to this clothing imagery and applies it to the subduing of the flesh. The clothing of oneself with Christ that initially takes place at baptism must be repeatedly applied over the entire course of a Christian life. Just as the Israelites, newly rescued from Egypt, had to live into God's gift of freedom, so the baptized must continually clothe themselves with Christ, conquering their sins with the help of his grace.

"Be Renewed in the Spirit of Your Minds"

Situated in the middle of Paul's moral exhortation in Ephesians we find one more application of the clothing imagery that loosely resembles the baptismal reference in Galatians. Significantly, this instance of clothing language appears not long after a reference to baptism. Toward the beginning of the second half of Ephesians, Paul urges his audience to maintain unity (Eph. 4:3). Among the factors contributing to this unity is baptism (4:5). Although the letter does not draw an explicit connection between baptism and clothing imagery, because of the connections in Galatians and Colossians it is at least plausible that such a connection may lie in the background, especially if the practice of using an actual baptismal garment had already begun by this time.

Regardless of whether early Christians were already using baptismal garments, the imagery of putting on "the new human being" appears in the context of a description of the new life believers begin at baptism (Eph. 4:17–32). Paul contrasts this new life with the former ways of his audience, when they walked "as the Gentiles live, in the futility of their minds" (4:17b). Formerly, the Ephesians had a darkened understanding and were alienated from God (4:18). Since their conversion, Paul reminds them, they have learned Christ (4:20), which has important consequences for how they lead their lives.

Negatively, their conversion entails a putting away of the "old human being" (see Eph. 4:22).[22] As in Colossians, the primary characteristic of this old human being is disordered desires, among which are sensuality, greed, and impurity (Eph. 4:19), as well as falsehood, theft, sins of speech, and hostility (4:25, 28–29, 31).[23] Positively, the Christian life involves putting on the new human being. Without being identical to it, the language of Ephesians resembles that of Colossians. In that letter Paul speaks of putting on the new human being, which is "according to the image of its creator" (Col. 3:10). Ephesians speaks of putting on the new human being "created according to [or in accord with] God" (Eph. 4:24, my translation). The "new human being" that Paul calls the Ephesians to put on ought to be characterized by "true righteousness and holiness" (4:24). Although Ephesians does not develop the imagery of clothing to the same extent that Colossians does, the letter nevertheless does present this "new human being" as a summation of the kind of life to which the Ephesians have been called. Similarly, the "old human being" serves as a shorthand description of the life they have set aside through baptism.

New Garment, New Life

A variant of the saying "Clothes make the man," one perhaps more popular in our own time, recommends that a person "dress for success." A person who shows up for a job interview in a ratty T-shirt or in clothes that he or she has clearly worn for several days will have a much lower likelihood of success than a person who dresses professionally. The sins that the desires of the flesh prompt us to commit are like the old ratty clothes worn to the interview. They diminish our human dignity, marring the image of God within us. In baptism the Lord has given us himself as a new garment, shining with the Christian virtues. Success in the Christian life is measured not by money or fame or power—things that inevitably fade away and are of no use when we

22. The verb translated as "putting away" (*apotithēmi*) is not the same as the word in Col. 3:9 (*apekduomai*). Nevertheless, the verb in Eph. 4:22 also appears in Acts 7:58 with reference to people laying aside their garments.

23. Paul uses the same verb to refer to both putting away the old human being and putting away falsehood.

die—but rather by the charity with which we treat God and neighbor. Baptism calls us to a new life, one in which we grow into the image of the Creator. As our growth in the natural life begins with conception, so our growth in the Christian life begins with a new birth by water and the Spirit marked by an enduring hope. To that new birth and to that hope we now turn.

10

Baptism and New Birth

And you shall be to me a kingdom of priests and a holy nation.

—Exodus 19:6a (ESV)

Various texts in the New Testament describe baptism with the imagery of new birth. As we saw in chapter 6, Jesus's late-night conversation with Nicodemus revolves around the notion of being born "again" or "from above" (John 3:1–15). Set firmly against the backdrop of several baptismal references, Jesus's language of being born "of water and the Spirit" makes most sense as a reference to baptism. A passing remark in Paul's Letter to Titus likewise alludes to baptism in a way that invokes both water and the Spirit, referring to a "washing of regeneration and renewal of the Holy Spirit" (Titus 3:5 ESV).[1] Perhaps the most extensive use of the image of new birth, however, appears in the First Letter of Peter, where such language appears three times over the course of the first two chapters (1 Pet. 1:3, 23; 2:2). The relatively extensive nature of this imagery, combined with the explicit reference to baptism in 1 Peter 3:21, led some twentieth-century interpreters to suggest that the entire letter concerns baptism in some way. The letter has been variously construed as the instructions for a baptismal liturgy, a baptismal homily, or, even more specifically, a baptismal homily for a paschal liturgy.[2]

1. One should note that the Greek words for "new birth" and "regeneration" in John and Titus differ from one another as well as from the language of 1 Peter. Nevertheless, the basic idea is the same.

2. The basic idea was first proposed in 1911 by the German scholar Richard Perdelwitz. For arguments in support of this reading in English, see, among others, F. L. Cross, *1 Peter: A*

Other scholars have understandably balked at such specific accounts of the nature and purpose of 1 Peter.[3] The evidence of the letter seems too vague to warrant such precise interpretations. In literary form, the text is a letter—with a greeting, opening prayer, and conclusion—not a homily, much less the first-century equivalent of a modern-day rite of baptism. Nevertheless, in light of the broader early Christian understanding of baptism as a new birth, 1 Peter offers an important explication of this new birth and what it entails for the life of the baptized. Fundamental to the baptismal theology of the letter is the significance of the rite for salvation. "Baptism . . . now saves you," the letter states (1 Pet. 3:21). This salvation has implications for both the present and the future. The new birth brought about by baptism imparts to the baptized a living hope for an incorruptible inheritance (1:3–12). Moreover, baptism involves a calling to a new kind of life, one characterized by holiness (1:16) and love (1:22), as the baptized become a part of a new royal and priestly people (2:9).[4]

"Baptism . . . Now Saves You"

As noted in chapter 2 above, 1 Peter 3:20–21, with its reference to Noah and his family, exercised considerable influence on early Christian interpretations of baptism. Containing the only explicit reference to baptism in the letter, these verses play an important role in understanding the baptismal theology of 1 Peter. The context of the verses emphasizes the priority of the saving acts of Christ's suffering, death, resurrection, and ascension, from which baptism draws its efficacy. Like much of 1 Peter, this section of the letter addresses the question of suffering, and it does so by appealing to Christ's example. The reference to Noah and his family is preceded by a description of Christ's saving work. That work includes his suffering, death, and resurrection, all of which have as their purpose "that he might bring us to God" (1 Pet. 3:18 ESV).

The initial reference to Christ's suffering, death, and resurrection leads into the example of Noah and his family. The details of these verses are murky

---

Paschal Liturgy (London: Mowbray, 1954); Oscar S. Brooks, "1 Peter 3:21—The Clue to the Literary Structure of the Epistle," *NovT* 16 (1974): 290–305.

3. G. R. Beasley-Murray, *Baptism in the New Testament* (Grand Rapids: Eerdmans, 1962), 251–58; David Hill, "On Suffering and Baptism in 1 Peter," *NovT* 18 (1976): 181–89.

4. The implications of baptism need not be limited to those verses that speak of the rite explicitly or allusively with the imagery of new birth. Nevertheless, in order to keep this chapter from becoming a full-blown commentary on the entire letter, I will limit it to an explication of these references and their surrounding context.

and have been the subject of much debate. On the surface, 1 Peter 3:19 seems to allude to the Christian tradition of the "harrowing of hell," the belief that in the interval between the crucifixion and the resurrection Christ descended into the realm of the dead and preached the gospel to the souls there. There are difficulties with such a reading, however. The letter seems to describe this preaching as taking place after Christ's resurrection: "But [Christ was] made alive in the spirit, in which also he went and made a proclamation to the spirits in prison" (1 Pet. 3:18b–19). The question is an intriguing one, but, when it comes to the letter's teaching on baptism, not much hangs on resolving the significance of this imagery.[5] More important for our purposes is the letter's mention of baptism in connection with Noah and his family.

As noted earlier, some early Christians saw in the number of human beings aboard the ark (eight) a figural anticipation of the resurrection, which was often associated with the "eighth day."[6] The rescue of these eight people "through water" leads Peter to speak of baptism, a water ritual that "now saves you" (1 Pet. 3:20–21).[7] The saving power of baptism stems not from its natural properties, however ("not as a removal of dirt from the body"), but rather from its connection with the resurrection ("but as an appeal to God for a good conscience, through the resurrection of Jesus Christ") (3:21). As in the Letters of Paul, so in 1 Peter baptism draws its power from Christ's resurrection and in this way offers hope to those who receive the sacrament, though the letter expresses this connection and hope in different ways, particularly with the imagery of new birth, as we will see. This brief, passing appeal to baptism ends as it begins, with another reference to Christ's victory, describing his ascension into heaven, his sitting at the right hand of God (a theme found throughout the New Testament and based on Ps. 110), and the subjection of "angels, authorities, and powers" to him (1 Pet. 3:22). The surrounding context of this baptismal reference makes clear that the water rite derives

5. On the various issues in the passage, see Cynthia Long Westfall, "The Relationship between the Resurrection, the Proclamation to the Spirits in Prison and Baptismal Regeneration: 1 Peter 3.19–22," in *Resurrection*, ed. Stanley E. Porter, Michael A. Hayes, and David Tombs, JSNTSup 186 (Sheffield, UK: Sheffield Academic, 1999), 106–35.

6. See chap. 2 above for details.

7. Although many modern scholars deny that 1 Peter was actually penned by the apostle, I will refer to the author as "Peter" for the sake of simplicity. This connection between baptism and salvation is also reflected in Mark 16:16, part of the longer ending of Mark. Although most scholars do not believe Mark 16:9–20 forms a part of the original version of Mark, the Catholic Church implicitly affirms its value as Scripture, as indicated by the fact that it serves as the lectionary reading for the Feast of St. Mark on April 25.

its power and efficacy from Christ's saving work. First Peter describes one of the primary effects of this saving work as the new birth that Christians experience at their baptism.

"A New Birth into a Living Hope"

After the opening greeting, 1 Peter moves into a prayer of blessing to God for the gifts of salvation that he has given believers. Such prayers are common in early Christian letters, as can be seen in most of Paul's letters.[8] Addressing an audience that seems to be enduring much suffering, the blessing focuses on the unshakable nature of the salvation God has prepared for Christians and for which they hope. The blessing has an implicit trinitarian structure, with the first part of the prayer focusing on God the Father and what he has done for believers (1 Pet. 1:3–5), the second part shifting to Christ and his coming revelation (1:6–9), and the third part highlighting the role of the Holy Spirit in inspiring the Old Testament prophets, who foretold the grace that believers would receive through Christ (1:10–12).[9] Significantly, the first act Peter ascribes to God is the new birth of believers: "Blessed be the God and Father of our Lord Jesus Christ! By his great mercy he has given us a new birth into a living hope through the resurrection of Jesus Christ from the dead" (1:3). While it is true that Peter nowhere explicitly describes baptism as a new birth, three factors suggest that this language at the very least alludes to baptism.

First, as noted in the introduction to this chapter, other passages in the New Testament also use the language of new birth to refer to baptism. Both the Gospel of John and Titus bring together references to water, the Spirit, and new birth, albeit with different Greek words for the image of new birth.[10] Second, one of the main themes of the opening benediction of 1 Peter is salvation—the word appears three times in a span of six verses (1 Pet. 1:5,

8. The famous exception to this structure is the Letter to the Galatians, which includes no prayer or thanksgiving. The blessing of 1 Peter most closely resembles the prayer of Eph. 1:3–14.

9. This presumes that 1 Pet. 1:10–12 constitutes a part of the benediction, a point on which interpreters disagree. The clear shift in 1:13 (marked by the transition word "therefore") suggests a new section. Moreover, the phrase "concerning this salvation" (v. 10) closely connects these verses with the earlier ones. It seems best, then, to take vv. 10–12 as part of the benediction. Part of the letter opening (1:2) has a similar trinitarian structure, though the order differs, with the Spirit mentioned before Christ.

10. John 3:1–8 uses the Greek adverb *anōthen*, which can mean both "again" and "from above." Titus 3:5 uses the noun *palingenesia*, which is frequently rendered "regeneration" in English.

9, 10). As we have seen, later in the letter Peter explicitly writes that baptism "now saves you" (3:21).[11] Finally, the image of new birth suggests a onetime change, the beginning of a new life. Especially in light of the connection between baptism and new birth in other texts of the New Testament, the event in a Christian's life that most obviously corresponds to this new beginning is the rite of baptism.

Taking the new birth of 1 Peter 1:3 as a baptismal reference, we can thus see the benediction at least in part as an explication of the gifts and the promises that God makes to those who receive baptism. This opening prayer emphasizes both the glory for which believers hope and the sufferings that necessarily precede the fulfillment of that glory. Although the language of 1 Peter differs from that of Paul, the basic structure resembles Paul's own understanding of the relationship between suffering and glory (see, e.g., Rom. 8:16–17).

Peter begins with the good news, the great hope that God has in store for the baptized. This hope finds its certainty in the resurrection of Christ as well as (implicitly) in his ascension. Peter describes this hope as "an inheritance that is imperishable, undefiled, and unfading, kept in heaven for you" (1 Pet. 1:4). For the time being, believers cannot see this inheritance in its fullness, but, Peter reminds his audience, God is guarding them until the time their salvation is to be revealed (1:5). Peter's emphasis on the imperishability of the inheritance Christians anticipate serves as a fitting contrast to their current condition of suffering and as a powerful motivation to endure the trials of this present life.

The purpose of these trials, Peter continues, is to prove the genuineness of believers' faith (1 Pet. 1:6–7). The various sufferings of the new life into which Christians are born through baptism are meant to lead to glory and honor at the last time, when Christ is revealed (1:5, 7). The present life of the baptized is a time of faith—1 Peter implicitly underscores the close relationship between baptism and faith—that results in joy even in the midst of suffering. It is by this faith that believers love Christ even though they have not seen him, and this love brings about an inexpressible joy that leads to salvation (1:8–9). The faith, suffering, and joy that characterize the life of the baptized anticipate the glory that will fully appear at Christ's return or revelation.[12]

11. The opening benediction uses the noun form *sōtēria*, whereas the baptismal reference uses the verb *sōzō*.

12. The New Testament uses a variety of images for Christ's return, but 1 Peter is not unique in speaking of this event as a kind of revelation. A similar idea appears in Col. 3:4 and Titus 2:13.

The salvation for which Christians hope did not spring from nowhere. Rather, the prophets of the Old Testament spoke about "the grace that was to be yours," seeking to discover when it would be revealed (1 Pet. 1:10–11). Unsurprisingly in light of the rest of the benediction, at the center of the salvation that the prophets foretold is a pattern of suffering and glory, first and foremost those of Christ (1:11). In their activity, Peter continues, the prophets were serving not themselves but rather those who are to receive the gospel, and behind this preaching activity the Holy Spirit is at work (1:12).

Before we continue, it is worth reiterating: 1 Peter 1:3–12 is not a straightforward exposition of baptism. In form, it is a benediction praising God for the great gifts he has given to his people. Nevertheless, the letter's reference to "a new birth into a living hope" likely alludes to baptism, and thus the benediction also at least implicitly describes the life of the baptized. It is a life characterized by faith: the Christian believes in Christ without seeing him in the present and rejoices in the glory to be revealed in the future. It is a life characterized by hope, in expectation that the present time of suffering and trial will one day give way to an imperishable and unfading inheritance. Finally, it is a life characterized by love. Without seeing Christ, the baptized love him, confident that the salvation promised to them will one day reach its complete fulfillment. Such a life could be encapsulated with the word "holiness," which serves as the context for the next reference to new birth in the letter.

"You Shall Be Holy, for I Am Holy"

In an important conversation in Evelyn Waugh's masterpiece *Brideshead Revisited*, Cordelia Flyte, speaking of the suffering of her brother, says to Charles Ryder, "No one is ever holy without suffering."[13] Holiness and suffering go hand in hand in the Christian life, and 1 Peter clearly reflects this reality. Much of the letter offers encouragement to Christians suffering some form of persecution (the exact nature of the persecution is unclear), and the opening chapters of the letter underscore the vocation to holiness, drawing on the language of the Old Testament to describe it. These exhortations to holiness offer the context for the other two references to new birth in the letter (1 Pet. 1:23; 2:2). The context of the passage leading up to 1 Peter 1:23

13. Evelyn Waugh, *Brideshead Revisited: The Sacred and Profane Memories of Captain Charles Ryder* (New York: Little, Brown, 1946), 355.

adds several important dimensions to the life that baptism entails. It is to be a life characterized by holiness and upright living. It is a life made possible by Christ's gift of self, a life purchased by his costly blood. And it is a life brought about through the power of the word of God.

Following the opening benediction, the letter expands on the themes of hope and imperishability, describing what the new life into which Christians have been born looks like. Peter calls his audience to a life of holiness in light of the hope laid up for them through the resurrection of Christ. The resurrection and the expectation of Christ's return, which Peter speaks of as Christ's revelation (1 Pet. 1:13), should empower Christians to change their lives. This hope for Christ's return leads to obedience, giving Christians a new vision of the world that allows them to subdue their passions: "Like obedient children, do not be conformed to the desires that you formerly had in ignorance" (1:14). Citing an important verse from the book of Leviticus, Peter summarizes this new life with the concept of holiness, exhorting his audience to a life of holy conduct. This holiness finds its basis in the relationship Christians have with the Lord, who alone is holy: "Instead, as he who called you is holy, be holy yourselves in all your conduct; for it is written, 'You shall be holy, for I am holy'" (1 Pet. 1:15–16, citing Lev. 11:44). The life of the baptized ought to reflect the holiness of the God who purifies his people through the sacrament.

This verse from Leviticus plays an important role in the New Testament. Both Matthew in the Sermon on the Mount (Matt. 5–7) and Luke in the Sermon on the Plain (Luke 6:17–49) subtly allude to this idea, interpreting it in different ways. Matthew's version interprets the holiness of which Leviticus speaks in terms of perfection, as Jesus teaches, "Be perfect, therefore, as your heavenly Father is perfect" (Matt. 5:48). Luke's version emphasizes the importance of compassion: "Be merciful, just as your Father is merciful" (Luke 6:36). In both Gospels the saying plays an important role, summing up the teaching that has preceded it (Matt. 5:21–47; Luke 6:27–35). Given the prominence of this idea in Jesus's teaching, it makes sense that it would also play an important role in describing what the life of the baptized entails.

The quotation from Leviticus is one of many allusions to the events of the exodus in this section of the letter (1 Pet. 1:13–2:10). First Peter 1:13 subtly alludes to Israel's escape from Egypt, as the exhortation refers to "girding up the loins of your mind" (my translation).[14] The expression to "gird one's

14. This is a more literal translation than the NRSV's "Prepare your minds for action."

loins" is common in the Old Testament, referring to the way ancient people would wrap up their garments around themselves to prepare for a hasty escape or to make a foray into battle. In the description of the Passover in Exodus 12, the Lord commands the Israelites to eat the Passover with "your loins girded" (12:11).[15] Although the expression is a common one, the other exodus images in the passage suggest that 1 Peter here intentionally alludes to that event. In addition to using the image of girded loins and the quotation from Leviticus, the letter describes Christ with language drawn from the Passover ritual, referring to him as a "lamb without defect or blemish" and speaking of the ransoming effect of his blood (1 Pet. 1:18–19). The Passover lamb was to have no blemishes (Exod. 12:5), and the Israelites were to smear its blood on the lintels of their doors to ask for God's protection at the time of the tenth plague (12:7, 13).

By drawing on this imagery from the exodus, 1 Peter describes the Christian life as a new exodus. As the Israelites spent time in the wilderness before they were allowed to enter the promised land, so Christians must conduct themselves in an upright manner during the "time of [their] exile" (1 Pet. 1:17). Continuing his contrast between perishable and imperishable things, Peter exhorts his audience, "You know that you were ransomed from the futile ways inherited from your ancestors, not with perishable things like silver or gold, but with the costly blood of Christ, like that of a lamb without defect or blemish" (1:18–19, modified).[16] The language of "ransom" again alludes to the exodus, as it is one of the primary images for God's saving activity in Exodus. In Exodus 6:6 the Lord says to Moses, "I will redeem you with an outstretched arm," and in the Song of the Sea in Exodus 15, Moses sings, "In your steadfast love you led the people whom you redeemed" (15:13a). In the Greek translation of both verses, the word frequently rendered as "redeem" or "redeemed" is the same word underlying 1 Peter's reference to being "ransomed."[17] The image is one of buying a person's freedom from slavery, which explains why Peter specifies that this purchase was made "not with

15. The expression in 1 Peter is *anazōsamenoi tas osphuas*, whereas in Exodus LXX it is *hai osphues hymōn periezōsmenai*. While the phrases are not identical, they both refer to the "loins" or waist, and they use related verbs for the image of girding.

16. For the translation of *timios* as "costly" rather than "precious," see Nathan Eubank, *Wages of Cross-Bearing and Debt of Sin: The Economy of Heaven in Matthew's Gospel*, BZNW 196 (Berlin: de Gruyter, 2013), 167–68.

17. The Greek verb in all three instances is *lutroō*. Throughout I will consistently replace the NRSV's "precious" with "costly."

perishable things like silver or gold" (1 Pet. 1:18). Rather, God purchases his people by the "costly blood of Christ" (1:19, modified).

The contrast between perishable money and the costly blood of Christ leads naturally to the source of Christ's imperishability and of the Christian hope: the resurrection. Emphasizing the eternal plan of God to offer Christ as a Passover lamb (1 Pet. 1:20), Peter notes that it is not simply Christ's death that offers believers hope but also his resurrection. God "raised [Christ] from the dead and gave him glory, so that your faith and hope are set on God" (1:21).

This reference to Christ's resurrection brings us to the letter's second reference to new birth, which serves as the basis for the conduct of the baptized. Although the word "holiness" does not appear in this section (1 Pet. 1:22–25), it may lie subtly in the background. Reminding his audience that they have been purified through their obedience, Peter exhorts them to "love one another earnestly from a pure heart" (1:22 ESV). The theme of the heart features prominently throughout much of the Old Testament, especially in Deuteronomy and several books influenced by the theology of Deuteronomy. The prophet Ezekiel also emphasizes the importance of the heart, particularly in relation to notions of purity. Ezekiel laments the way the nations held the name of the Lord in contempt because of Israel's behavior (Ezek. 36:20–21). Following this lament, however, the Lord declares that he will vindicate the holiness of his name (36:22–23), and he promises through the prophet that he will purify his people with clean water and give them a new heart: "I will sprinkle clean water upon you, and you shall be clean from all your uncleannesses, and from all your idols I will cleanse you. A new heart I will give you, and a new spirit I will put within you; and I will remove from your body the heart of stone and give you a heart of flesh" (36:25–26). According to Ezekiel, God reveals his holiness in part by purifying his people and giving them new hearts. The exhortation to "love one another earnestly from a pure heart," then, serves as a manifestation of God's holiness. This fraternal love is at the center of the holiness to which Peter calls his audience (1 Pet. 1:15–16).

The source of this holiness lies in the new birth that Christians undergo. Here Peter closely associates this new birth with the word of God: "You have been born anew, not of perishable but of imperishable seed, through the living and enduring word of God" (1 Pet. 1:23). As noted above, throughout the New Testament the language of rebirth or new birth frequently refers to baptism. The way Peter speaks here of this new birth as coming about through the word of God suggests a close connection between baptism and the word. Water brings about salvation not because of its natural properties but by its transformation through the power of the word. The imperishable word of God that abides forever (1 Pet. 1:24–25, citing Isa. 40:6, 8) gives perishable water the power to cleanse the hearts of believers, making them into a holy people. As Peter clarifies, the "word" refers to the gospel, the good news of Christ's death and resurrection.[18] Having reminded his audience of their new status, Peter further develops his exhortation, continuing the twin themes of holiness and new birth.

"But You Are a Chosen Race, a Royal Priesthood, a Holy Nation"

First Peter 2 specifies the nature of the holiness into which believers have been born. Unsurprisingly, two of the key images of this holiness relate to central institutions in ancient Israel: the priesthood and the temple. The opening of this chapter prepares for this imagery by exhorting believers to put away vices that preclude one from participating in temple worship: "Rid yourselves, therefore, of all malice, and all guile, insincerity, envy, and all slander" (1 Pet. 2:1). This verse loosely resembles two psalms that specify the qualifications for entering the temple:

> O Lord, who may abide in your tent?
> Who may dwell on your holy hill?
> Those who walk blamelessly, and do what is right,
> and *speak the truth from their heart*;
> who *do not slander* with their tongue,
> and do no *evil* to their friends,
> nor take up a reproach against their neighbors. (Ps. 15:1–3)
>
> Who shall ascend the hill of the Lord?
> And who shall stand in his holy place?
> Those who have clean hands and *pure hearts*,
> who do not lift up their souls to what is false,
> and do not swear *deceitfully*. (Ps. 24:3–4)

18. It is worth noting that 1 Peter uses the verbal form of "gospel" (*euangelizō*) rather than the noun form. Nevertheless, particularly with his repeated contrast between the perishable and the imperishable, the word of which he speaks seems most likely to refer to the message of the resurrection.

The Priesthood of All Believers

Many Catholics are unaware that the priesthood of all believers is a part of the Church's long-standing teaching. The idea was well known in the early Church, sometimes being combined with the royal dimension of the Christian vocation. St. Leo the Great writes,

> All who have been regenerated in Christ are made kings by the sign of the cross and consecrated priests by the anointing of the Holy Spirit. Apart from the particular service that our ministry entails, all Christians who live spiritual lives according to reason recognize that they have a part in the royal race and the priestly office. What could be more royal than the soul in subjection to God ruling over its own body? What could be more priestly than dedicating a pure conscience to the Lord and offering spotless sacrifices of devotion from the altar of the heart?[a]

a. Leo the Great, *Sermon* 4.1, in *Sermons*, trans. Jane Patricia Freeland and Agnes Josephine Conway, FC 93 (Washington, DC: Catholic University of America Press, 1996), 25.

In the preceding chapter Peter speaks of loving one another "from a pure heart" (1 Pet. 1:22 [NRSV marginal note]). His references to "guile," "insincerity," and "slander" also loosely resemble the description of these two psalms.[19] The exhortation to renounce these vices fittingly prepares the way for Peter's description of the Church as both a priesthood and a temple.

Once more, Peter draws on the imagery of new birth to speak of his audience's situation and to exhort them to growth. Given the connection between baptism and temple imagery elsewhere in the New Testament, it is reasonable to interpret the new-birth imagery in a baptismal sense. Peter urges his audience, "Like newborn infants, long for the pure, spiritual milk, so that by it you may grow into salvation" (1 Pet. 2:2). Shifting from an organic image of growth, Peter then describes the baptized by using the architectural image of a building, though without losing sight of the organic dimension: "Come to

19. First Peter refers to loving "from a pure heart" (*ek katharas kardias*) and putting away "all wickedness" (*pasan kakian*), "all deceit" (*panta dolon*), and "slander" (*katalalias*). The Greek version of Ps. 15 (14 LXX) describes the righteous man as speaking the truth "in his heart" (*en kardia autou*), not "deceiving" (*edolōsen*) with his tongue, and not doing "evil" (*kakon*) to his neighbor. Psalm 24 (23 LXX) describes the man as being "pure in heart" (*katharos tē kardia*) and not swearing "deceitfully" (*epi dolō*) to his neighbor.

him, a living stone, though rejected by mortals yet chosen and costly in God's sight, and like living stones, let yourselves be built into a spiritual house, to be a holy priesthood, to offer spiritual sacrifices acceptable to God through Jesus Christ" (2:4–5, modified). These brief but dense verses contain numerous dimensions of the effects of baptism.

The opening statement underscores the primacy of Christ in the order of salvation. Christ himself is *the* living stone who was rejected by human beings but has become the foundation of a new temple. The baptized resemble Christ in that they are "like living stones" belonging to a new temple, a "spiritual house." In other words, by their new birth the baptized have become a part of the new dwelling place of God. Rather than living in a house made of lifeless stones, God now dwells in a living temple made up of those he has chosen to be like Christ, the living stone. But Christians are not merely inert stones in an unmoving building—we are living stones, called also to be a "holy priesthood." An essential aspect of that priesthood involves offering "spiritual sacrifices." The word "sacrifice" appears only here in the letter, but in light of both the message of the letter as a whole and the way Peter presents Christ as an example, suffering seems to be at the heart of these sacrifices.

The end of 1 Peter 2 appeals to Christ's suffering both as an example and as the act that bore away our sins. Peter exhorts his audience, "For to this you have been called, because Christ also suffered for you, leaving you an example, so that you should follow in his steps" (2:21). He goes on to describe Christ's suffering with imagery drawn from the famous "Suffering Servant Song" of Isaiah 53.[20] Christ refused to respond to evil with evil (1 Pet. 2:22–23). Even more importantly, "he himself bore our sins in his body on the cross, so that, free from sins, we might live for righteousness" (2:24a). The following chapter once again connects the suffering of Christians with that of Christ. Reminding his readers that the Christian life sometimes means suffering for doing good (3:17), Peter grounds this claim in Christ's own experience: "For Christ also suffered for sins once for all, the righteous for the unrighteous, in order to bring you to God" (3:18a). The phrase "for sins" points to the sacrificial nature of Christ's death, a sacrifice that is completed through his resurrection and ascension into heaven. Peter appeals to Christ's suffering as an example once more in the following chapter: "Since therefore Christ suffered in the flesh,

20. The nature of the Servant Songs in Isaiah—including whether they are even a legitimate category—is complex and much disputed. For an extensive bibliography on the question, see Joseph Blenkinsopp, *Isaiah 40–55: A New Translation with Introduction and Commentary*, AB 19A (New York: Doubleday, 2002), 166–74.

arm yourselves also with the same intention (for whoever has suffered in the flesh has finished with sin)" (4:1). Those who belong to the "holy priesthood" established by baptism offer up their sufferings as "spiritual sacrifices" (2:5) in imitation of and union with Christ, the living stone, who suffered for our sake.

Peter grounds the connection between spiritual sacrifices and suffering and rejection in a series of scriptural quotations (Isa. 28:16; Ps. 118:22; Isa. 8:14) tied together by the keyword "stone" (1 Pet. 2:4–8). The first citation serves as the source for Peter's description of Christ as "a living stone . . . chosen and costly" and emphasizes the importance of faith in Christ. The second citation, from Psalm 118, features prominently in the accounts of Jesus's last days in Jerusalem in Matthew, Mark, and Luke. At the end of the parable of the tenants, which not so subtly indicts the Jewish leaders for rejecting the Son, Jesus interprets the parable through Psalm 118. As the rejected Son, Jesus is also the rejected stone, which will serve as the foundation of a new temple (Matt. 21:33–46 and parallels). This image seems to have had a significant impact on early Christian thought. The final citation, Isaiah 8:14, is the most intriguing, particularly if one considers the context of the verse. Exhorting Isaiah not to behave like the rebellious people in whose midst he lives, the Lord says of himself to Isaiah, "He [the LORD] will become *a sanctuary*, a stone one strikes against; for both houses of Israel he will become a rock one stumbles over" (Isa. 8:14a). For Peter, Christ, the incarnate Lord, is the foundation of this new sanctuary, into which the baptized are built up through faith.[21]

Peter brings the first part of the exhortation (1 Pet. 1:13–2:10) to a close with a reminder of the new identity of the baptized, drawing on both Exodus and Hosea. He tells them, "But you are a chosen race, a royal priesthood, a holy nation, God's own people, in order that you may proclaim the mighty acts of him who called you out of darkness into his marvelous light" (2:9). This imagery of a royal priesthood and a holy nation first appears in Exodus 19:6. In light of the early Christian interpretation of the crossing of the Red Sea as a prefiguration of baptism (see, e.g., 1 Cor. 10:1–5), this identification of the baptized as a royal priesthood is fitting. As Israel passed through the Red Sea and became God's royal priesthood at Sinai, so Christians, passing through the waters of baptism, become God's new royal priesthood. The imagery of light may also suggest a baptismal context. One of the most popular names

21. On the connection between the two Isaiah texts in Romans and in 1 Peter, see J. Ross Wagner, *Heralds of the Good News: Isaiah and Paul in Concert in the Letter to the Romans* (Leiden: Brill, 2002), 126–36.

for baptism in the early centuries of the Church was "illumination," perhaps due to texts like this one and others. The New Testament frequently depicts conversion as a transition from the realm of darkness to the realm of light, and baptism is an important moment in that transition.

The phrase "God's own people" leads naturally into another allusion to Scripture, the words of the prophet Hosea. Describing their newfound status in Christ, Peter writes,

> Once you were not a people,
>   but now you are God's people;
> once you had not received mercy,
>   but now you have received mercy. (1 Pet. 2:10)

This language comes from Hosea 2:23, which speaks of the mercy God would show to the people of Israel after their punishment. God promises through Hosea that he will at first reject his people, but later show mercy and welcome them back as his people. Once again, the surrounding context of this allusion is illuminating. As is often the case in the Prophets, Hosea describes this act of mercy with imagery drawn from the exodus. God speaks of alluring Israel into the desert and compares this act to the time when he brought Israel out of Egypt (Hosea 2:14–15). This act of redemption will result in a relationship of intimacy between God and his people (2:16–20). Peter takes this promise and reapplies it to all those who believe in Christ. The new exodus and the new Passover that Christ has enacted extend not only to those who are descended from Abraham biologically but also to all those who have come to faith in Christ and have been washed in the waters of baptism.

"Who Shall Ascend the Hill of the Lord?"

In ancient Israel, as in many ancient Near Eastern and Greco-Roman cultures, only those who were ritually pure could participate in temple worship.[22] Given the way the New Testament associates baptism with temple theology, it should come as no surprise that several texts also speak of the sacrament in terms of purification. To this dimension of baptism we now turn.

22. For a recent treatment of this question in the New Testament with comparisons to both the ancient Near East and the Greco-Roman world, see Matthew Thiessen, *Jesus and the Forces of Death: The Gospels' Portrayal of Ritual Impurity within First-Century Judaism* (Grand Rapids: Baker Academic, 2020).

11

Baptismal Purity

> Then Moses brought Aaron and his sons forward, and washed them with water.
>
> —Leviticus 8:6

The power of water to cleanse is remarkable. Deeply ingrained stains require stronger cleaning agents for their removal, but most blemishes, if caught quickly enough, disappear with a thorough application of water, and even deep-set stains benefit from a presoak in water. This natural capacity of water for cleansing makes it a fitting symbol for the spiritual purification with which it is frequently associated throughout Scripture. As we saw in chapter 4, water plays a prominent role in the removal of ritual impurity brought about by various bodily discharges and other actions. Moreover, some of the writings of the Psalms and the Prophets apply cleansing imagery to the removal of sin. The New Testament does not simply adopt the purity system of the Old Testament wholesale, but it does share some of its images and describes practices analogous to aspects of that system.[1]

Purity language appears frequently in the writings of the New Testament, most often in contexts that relate to behavior. Outside the Gospels, the New

1. For a compelling argument that Jesus himself took purity quite seriously, see Matthew Thiessen, *Jesus and the Forces of Death: The Gospels' Portrayal of Ritual Impurity within First-Century Judaism* (Grand Rapids: Baker Academic, 2020).

Testament speaks primarily of moral impurity.[2] This emphasis on moral impurity—rather than ritual impurity—nevertheless still had important ramifications for the liturgical life of the early Christians. Several texts describe baptism as a kind of cleansing, particularly with respect to sin. The removal of impurity, however, is not the only setting for which the Old Testament prescribes the use of water. The ordination rite for Aaron and his sons also involves a cleansing of the priests-to-be with water, preparing them to minister in the holy place. Both these ritual uses of water—for the removal of impurity and for the ordination of priests—have something in common. They both prepare a person to enter some part of the temple. The washing imagery associated with baptism in the New Testament likewise relates to participation in the new temple, with the primary difference being the New Testament's emphasis on moral rather than ritual purity.

Sanctified for Service in the Temple

We return once more to Paul's reminder to the Corinthians of their new status in 1 Corinthians 6:11. Even though this passage does not explicitly use the language of "baptism," it contains a wealth of baptismal imagery and theology.[3] Here we will focus on three aspects of this verse: the surrounding context that focuses on moral purity, the meaning of the "sanctification" the Corinthians have received, and the relation of that sanctification to their status as temples of the Holy Spirit (1 Cor. 6:19).

Paul's reference to the Corinthians' being "washed" sits in the middle of several references to what could be called moral impurity. In the verses leading up to this washing, Paul reminds the Corinthians, "Do you not know that wrongdoers will not inherit the kingdom of God?" (1 Cor. 6:9a). He follows this reminder with a list of ten categories of sin that exclude a person from the kingdom of God. Such sins formerly characterized the lives of Paul's Corinthian converts (6:11a), but now that they have passed through the cleansing waters of baptism, their lives have changed and they must remain in this

2. On Paul's understanding of impurity, see Jonathan Klawans, *Impurity and Sin in Ancient Judaism* (New York: Oxford University Press, 2000), 150–56.

3. For a more detailed discussion of this passage, see Isaac Augustine Morales, "Washed, Sanctified, Justified: 1 Corinthians 6 and Baptismal Participation in Christ," in *A Scribe Trained for the Kingdom of Heaven: Essays on Christology and Ethics in Honor of Richard B. Hays*, ed. David M. Moffitt and Isaac Augustine Morales (Lanham, MD: Fortress Academic, 2021), 91–108.

new state. The instruction that follows the baptismal reference specifically warns the Corinthians regarding the dangers of sexual immorality (6:12–20). Although Paul's primary focus throughout seems to be on moral purity, it is worth noting that in this passage he singles out sexual perversion.[4] Most likely the primary reason for this emphasis stems from the Corinthians' struggle (or lack thereof) in this area. However, it is perhaps also worth considering whether at a subconscious level Paul also may have had in mind the impurity that sexual activity brings about according to the Jewish purity system (see Lev. 15:18). Particularly in light of his appeal to the Corinthians' status as temples of the Holy Spirit, it is possible that—even though Paul rarely speaks of ritual purity in his letters—the problem of sexual immorality would lead him to voice his concerns about the temple. Nevertheless, the point remains that Paul's primary concern in addressing his churches is moral purity rather than ritual purity.

Before we turn to the sanctification language, it is worth noting that this pairing of warnings against sexual perversion and baptismal language also appears in 1 Corinthians 10. There Paul appeals to the wilderness generation as a negative example for the Corinthians. Interpreting the crossing of the Red Sea as a figural foreshadowing of baptism (1 Cor. 10:2), he warns them not to fall as the wilderness generation did. This connection between baptismal language and sexual morality further supports a baptismal interpretation of the washing language in 1 Corinthians 6.

At the center of Paul's threefold reminder to the Corinthians about their baptism in 1 Corinthians 6:11 lies the word "sanctified." As many have noted, for the ancient Israelites and Jews, holiness and purity were not identical.[5] One could be pure or clean without being holy. Attaining holiness—that is, fitness for use or service in the temple—required a further action or ritual.[6] By reminding the Corinthians that they were not only washed but also sanctified, Paul implies that through baptism they have been prepared for temple

4. The Greek word for "prostitute" is *pornē* (1 Cor. 6:15–16), and Paul urges the Corinthians to flee from *porneia* (6:18).

5. For a recent, succinct discussion, see Thiessen, *Jesus and the Forces of Death*, 9–20. See also Richard D. Nelson, *Raising Up a Faithful Priest: Community and Priesthood in Biblical Theology* (Louisville: Westminster John Knox, 1993), 21.

6. See Nelson, *Raising Up a Faithful Priest*, 21: "To sanctify was to move something or someone from the realm of the common to the sphere of the holy. The sanctuary, its altar and vessels, and its priests were transferred into a holy state through such a ritual (Exod. 30:22–30; 40:9–13; Lev. 8:10–12, 30)."

service. One possible background for this imagery appears in the Old Testament ordination rite for Aaron and his sons.[7]

Most ritual purifications in the Old Testament were self-administered. A person who contracted impurity through a variety of circumstances—skin diseases, bodily discharges, contact with a corpse—would wash himself or herself with water, sometimes multiple times, as part of the process of removing the impurity. One rite described in Leviticus, however, involved one person washing another: the rite of ordination in Leviticus 8. The ordination of Aaron and his sons included several elements, one of which was a ritual washing: Moses washed Aaron and his sons with water (Lev. 8:6). Three aspects of this rite serve as intriguing parallels with Christian baptism. First, in contrast to the ritual washings for removing impurity, the washing of Aaron and his sons took place only once.[8] Second, the purpose of this rite was to consecrate Aaron and his sons for service in the temple—in other words, it sanctified them, much as baptism sanctifies the baptized. Third, following their washing, Aaron and his sons received new garments for their service in the temple (Lev. 8:7–9).[9] Given these similarities in symbolism, a priestly dimension to the rite of baptism seems plausible.[10] The language of "sanctification" or holiness in Paul's reminder further supports such an interpretation. As Peter Leithart argues, to be "holy" means to become God's property, and this is precisely what Paul tells the Corinthians later in the same passage: "You are not your own, for you were bought with a price" (1 Cor. 6:19b–20a ESV).[11] By the sanctifying bath of baptism, the Corinthians have become God's property, his priests.

Interpreting the washing reference of 1 Corinthians 6:11 in a priestly light also helps to make sense of Paul's use of temple imagery in verse 19. As we saw in the previous chapter, 1 Peter moves seamlessly between describing the Church as a temple and describing the Church as a priesthood. In the New Covenant, priesthood and temple overlap in a much more intimate way, as the people of God simply *are* both temple and priests, the dwelling place of the Spirit and those who serve in that temple.

7. This is the central thesis of Peter J. Leithart, *The Priesthood of the Plebs: A Theology of Baptism* (Eugene, OR: Wipf & Stock, 2003).

8. Leithart, *The Priesthood of the Plebs*, 95.

9. Leithart (*The Priesthood of the Plebs*, 102–8) argues that this ritual also lies behind Paul's imagery of being "clothed with Christ" in Gal. 3:27.

10. On 1 Cor. 6, see Leithart, *The Priesthood of the Plebs*, 108–11.

11. Leithart, *The Priesthood of the Plebs*, 109.

Baptism as Priestly Anointing

The inclusion of the act of anointing with oil as part of the rite of baptism, dating back to the early centuries of the Church, would easily lead to a priestly interpretation of the sacrament. In his treatise *On Baptism*, Tertullian writes,

> After this, when we have issued from the font, we are thoroughly anointed with a blessed unction,—(a practice derived) from the old discipline, wherein on entering the priesthood, men were wont to be anointed with oil from a horn, ever since Aaron was anointed by Moses. Whence Aaron is called Christ, from the chrism, which is the unction; which, when made spiritual, furnished an appropriate name to the Lord, because He was anointed with the Spirit by God the Father; as written in the Acts: For truly they were gathered together in this city against Your Holy Son whom You have anointed. Thus, too, in our case, the unction runs carnally, (i.e., on the body,) but profits spiritually; in the same way as the act of baptism itself too is carnal, in that we are plunged in water, but the effect spiritual, in that we are freed from sins.[a]

a. Tertullian, *On Baptism* 7 (*ANF* 3:672).

"Have Your Sins Washed Away"

In chapter 7 we considered the connection between baptism and the name of the Lord in the Acts of the Apostles. In his Pentecost speech Peter suggests that there is a connection between baptism and the reception of the Holy Spirit, and for the most part Acts bears out this connection. With a few exceptions, the administration of water baptism leads to the reception of the Holy Spirit. In that same speech Peter speaks of another consequence of baptism: the forgiveness of sins. In fact, the two effects of baptism seem to go together. Peter tells the crowds in Jerusalem, "Repent, and be baptized every one of you in the name of Jesus Christ so that your sins may be forgiven; and you will receive the gift of the Holy Spirit" (Acts 2:38). Some Protestant interpreters have suggested that there is no causal relationship between baptism and the forgiveness of sins. Rather, baptism is simply a sign of hope that the believer will receive forgiveness.[12] Those who

12. A classic statement of this position is found in Markus Barth, *Die Taufe—Ein Sakrament? Ein exegetischer Beitrag zum Gespräch über die kirchliche Taufe* (Zürich: Evangelischer A.G. Zollikon, 1951).

interpret the text in this way point to the similar case of the baptism of John, in which the emphasis falls primarily on repentance (Luke 3:3). Such a reading, however, strains the way Acts brings together baptism and the forgiveness of sins.

In the Pentecost speech Peter seems to suggest that the forgiveness of sins is the result of repentance and baptism. On its own, one could perhaps see this speech as placing the emphasis on repentance, with the rite of baptism serving merely as a sign. The last reference to baptism in Acts, however, makes such an interpretation difficult to sustain. In the second account of Paul's conversion and his subsequent meeting with Ananias, he recounts Ananias's words to him: "And now why do you delay? Get up, *be baptized, and have your sins washed away*, calling on his name" (Acts 22:16). Unlike Peter in his speech, Ananias says nothing about repentance here. This is not to say that there was no repentance in Paul's case; clearly, as a result of Christ's self-revelation to him, Paul changed his ways, abandoning his mission to destroy the Church. Nevertheless, Ananias's command locates the washing away of Paul's sins in the act of baptism itself. Indeed, he uses the literal act as an image of the cleansing of sins.

As in 1 Corinthians, here the washing imagery most likely draws on the Old Testament notion of moral impurity. In the opening chapter of Isaiah, God urges the Israelites,

> Wash yourselves; make yourselves clean;
> remove the evil of your doings
> from before my eyes;
> cease to do evil,
> learn to do good. (Isa. 1:16–17a)

While the language of Acts 22 is not identical with that of Isaiah, the two words for washing are closely related.[13] More importantly, both texts speak of the washing away of sins. In light of the New Testament's shift from categories of ritual impurity to moral impurity, the washing imagery of Acts 22:16 also supports the suggestion that the notion of calling on the name of the Lord relates to temple imagery.

It is important to recall that in ancient Israel, individual sins did not prevent a person from entering the temple. On the contrary, certain rites for obtaining forgiveness of sins *required* that the sinner enter the temple. On the other

13. Acts uses the compound verb *apolouō*, whereas Isaiah uses a form of the verb *louō*.

hand, some texts do speak of God's abandonment of the temple and the expulsion of Israel from the land as a consequence of their sins.[14] In light of this connection between sin and the destruction of the temple, as well as the New Testament shift with respect to purity, it makes sense that the notion of moral purity and temple imagery should go together. This combination appears in 1 Corinthians 6, and in Acts 22 we see a similar cluster of ideas. Elsewhere in the Pauline Epistles the connection between washing and temple imagery is not so clear. Nevertheless, the language of washing in Titus and Ephesians does relate to other ideas commonly associated with baptism.

"The Washing of Regeneration"

The Letter to Titus makes a brief allusion to baptism, referring to the "water of rebirth"—more literally, the "water of regeneration" (Titus 3:5). As is commonly the case in the Pauline Letters, Titus does not give a systematic account of the meaning of baptism. Nevertheless, as in the case of 1 Corinthians 6:11, the washing reference in Titus 3:5 is surrounded by a constellation of images and ideas elsewhere associated with baptism: a former life of slavery to the passions, justification, inheritance and eternal life, and warnings against division. Once again, the cleansing language in this passage concerns sin rather than the sources of ritual impurity.

The verses leading up to Titus 3:5 include a moral exhortation juxtaposed with a description of the believers' former way of life. The exhortation begins with a call to submit to authorities and rulers, but the greater part of this instruction focuses on behaviors that contribute to unity. Paul urges Titus to remind those entrusted to him "to be ready for every good work, to speak evil of no one, to avoid quarreling, to be gentle, and to show every courtesy to everyone" (3:1b–2). Sins of division frequently come in for criticism in Paul's Letters, and exhortations to unity often appear in the context of baptismal references, because unity is one of the most important effects of baptism.[15] Paul balances this exhortation with a reminder of the way of life that he and his fellow believers used to follow: "For we ourselves were once foolish, disobedient, led astray, slaves to various passions and pleasures, passing our days in malice and envy, despicable, hating one another" (3:3). Once again,

14. For God's abandonment of the temple, see Ezek. 8–11, esp. 10:18–22. For the expulsion of Israel from the land, see esp. Lev. 26 and Deut. 28. See Klawans, *Impurity and Sin*, 27.

15. See chap. 12 below.

we see an accent on division with the sins of malice, envy, and hatred. At the heart of the problem, however, is the notion of being "slaves to various passions and pleasures." One implication of this statement seems to be that through baptism believers have been liberated from this slavery. A similar idea appears in the context of a more explicit reference to baptism in Romans 6. There Paul exhorts his audience not to allow sin to reign over them (6:12–14). Through baptism believers are set free from sin and made slaves of righteousness (6:18). Through the "washing of regeneration" (Titus 3:5 ESV) believers receive this liberation, becoming new creatures free from the enslaving power of the passions.

The fundamental source of this liberation is God's mercy manifested in Christ: "But when the goodness and loving kindness of God our Savior appeared, he saved us, not because of any works of righteousness that we had done, but according to his mercy" (Titus 3:4–5a). Although the word "grace" does not appear until verse 7, the whole passage serves as a fitting encapsulation of Paul's theology of grace. God acts to save us, not because of any works of righteousness that we have done, but purely out of mercy for his beloved creatures. Paul further specifies the source of this salvation at the end of the verse: "He saved us . . . by the washing of regeneration and renewal by the Holy Spirit" (3:5 ESV). Like 1 Peter, Titus suggests that baptism actually brings about salvation.

The grammar of the last phrase of the verse is ambiguous, and some have taken it to suggest that Paul makes a distinction between the "washing of regeneration" and the "renewal by the Holy Spirit." On this reading, the washing of baptism is not the source of the renewal that the Holy Spirit effects. Such a reading, however, faces at least two difficulties. First, even if one does separate the renewal of the Holy Spirit from baptism, Paul's statement still describes this washing as the means by which God saves. There is only one preposition governing both the washing and the renewal of which the letter speaks. Additionally, one can also construe the grammar differently, such that the washing and the renewal go hand in hand. Some interpreters suggest that the words "regeneration" and "renewal" are effectively synonymous, though each word brings out a different aspect of the reality described.[16] The close connection between the two terms underscores the role of the Holy Spirit in baptism and the regeneration it produces. Water saves not by any natural

16. See G. R. Beasley-Murray, *Baptism in the New Testament* (Grand Rapids: Eerdmans, 1962), 210–11.

property of its own but because God has chosen it as a means of conveying grace to his people by the power of the Holy Spirit.

The outpouring of the Spirit through this washing has other important effects. Elaborating on the gift of the Holy Spirit, Paul writes that through this gift, made possible by Jesus Christ, the baptized receive justification "by his grace" and become "heirs according to the hope of eternal life" (Titus 3:6–7). The three ideas of justification, inheritance, and eternal life all have a connection with baptism in other parts of the New Testament. The close association between washing and justification is characteristically Pauline; we have seen it in Romans 6 and 1 Corinthians 6, though expressed differently in each context. Moreover, the emphasis on grace is in keeping with Paul's understanding of the gift of salvation (see esp. Rom. 6). Baptism and inheritance also appear together in another of Paul's appeals to the rite in Galatians 3. There he refers to the Galatians' new status as "heirs," one of the important outcomes of their baptism (3:29; see also 4:1, 7). Through baptism the Galatians—indeed, all those baptized—have become sons of God in Christ (3:26–27) and, in this way, heirs.

Titus offers a description of this inheritance that has more in common with the writings of John: the baptized are now heirs "according to the hope of eternal life" (Titus 3:7). In Jesus's late-night conversation with Nicodemus, Jesus speaks of a new birth from above by which a person can enter the kingdom of God (John 3:3–5). The use of the phrase "kingdom of God" is uncharacteristic of John's Gospel, but by the end of the conversation Jesus shifts to the more common phrase "eternal life" to speak of what those who believe will receive (3:15). John seems to signal here that what he describes as "eternal life" is roughly equivalent to what Matthew, Mark, and Luke more frequently refer to as the "kingdom of God" or the "kingdom of heaven."[17] Baptism, then, is for John the gateway to the kingdom and to eternal life, and the Letter to Titus seems to share this understanding.

Toward the end of this section of Titus, Paul returns once more to the problem of division. After exhorting Titus to encourage believers "to devote themselves to good works" (Titus 3:8), Paul warns him against quarreling and division. This warning has both a specific and a more general dimension. Specifically, Paul instructs Titus to avoid arguments about genealogies and the law (most likely the law of Moses), calling these disputes "unprofitable

17. See Richard J. Bauckham, *Gospel of Glory: Major Themes in Johannine Theology* (Grand Rapids: Baker Academic, 2015), 192.

and worthless" (3:9). In the final instruction before the closing of the letter, Paul extends his warning to any person who causes division: "After a first and second admonition, have nothing more to do with anyone who causes divisions, since you know that such a person is perverted and sinful, being self-condemned" (3:10–11). The cleansing waters of baptism are opposed to "slavery to the passions" (see 3:3), above all the passions that fracture the unity of the body of Christ.[18]

"The Washing of Water by the Word"

Most of the passages we have considered thus far focus, at least implicitly, on the baptism of individuals. Though baptism always has implications for the Church as a whole, it is individuals who receive the actual rite. Ephesians 5, however, offers a unique perspective on the nature of baptism. In the context of a discussion of the relationship between husbands and wives, Paul speaks of Christ washing the Church, his bride, "with the washing of water by the word" (Eph. 5:26).[19] Here Paul implicitly suggests that, in addition to the personal dimension of baptism, it also has a collective dimension. Despite the difference in perspective, Paul's allusion to baptism in Ephesians shares several features with other baptismal texts. In addition to the imagery of washing, Ephesians closely associates baptism with Christ's gift of self, and the language Paul uses to describe the effect of baptism describes the Church in ways reminiscent of the offerings in the Jewish temple. Ephesians also develops the theology of baptism in new ways in light of the marital relationship between Christ and the Church.

This baptismal reference—the second in Ephesians—appears in the context of Paul's adaptation of the "household codes."[20] These codes predate the New Testament by quite some time, extending back at least to the time of Aristotle; as the name implies, they offer prescriptions for governing one's household.[21] Many people in modernity find these codes offensive for at least two reasons. First, the codes implicitly condone the existence of slavery, a widespread institution in the Roman Empire (and in antiquity more

18. For more on the importance of unity as a result of baptism, see the following chapter.

19. On the strangeness and uniqueness of the image, see Lars Hartman, *"Into the Name of the Lord Jesus": Baptism in the Early Church*, SNTW (Edinburgh: T&T Clark, 1997), 105–6.

20. The first and only explicit use of baptismal language appears in Eph. 4:5.

21. Aristotle, *Politics* 1.

generally). Second, they are by nature hierarchical, suggesting a proper order in the household, and one aspect of this hierarchy is the subordination of wives to their husbands.

While we understandably would like the New Testament to criticize the institution of slavery, a few points are worth bearing in mind. First, at the time of the writing of the New Testament, Christians were a minuscule minority in the Roman Empire with no power. It would have been impossible for Christians to abolish slavery in that time and cultural context. Second, despite the ongoing existence of slavery, Christianity was open to all, slave or free. Moreover, Christ himself identified with those who serve (Mark 10:45), and Christians described his incarnation in a similar way (Phil. 2:6–11). Third, although it took time for attitudes toward slavery to change, they did so largely in light of Christian reflection on biblical principles.[22]

With respect to the hierarchical nature of the codes, it is important to note that Paul does not simply adopt them wholesale. Rather, Paul transforms them in light of the gospel, presenting Christ as the model for how to live them out. While it is true that Ephesians says, "Wives, be subject to your husbands as you are to the Lord" (Eph. 5:22), the verse that immediately precedes this teaching directs believers to "be subject *to one another* out of reverence for Christ" (5:21). The way of the gospel excludes domineering (see also Mark 10:42–45). This is why Paul presents Christ as the model for how husbands ought to treat their wives. The "subjection" of wives to their husbands does not mean that the latter can do whatever they want. Rather, husbands must love their wives "as Christ loved the church" (Eph. 5:25).

This description of Christ's love for the Church leads seamlessly into the baptismal allusion of Ephesians 5:26. Paul thus connects baptism with Christ's self-offering, suggesting that through the rite the baptized receive the effects of Christ's gift. The phrasing that describes Christ's love for the Church is nearly identical to an earlier verse in the same chapter. In Ephesians 5:2 Paul writes, "And live in love, *as Christ loved us and gave himself up for us*, a fragrant offering and sacrifice to God." In his instructions to husbands, he writes, "Husbands, love your wives, *just as Christ loved the church and gave*

22. For a brief description of an all-too-rare exception in the early Church, see the discussion of St. Gregory of Nyssa's critique of slavery as an institution in David Bentley Hart, *Atheist Delusions: The Christian Revolution and Its Fashionable Enemies* (New Haven: Yale University Press, 2009), 177–82.

himself up for her" (5:25).[23] The waters of baptism draw their strength from Christ's love, made manifest in his crucifixion.

The goal of Christ's gift is to sanctify the Church, an act he accomplishes in part through baptism, which Paul describes as "the washing of water by the word" (Eph. 5:26). The juxtaposition of holiness language ("in order to make her holy") with cleansing imagery naturally evokes the temple, where holiness and purity belong together. Only those who are pure may enter the temple precincts. Just as importantly, Paul refers to baptism not as any kind of washing, but as a washing "by the word." Baptism draws its power not only from Christ's gift of self but also from "the word." Paul does not specify whether that word is a formula or some other exchange of words. Regardless, baptism is not simply a natural cleansing. Rather, "the word," which most likely refers to a description of Christ's gift of self, invests the water with the power to sanctify those who receive baptism.

Paul describes the purpose of this washing: "so as to present the church to himself in splendor, without a spot or wrinkle or anything of the kind—yes, so that she may be holy and without blemish" (Eph. 5:27). At least two contexts inform the language Paul uses to describe the Church's state that results from "the washing of water by the word" (v. 26). First, in light of the marital imagery that surrounds the passage, these words most likely reflect some of the Old Testament passages that describe God's relationship with Israel in marital terms.[24] In Ezekiel, God speaks of washing Israel, personified as a woman, with water and making her beautiful through various adornments (Ezek. 16:8–13). In the Song of Songs, Solomon says to his beloved, "You are altogether beautiful, my love; there is no flaw in you" (Song 4:7). In the Septuagint the word for "flaw" is related to Paul's language of Christ presenting the Church as "without blemish."[25] Given the emphasis on holiness in these verses, it seems likely that Paul also has in mind a cultic connotation for the language of being "without blemish." In the Pentateuch and in Ezekiel's vision of the new temple, the word "without blemish" frequently appears in connection

23. A similar variation of the phrase also appears in Galatians, where Paul says of Christ that he "loved me and gave himself for me" (Gal. 2:20b). Christ's love is both personal and corporate—he loves me, and he loves the Church. On the connection between Eph. 5:26 and 5:2, see Nils Alstrup Dahl, "The Concept of Baptism in Ephesians," in *Studies in Ephesians: Introductory Questions, Text- & Edition-Critical Issues, Interpretation of Texts and Themes*, WUNT 131 (Tübingen: Mohr Siebeck, 2000), 413–40, here 420–21.

24. Dahl, "The Concept of Baptism," 421–22.

25. The Song of Songs speaks of the beloved having no *mōmos* ("flaw" or "blemish"); in Eph. 5:27 Paul describes the Church as being *amōmos* ("without blemish").

with the offerings of bulls and lambs.[26] The offerings that the Israelites were to bring to the temple were to be spotless, without blemish. Baptism, then, also prepares the Church to make of herself an offering reflecting Christ's own self-offering.

"To Enter the Sanctuary"

Few texts in the New Testament draw on Israel's liturgical traditions more explicitly than the so-called Letter to the Hebrews.[27] At the heart of this writing are, first, the new priesthood that Christ has established through his passion, death, resurrection, and ascension and, second, the access to the heavenly sanctuary that his saving work makes possible. In light of these priestly interests, it would make sense if Hebrews spoke of baptism in priestly terms, reflecting the Christian understanding of the priesthood of all believers.[28] Hebrews twice uses language relating to washing or baptism. In chapter 6 the author speaks of "instruction about baptisms, laying on of hands, resurrection of the dead, and eternal judgment" (Heb. 6:2). Though tantalizing, the text is also a bit vague. It is unclear what "baptisms" (plural) the author has in mind. Nevertheless, it is worth noting that Hebrews associates these baptisms with resurrection and eternal judgment, ideas associated elsewhere in the New Testament with baptism (see, e.g., Col. 2:11–12). Moreover, a few verses later the text speaks of enlightenment and the reception of the Holy Spirit (Heb. 6:4), ideas also frequently connected with baptism in the early Church.[29]

Hebrews speaks of washing again a few chapters later, referring to "bodies washed with pure water" (Heb. 10:22b). Both the context and the language of the reference suggest that baptism corresponds in some way to the Old Testament priesthood. But whereas in the Old Testament only a certain subset of the tribe of Levi received the priesthood and the privilege of ministering in the temple, in the New Covenant all the baptized belong to this new priesthood, whose head is Christ.

26. Lev. 1:3, 10; 3:1, 6; Num. 19:2; Ezek. 43:22–23, 25; 45:18. Examples could be multiplied ad nauseam.

27. Although the text has had this name for centuries, modern scholars agree that, in format, Hebrews does not conform to any of the common styles of ancient letters.

28. See the discussion of 1 Peter in the previous chapter, especially the sidebar "The Priesthood of All Believers."

29. For references to baptism as "illumination" in the early Church, see Justin Martyr, *First Apology* 61; Clement of Alexandria, *The Instructor* 1.6; Gregory of Nazianzus, *Oration* 40.

One of the primary images of Hebrews is the heavenly temple and the access believers have to that temple. The writer, like many of his contemporary Jews, believed that there was a heavenly temple of which the earthly temple was a reflection or imitation.[30] Through Christ's self-offering, which culminates in his ascension into the heavenly temple, he grants his followers access to this heavenly temple.[31] This access serves as the context for the baptismal reference in Hebrews 10:22. The passage begins at verse 19 with a reference to the holy places (rendered in the NRSV as "sanctuary"): "Therefore, my friends, since we have confidence to enter the sanctuary by the blood of Jesus, by the new and living way that he opened for us through the curtain (that is, through his flesh) . . ." (10:19–20). In ancient Israel only priests were allowed to enter certain parts of the temple, and only after performing certain rites. One of these rites, the rite of ordination described in Exodus 29 and Leviticus 8, shares a number of similarities with the way that Hebrews describes baptism.[32]

The writer of Hebrews exhorts his audience, "Let us approach with a true heart in full assurance of faith, with our hearts sprinkled clean from an evil conscience and our bodies washed with pure water" (Heb. 10:22). Some scholars have suggested that the background to this imagery is to be found in the ordination rites of the Old Testament.[33] Both sprinkling and washing played a role in the ordination of priests in ancient Israel. The first set of instructions for the ordination of Aaron and his sons in the Pentateuch includes, among other things, a washing and a sprinkling with blood. The Lord commands Moses to wash Aaron and his sons with water at the entrance of the tabernacle (Exod. 29:4).[34] Later on in the description of the rite, God tells Moses, "Then you shall take some of the blood that is on the altar, and some of the anointing oil, and sprinkle it on Aaron and his vestments and on his sons and his sons' vestments with him; then he and his vestments shall be holy,

30. See Jonathan Klawans, *Purity, Sacrifice, and the Temple: Symbolism and Supersessionism in the Study of Ancient Judaism* (Oxford: Oxford University Press, 2006), 111–44. This notion of a correspondence between the earthly temple/tabernacle and the heavenly temple goes back to Exodus, where the Lord tells Moses, "In accordance with all that I show you concerning the pattern of the tabernacle and of all its furniture, so you shall make it" (Exod. 25:9).

31. See, e.g., Heb. 4:14. On the importance of the ascension in Hebrews, see David M. Moffitt, *Atonement and the Logic of Resurrection in the Epistle to the Hebrews*, NovTSup 141 (Leiden: Brill, 2011).

32. I owe this point to Leithart, *The Priesthood of the Plebs*, 99–100, who in turn depends on W. F. Flemington, *The New Testament Doctrine of Baptism* (London: SPCK, 1964), 98–99.

33. See again, e.g., Flemington, *The New Testament Doctrine of Baptism*, 98–99.

34. The Septuagint text of Exodus uses the same verb (*louō*) found in Heb. 10:22.

as well as his sons and his sons' vestments" (29:21).[35] Throughout Hebrews, sprinkling imagery refers most frequently to the sprinkling of blood, either that of animals or that of Jesus (Heb. 9:19, 21–22; 12:24).[36] The sprinkling of Hebrews 10:22, then, seems most likely to be a metaphorical sprinkling with the blood of Jesus, particularly in light of the reference to his blood in verse 19. The combination of sprinkling with washing would suggest that the writer of Hebrews interprets baptism as a rite that corresponds to the ordination of the Aaronic priests in the Old Testament. Baptism now gives all believers access to the "sanctuary," a right that in the Old Covenant was limited to Israel's priests; it equips believers to minister in the heavenly temple and initiates those who receive it into the "royal priesthood" (1 Pet. 2:9) of the New Covenant.

The baptismal reference in Hebrews is not just connected with priestly imagery but is also followed by other themes commonly associated with baptism in the New Testament.[37] Hebrews emphasizes the importance of faith and hope (Heb. 10:22–23). The text also exhorts the baptized to an upright life (10:24; cf. Rom. 6). Moreover, there is a connection between baptism, the moral life, and liturgical gathering in anticipation of Christ's return, as the writer urges his audience, "Let us consider how to provoke one another to love and good deeds, not neglecting to meet together, as is the habit of some, but encouraging one another, and all the more as you see the Day approaching" (Heb. 10:24–25). Those incorporated into the new priesthood anticipate the day of the Lord's return by leading an upright life and gathering for worship in the holy places.

"That They May All Be One"

Toward the end of John's Gospel, shortly before the passion narrative, Jesus offers a prayer that interpreters have come to call the "high priestly prayer" because it reflects Jesus's priestly role (see John 17). At the heart of that prayer Jesus asks the Father, on behalf of his disciples and all who will believe in him, "that they may all be one. As you, Father, are in me and I am in you,

35. Again, the verb in the Greek of Exod. 29:21 (*rhainō*) is closely related to the verb in Hebrews (*rhantizō*). Leviticus 8 describes the same ritual using similar language (8:5–6, 30), with v. 30 using the compound verb *prosrhainō* instead of the simple verb *rhainō*.

36. Leithart, *The Priesthood of the Plebs*, 100.

37. Flemington, *The New Testament Doctrine of Baptism*, 98–99.

may they also be in us" (17:21). Jesus's priesthood is ordered to healing and reconciliation, to bringing about unity where once there was division. In light of the nature of baptism as a participation in Christ's own priesthood, it makes sense that this sacrament should also be ordered to unity. Just such a theme appears at several points in the Pauline Letters, and this theme will serve as the subject of the final chapter of our study.

12

Baptismal Unity

Hear, O Israel: The LORD our God, the LORD is one.

—Deuteronomy 6:4 (ESV)

Most of the New Testament images of baptism we have considered thus far appear to focus primarily on the individual. Dying and rising with Christ, being clothed with Christ, new birth, purification rituals—all of these images apply naturally to the individual. Baptism, however, is not a private affair. Baptism is not just administered by another person.[1] The effects of baptism have implications for the whole Church. This communal dimension is implicit in 1 Peter, which speaks of believers as "living stones" being built into a dwelling place for God (1 Pet. 2:4–5). But no one speaks more clearly or explicitly about the union to which baptism is ordered than the apostle Paul. Unity is one of the primary themes of his letters as a whole, and this unity is frequently connected with baptism. Indeed, nearly all the clear references to baptism in the Pauline Epistles address the problem of division and the goal of unity.

"There Is One Body and One Spirit"

Toward the beginning of the second half of Ephesians, Paul exhorts his audience "to maintain the unity of the Spirit in the bond of peace" (Eph. 4:3). He

1. *Acts of Paul and Thecla* 34 does make reference to Thecla baptizing herself, but this is an outlier in the tradition.

underscores the importance of this unity with a series of "ones" at the heart of the Christian life: "There is *one* body and *one* Spirit, just as you were called to the *one* hope of your calling, *one* Lord, *one* faith, *one* baptism, *one* God and Father of all, who is above all and through all and in all" (4:4–6). This emphasis on unity pervades Ephesians, as it does many of Paul's letters.[2] It should come as no surprise that the apostle appeals to baptism as a source of unity, since he frequently points to baptism as that which unites believers in Christ.[3] The unity of which Paul speaks in Ephesians has two dimensions described under two images. First, he emphasizes the unity of Jew and Gentile in Christ. In this regard Ephesians develops ideas present in Romans and Galatians. To elaborate on this unity, Paul draws on temple imagery, speaking both of the destruction of the dividing wall that once separated Jews and Gentiles and of the status of believers as the new dwelling place of God built on Christ (Eph. 2:11–22). Second, Paul also notes that unity does not mean uniformity. Rather, within the Church different members receive different gifts, all "for building up the body of Christ" (4:12). The primary image for this diversity of tasks is the body of Christ. The body and temple images come together, however, in that both are grounded in Christ himself, the "new human being [*anthrōpos*]" (see Eph. 2:15; 4:24).[4]

Twenty-first-century Christians may have difficulty understanding the significance of the reconciliation of Jews and Gentiles, which consumes so much of Paul's thought. If we consider the sad divisions that plague so much of our world today, perhaps we can begin to understand why Paul devotes so much of his energy to this question. Perhaps even more importantly, we must understand the division in light of the promises God made to Abraham and his descendants in Genesis. Paul always frames his understanding of the inclusion of the Gentiles within the promises God made to Israel's ancestors, and Ephesians is no exception.

Toward the middle of Ephesians 2, Paul turns to the healing of this division between Jew and Gentile. He begins by first describing the condition of the

2. Numerous texts reflect Paul's concern for unity. See, e.g., Rom. 14; 1 Cor. 1:10–17; 11:17–34; 12:12–31; Phil. 2:1–4.

3. See the discussion of other baptismal texts later in this chapter. This connection between baptism and unity helps to explain Paul's frustration in 1 Cor. 1:10–17. The Corinthians seem to have taken baptism, a fundamental source of unity, and turned it into a cause of division by their allegiance to their favorite leader, perhaps in part on the basis of which leader baptized them (1:13).

4. This use of temple and body imagery is not unique to Ephesians. In 1 Corinthians, Paul speaks of the Corinthian church as both temple of God (1 Cor. 3) and body of Christ (1 Cor. 12), and in both instances the images serve to foster unity, with the latter explicitly connected with baptism (12:13).

Gentiles prior to the coming of Christ. In times past, he notes, the Gentiles were without Christ and excluded from the covenants God had made with Israel, "without God in the world" (2:12). What the Gentiles receive in Christ, then, does not bypass the promises made to Abraham, as though God had chosen simply to start over from scratch. Rather, Paul teaches them, "But now in Christ Jesus you who once were far off have been brought near by the blood of Christ" (2:13). By incorporating the Gentiles into Abraham's family through the saving work of Christ, God has done away with the source of division between Jews and Gentiles. Although there is an element of continuity in the inclusion of the Gentiles, Paul also describes a newness in this event. Moreover, this new event brings about not only reconciliation of Jews and Gentiles with each other in Christ but also reconciliation between both groups and God:

> For [Christ] is our peace; in his flesh he *has made both groups into one* and has broken down the dividing wall, that is, the hostility between us. He has abolished the law with its commandments and ordinances, *that he might create in himself one new human being in place of the two*, thus making peace, and *might reconcile both groups to God in one body* through the cross, thus putting to death that hostility through it. (Eph. 2:14–16, modified)

Through his death, Christ has done away with the need to observe some of the commandments of the law of Moses that set Jews apart from Gentiles, thus bringing the two groups (Jews and Gentiles) into one new human being.[5] Paul describes this healing as a new creation, bringing into being a new human being (*anthrōpos*) through Christ's reconciling work on the cross. In addition, through his saving work Christ "reconcile[s] both groups to God in one body" (2:16). Paul's use of the language of the "body" anticipates the way he will discuss the unity of believers in Ephesians 4, a passage that grows in part out of his reference to baptism in 4:5.

The result of the creation of this "new human being" is that the Gentiles are no longer "strangers and aliens" (Eph. 2:19). The newness of God's action in Christ does not do away with the promises to Abraham but rather extends

5. There is some tension between the statement in Eph. 2:15 regarding the abolishing of the law and passages in which Paul reaffirms the value of the law. For example, in Romans Paul writes, "Do we then overthrow the law by this faith? By no means! On the contrary, we uphold the law" (Rom. 3:31). Without denying the difficulty of holding these two texts together, it is worth noting that in Romans Paul can both affirm the goodness of the law (7:12) and at the same time suggest that certain practices commanded by the law are now matters of indifference (see, e.g., Rom. 14).

them to all peoples. The agent of this newness is the Spirit, by whom all believers have "access" to the Father (2:18) and whom Paul closely associates with baptism (4:4–5). The goal of this new humanity is worship. The Gentiles who have believed in Christ have become a part of God's household and are now "being built together [with Jewish believers] into a dwelling place for God by the Spirit" (2:22 ESV).

Paul returns to the theme of unity in Ephesians 4. Following his opening exhortation to unity, he describes what that unity should look like. It is not a unity that flattens out differences but rather one that celebrates the many gifts Christ has bestowed upon the Church: "But each of us was given grace according to the measure of Christ's gift" (4:7). Christ distributes those gifts as he sees fit with one purpose in mind: "to equip the saints for the work of ministry, for building up the body of Christ" (4:12).[6] In other words, although not all members of the Church are leaders (the various groups listed in 4:11), all do have a task of ministry, and that ministry serves the good of the Church.

The purpose of the various ministries in which believers engage is to contribute to the unity and growth of the body of Christ (Eph. 4:13). Baptism is the beginning of a lifelong task of growing in maturity by being more closely united to Christ, a maturity that entails not being deceived by the lies of this world (4:14–15). Holding fast to the truth should contribute to growth in love: "But speaking the truth in love, we must grow up in every way into him who is the head, into Christ, from whom the whole body, joined and knit together by every ligament with which it is equipped, as each part is working properly, promotes the body's growth in building itself up in love" (4:15–16). The ultimate purpose of baptism, like the ultimate purpose of the Christian life, is to grow in love. This love has both an inward dimension (love among the baptized) and an outward dimension (adding to the body of Christ by sharing the gospel with others).

"All of You Are One in Christ Jesus"

Whereas the most explicit reference to baptism in Ephesians (Eph. 4:4–6) speaks of unity in general terms, other passages in Paul speak of more specific

6. When Paul speaks of "saints," he does not mean saints in the sense of canonized saints. Rather, "saint" or "holy one" is Paul's preferred term for the baptized. Nevertheless, there is continuity between the two uses of the word. The canonized saints in heaven are those who have fully lived out their baptismal call to holiness and now enjoy beatitude in God's presence as they await the general resurrection.

Baptism and Overcoming Oppositions

In three different places in the Pauline Epistles, the apostle speaks of the openness of the gospel to all. Even pairs that were traditionally hostile to one another are reconciled and made one through Christ:

> There is no longer Jew or Greek, there is no longer slave or free, there is no longer male and female; for all of you are one in Christ Jesus. (Gal. 3:28)
>
> For in the one Spirit we were all baptized into one body—Jews or Greeks, slaves or free—and we were all made to drink of one Spirit. (1 Cor. 12:13)
>
> In that renewal there is no longer Greek and Jew, circumcised and uncircumcised, barbarian, Scythian, slave and free; but Christ is all and in all! (Col. 3:11)

Although some interpreters have suggested that Paul is quoting a formula, the variation across the three passages seems to suggest that there is no set formula. Rather, Paul has a basic idea that he can formulate in different ways depending on the needs of the people he is addressing.

divisions that are overcome by baptism. Galatians, 1 Corinthians, and Colossians all have some variation on this pattern, with each letter drawing different conclusions from it. Each of these texts addresses at least one aspect of the unity discussed in Ephesians: ethnic reconciliation (especially between Jew and Gentile), diversity of gifts, and the practical implications of baptism. Ephesians, then, could be seen as a summation of the other three letters with respect to the goal and the effects of baptism. Before considering each letter's approach to baptismal unity in detail, it will be helpful to consider their statements regarding these paired opposites side by side, in order to notice both the similarities and the differences in the way each letter frames the oppositions overcome in baptism (see the sidebar "Baptism and Overcoming Oppositions").

Perhaps the most famous instance of this pattern appears in Galatians. As noted in chapter 9, one of the primary challenges Paul addresses in this letter is the status of Gentile Christians and whether they need to practice circumcision in order to be welcomed into the people of God. This context is crucial for understanding Paul's statement in Galatians 3:28.[7]

It would be hard to overestimate the significance of circumcision as a central part of the problem Paul addresses in Galatians. The topic appears numerous times throughout the letter. It serves as the primary point of debate at the meeting Paul attends with Peter, James, and John (Gal. 2:3, 7–9). The trouble Paul describes at Antioch arose with the arrival of the "circumcision party" (see Gal. 2:12). Circumcision plays an important role in Paul's understanding of the law and all that it entails (5:2–3), and shortly thereafter he insists that in Christ the practice of circumcision is of no value (5:6). Twice Paul links his opponents' insistence on circumcision with a desire to avoid offense and/or persecution (5:11; 6:12). Finally, in the letter closing, written in Paul's own hand, he returns once more to the question of circumcision, contrasting both circumcision and uncircumcision with new creation (6:12–15).

This emphasis on circumcision sheds considerable light on Paul's list of paired opposites in Galatians 3:28. Based on the pattern noted above, wherein the relativizing of binaries appears in a baptismal context, some interpreters have suggested that the series of negations in Galatians 3:28 stems from a baptismal formula.[8] There are several problems with such an explanation, however. Perhaps most significantly, the considerable variation in the formulations of Galatians 3:28, 1 Corinthians 12:13, and Colossians 3:11 speaks against a fixed formula.[9] Rather, it seems that Paul works with a general principle and applies it in different ways appropriate to the circumstances he is addressing. In Galatians, one of the main issues he is dealing with is circumcision, and

7. On the importance of paying attention to the context of each of the variations on these oppositional pairs, see Troy W. Martin, "The Covenant of Circumcision (Genesis 17:9–14) and the Situational Antitheses in Galatians 3:28," *JBL* 122 (2003): 111–25, esp. 112–14. I have relied on Martin's article for much of what follows, though I disagree with his proposed historical reconstruction of the situation Paul is facing. It seems highly unlikely that the Galatians were abandoning the faith to return to paganism, as Martin suggests, rather than considering the practice of circumcision. See Martin, "The Covenant of Circumcision," 116, and his earlier article "Apostasy to Paganism: The Rhetorical Stasis of the Galatian Controversy," *JBL* 114 (1995): 437–61.

8. J. Louis Martyn, *Galatians: A New Translation with Introduction and Commentary*, AB 33A (New York: Doubleday, 1997), 378–83; Frank J. Matera, *Galatians*, SP 9 (Collegeville, MN: Liturgical Press, 1992), 142.

9. See Martin, "The Covenant of Circumcision," 111–15. In this respect, there is a similarity between Paul's use of binaries and the various baptismal "formulae" found in the Acts of the Apostles ("in the name of Jesus Christ," "in the name of the Lord," "in the name of the Lord Jesus").

his choice of all three pairs of opposites (Jew-Greek, slave-free, male-female) can be explained in light of this question.

Behind all three of these pairs lies God's establishment of the covenant of circumcision with Abraham in Genesis 17:9–14.[10] The description of this covenant has implications for each of the groups mentioned in Galatians 3:28, either explicitly or implicitly. The covenant first explicitly singles out the males among Abraham's descendants, who alone must undergo the procedure of circumcision. Thus, God tells Abraham, "This is my covenant, which you shall keep, between me and you and your offspring after you: *Every male among you* shall be circumcised. You shall circumcise the flesh of your foreskins, and it shall be a sign of the covenant between me and you" (Gen. 17:10–11). Although the covenant does not exclude women, only the males among Abraham's descendants receive the sign of the covenant.

This covenant also explicitly addresses the status of slaves in an Israelite household. Circumcision is not limited to Abraham's biological descendants but also must be administered to slaves of the household. Thus, God's instructions to Abraham continue:

> Throughout your generations every male among you shall be circumcised when he is eight days old, including the slave born in your house and the one bought with your money from any foreigner who is not your offspring. Both the slave born in your house and the one bought with your money must be circumcised. So shall my covenant be in your flesh an everlasting covenant. (Gen. 17:12–13)

Circumcision thus applies to all male slaves in an Israelite household, whether they are born in that household or purchased. By contrast, free persons who do not belong in any way to Abraham's descendants are not required to be circumcised. Numerous texts refer to the "sojourner" in Israel (see, e.g., Lev. 16:29; 17:8–10; 19:10)—that is, to foreigners who happen to dwell in the midst of the Israelites.[11] The Pentateuch envisions only one situation in which foreigners must accept circumcision—namely, if they want to participate in the Passover (see Exod. 12:48–49). The fact that foreigners must be circumcised in order to partake of the Passover implies that ordinarily they are not expected to do so. Once again, the covenant with Abraham maps onto the pair of slave and free that Paul highlights in Galatians 3:28.

10. Martin, "The Covenant of Circumcision," 116–21.
11. Martin, "The Covenant of Circumcision," 117–18.

The categories "Jew" and "Greek" do not explicitly appear in Genesis 17. On the level of the narrative, at the time of the establishment of the covenant of circumcision not a single Jew exists because Abraham's great-grandson Judah, from whom the Jews receive their name, does not yet exist. Nevertheless, in a first-century context Jews saw themselves as the descendants of Abraham; Greeks, for the most part, did not.[12] Since the covenant distinguishes between Abraham's descendants and free foreigners, then, Paul's decision to pair "Jew" and "Greek" in Galatians 3:28 also makes sense in light of the covenant.[13]

The common denominator in all three pairs Paul highlights is their relation to circumcision. Under the covenant of circumcision, the first group in each of the pairs (Jew, slave, male) had to receive circumcision, whereas the second group (Greek, free, female) did not. By contrast, in the New Covenant established by Christ (see 2 Cor. 3:6), circumcision is required of no one. Baptism is open to all. As Troy Martin puts it, "Christian baptism ignores the distinctions required by the covenant of circumcision and provides a basis for unity in the Christian community."[14] By their common baptism, members of all the groups Paul lists find their more fundamental identity in Christ, an identity that relativizes the distinctions that often serve as a source of division and conflict.

"The Body Does Not Consist of One Member but of Many"

First Corinthians addresses a different situation than Galatians does. Whereas in Galatians the primary question concerns the role of the law of Moses and of circumcision, in 1 Corinthians Paul faces a church in chaos, including factionalism based on an obsession with eloquence and, perhaps, spiritual gifts (1 Cor. 1–4); general confusion in the realm of sexual ethics (1 Cor. 5–7); liturgical abuses both within and outside Christian worship settings concerning temples, spiritual gifts, and the celebration of the Eucharist (1 Cor. 8–14); and a fundamental misunderstanding of the Christian hope

12. For a rare exception, see 1 Macc. 12:20–21.

13. It is worth noting that Paul frequently uses the word "Greek" generically to refer to non-Jews. Thus, in Romans Paul uses the phrase "the Jew first and also the Greek" (Rom. 1:16; 2:9–10) without intending to exclude the Roman, the Egyptian, the Ethiopian, or the member of any other ethnic group.

14. Martin, "The Covenant of Circumcision," 121.

(1 Cor. 15).[15] Despite the difference in context and problems, Galatians and 1 Corinthians share at least one thing in common: both letters appeal to baptism as a source of Christian unity. Galatians does so by emphasizing that baptism is open to all; 1 Corinthians does so by underscoring the interdependence of the baptized. The unity that baptism brings about does not do away with the diversity of those who come to Christ. Rather, it knits them together into one body made of many members, each of which has a function that contributes to the good of the whole (1 Cor. 12:21–26).

Early on in 1 Corinthians, Paul contrasts the unity that baptism symbolizes and accomplishes with the division plaguing the church at Corinth. Chastising the Corinthians for their allegiance to their favorite Christian leader (or the rejection by some of any merely human leader at all; see 1 Cor. 1:12), Paul poses three rhetorical questions: "Has Christ been divided? Was Paul crucified for you? Or were you baptized in the name of Paul?" (1:13). Implicit in these questions is a close connection between the crucifixion, baptism, and unity. The division in Corinth undercuts one of the central purposes of baptism: the creation of an interconnected and interdependent body. By aligning themselves with one leader over and against the others and their partisans, the Corinthians are effectively, albeit metaphorically, cutting off a limb (1 Cor. 12).

In 1 Corinthians 12 Paul addresses the nature and purpose of spiritual gifts, which seem to have been a major source of division among the Corinthians.[16] The entire chapter focuses on the relationship between unity and diversity, particularly when it comes to gifts such as prophecy, speaking in tongues, and healing, among others (for the list of gifts, see 12:8–10, 28). Paul approaches the problem from a variety of angles, one of which includes the role of baptism (12:13). In order to understand the significance of this baptismal reference, it is helpful to place it in its broader context.

Paul first grounds the notion of unity in diversity in the source of the gifts over which the Corinthians seem to be obsessed. These gifts have their origin in the one God: "Now there are varieties of gifts, but the same Spirit;

15. For such a division of the letter, as well as the description of the Corinthian situation as one of "chaos," see Michael J. Gorman, *Apostle of the Crucified Lord: A Theological Introduction to Paul and His Letters*, 2nd ed. (Grand Rapids: Eerdmans, 2017), 273–84. The similarities between the Corinthian situation and the modern Church confirm the old adage "The more things change, the more they stay the same." Or as Qoheleth would put it, "There is nothing new under the sun" (Eccles. 1:9).

16. The discussion of gifts actually extends through 1 Cor. 14, but Paul appeals to baptism only in 1 Cor. 12.

and there are varieties of service, but the same Lord; and there are varieties of activities, but it is the same God who activates all of them in everyone" (1 Cor. 12:4–6).[17] The repetition of the word "same" underscores the common source of the various gifts the Corinthians have received. The variety of these gifts, Paul insists, ought not to obscure the unity of their source. Moreover, these gifts have a purpose that corresponds to both the diversity within the Church and the unity of believers: "To each is given the manifestation of the Spirit *for the common good*" (12:7). Not everyone receives the same gift—some receive wisdom, others knowledge, others faith, among other gifts (12:8–10). But the reception of these gifts should not be cause for boasting; rather, those who receive the gifts are called to use them for the good of the whole. To use another of Paul's favorite images in 1 Corinthians, the gifts are ordered to the "building up" of the Church (see 8:1). By reiterating that these gifts come from the Spirit (12:11) and not from natural ability, Paul subtly undercuts any arrogance or pride that could stem from the exercise of the gifts.

In 1 Corinthians 12:12 Paul shifts to the image of a body, an image he has already introduced a few chapters earlier in the letter. There he grounds the Corinthians' unity in the Eucharist: "Because there is one bread, we who are many are one body, for we all partake of the one bread" (10:17). In light of this sacramental context of the body imagery, it is not surprising that in chapter 12 Paul appeals to this image once again in a sacramental context.[18] Thus, he writes, "For in the one Spirit we were all baptized into one body—Jews or Greeks, slaves or free—and we were all made to drink of one Spirit" (12:13). Here we see a set of binaries similar to the one found in Galatians 3:28, but there are important differences between the two sets that stem from the situation Paul is addressing.

As noted above, the primary problem Paul is facing in Galatians is the question of circumcision and whether Gentiles need to undergo this rite to become a part of the people of God. In 1 Corinthians, by contrast, circumci-

17. Some see in these verses an early, implicit trinitarian understanding of God, with the references to one Spirit, one Lord (Christ), and one God (the Father; on this distinction between Christ and the Father, see 1 Cor. 8:6). See Gordon D. Fee, "Christology and Pneumatology in Romans 8:9–11—and Elsewhere: Some Reflections on Paul as a Trinitarian," in *Jesus of Nazareth: Lord and Christ; Essays on the Historical Jesus and New Testament Christology*, ed. Joel B. Green and Max Turner (Grand Rapids: Eerdmans, 1994), 312–31, esp. 329n52.

18. As I have argued above, the connection between baptism and the body is also likely in the background of 1 Cor. 6:9–20.

sion barely makes an appearance.[19] This may explain why Paul does not use the male-female pair in 1 Corinthians 12:13: the situation does not seem to require it. This may also explain why the pairs in 1 Corinthians appear in the plural ("Jews or Greeks, slaves or free"), whereas in Galatians they appear in the singular. In 1 Corinthians Paul is addressing the relationship between diversity (which implies plurality) and unity, whereas in Galatians he is addressing whether anyone has to undergo the rite of circumcision, which is necessarily an individual act in practice.[20]

Following the baptismal reference, Paul develops the imagery of the body at greater length. Once again, the emphasis falls on plurality, as he begins, "Indeed, the body does not consist of one member but of many" (1 Cor. 12:14). Plurality alone does not suffice, however, to make his point. Rather, with the body analogy Paul can speak of the interdependence of the members of the body of Christ. Generally speaking, the limbs and members of a body cannot function well independently of one another—indeed, in an important sense they cannot exist independently of one another.[21] Once it is cut off from the body, a severed "hand" is a hand only by analogy, since it can no longer perform its function. Using comic imagery, Paul brings home the point by asking what a body would be like if it were only an eye or only an ear (1 Cor. 12:17). Important functions would be impossible. Just as a body needs many parts to perform many functions, so too the Church needs people with different gifts for different activities. The image of the body thus serves to address one of the primary problems facing the Corinthian church—namely, divisions based on arrogance and pride. For this reason Paul further suggests that God gives more honor to those parts of the body that many consider unimportant (12:24–25). This teaching restates in a different way a point Paul makes earlier in the letter: that God favors the foolish and the weak to shame the wise and the strong (1:26–31). Paul further underscores the incompatibility of baptism with factionalism, reminding the Corinthians, "Now you are the body of Christ and individually members of it" (12:27).

19. In 1 Corinthians the noun "circumcision" (*peritomē*) appears once (7:19), compared with seven occurrences in Galatians, a letter less than half the length of 1 Corinthians. The verb (*peritemnō*) appears twice in 1 Corinthians (7:18), and it is not a central part of the argument, whereas the verb appears five times in Galatians and at crucial points.

20. See Martin, "The Covenant of Circumcision," 113.

21. This is, of course, an exaggeration. The eyes of a person can continue to function and exist even if other limbs have been cut off. Nevertheless, the body will suffer from the loss. Similarly, the Church can survive if an organ is removed, but it will be worse off for the loss.

All the baptized make up one body, not several bodies headed by different leaders.

Paul brings his discussion of the gifts to a preliminary conclusion by reiterating the need for a variety of gifts and tasks in the Church (1 Cor. 12:27–31). The discussion of these vocations in the context of the baptismal reference of 12:13 brings out another important aspect of baptism. The rite does not simply initiate a person into the Church generically. Rather, God brings people into the Church with a particular purpose in mind. Paul refers to the different activities as "gifts," and he notes that God is the one who appoints people to particular vocations. One of the most important tasks of the Church—both for its own sake and for that of the whole world—is to help the baptized discover what gifts God has appointed to each of them.

"Christ Is All and in All"

The third set of binaries in the Pauline Epistles (Col. 3:11) stands a bit removed from Paul's only explicit mention of baptism in Colossians (2:12). Nevertheless, there are good reasons to interpret the list of 3:11 as a baptismal reference or allusion. First, there is the fact that in both Galatians and 1 Corinthians this pattern appears immediately in connection with baptism. Although it seems unlikely that there was any set "formula" that accompanied baptism, Paul seems to have associated the basic idea of overcoming opposites with the rite.[22] Second, as I argue above, much of Colossians 2–3 can be seen as an exposition of the significance of baptism, particularly because of the way it develops the imagery of dying and rising with Christ. Moreover, the reference to binaries in Colossians is followed by clothing imagery, which is also frequently associated with baptism.[23]

The binaries in Galatians relate primarily to the question of circumcision as an entrance requirement for joining the people of God. The binaries of 1 Corinthians figure into Paul's insistence on the need for plurality and diversity within the Church. What, then, is the purpose of the binaries in Colossians? Like both earlier letters, Colossians includes references to the Jew-Greek distinction and the slave-free distinction. In two respects, however, the formulation of Colossians resembles that of Galatians more than that of 1 Corinthians.

22. For a critique of the baptismal-formula hypothesis, see again Martin, "The Covenant of Circumcision," 111–15.

23. On dying and rising with Christ, see chap. 8 above; on clothing imagery, see chap. 9.

Baptism and Racial Reconciliation

The racial tensions that have plagued American society in recent years are, sadly, only the latest in a long history of animosity springing from ethnic and other divisions. From the hatred many ancient people felt for the Jews to the modern-day slave trade to the strife between tribes in Rwanda, these and other tensions seem to be an inherent part of human nature. The gift of baptism calls us to a better way. Baptism reminds us, first, of our common dignity as human beings made in the image and likeness of God. Even more importantly, though, baptism reminds us that the gift of salvation does not discriminate. The invitation to find life in Christ is open to all, and with it comes the recognition of our call to love even those most different from us. We can do so only by daily living out the baptismal vocation to die to self—to our selfish desires and inclinations—and so to live for Christ through love of God and neighbor.

First, as in Galatians, the pairs in Colossians appear in the singular rather than in the plural. Second, the phrase that closes the list of binaries, "Christ is all and in all" (Col. 3:11b), comes close to the statement that precedes the list of binaries in Galatians: "As many of you as were baptized into Christ have clothed yourselves with Christ" (Gal. 3:27). In this regard, it is significant that the binaries in Colossians are preceded by a reference to putting on the "new human being [*anthrōpos*]" (see Col. 3:10) and are followed by an exhortation to put on various virtues (Col. 3:12–14). On the other hand, Colossians resembles 1 Corinthians in that it does not include the male-female pair.[24]

At the heart of Paul's treatment of the distinctions common in his society is his vision of Christ as the key to understanding the universe. His reference in Colossians 3:10 to the "image of its creator," as well as the language of "all" repeated twice in verse 11, points back to 1:15–20, perhaps the most important passage in the letter. There Paul speaks both of Christ's status as the image of God and of Christ's role in sustaining all things in existence.[25]

24. This point supports Martin's argument that the male-female pair in Galatians appears because of its relevance to the question of circumcision. See again Martin, "The Covenant of Circumcision," 118.

25. On Christ as the image, see Col. 1:15; on his role in sustaining all things, see 1:17.

The relationship that baptism establishes between the baptized and Christ thus carries more weight than the ethnic and social differences on which many people—in both Paul's day and our own—tend to focus.

N. T. Wright has wisely suggested that the categories Paul relativizes in Colossians 3:11 relate to the sins he condemns in 3:8.[26] Many of the sins Paul lists ("anger, wrath, malice, slander, and abusive language") contribute to and reinforce the divisions that plague human society. Conversely, the divisions and the tensions between the groups Paul refers to would naturally grow into those very sins. In his appeal to baptism, Paul reminds his readers of two things. First, the image in which they were made and according to which they are being refashioned is not the exclusive right of any particular ethnic group or social class. Rather, as Genesis 1:26–28 suggests, *all* human beings are made in the image and likeness of God.[27] Second, and perhaps even more importantly, the conflict that sin introduced into the world can now be overcome through the saving work of Christ. If, as Paul says, "Christ is all and in all!" (Col. 3:11b), a reality brought about by baptism (cf. Gal. 3:26–28), then among Christians there is no place for the conflict that plagues our broken world, much less for looking on others with disdain because of their social or ethnic background.

Whereas the sins Paul lists in Colossians 3:8 relate to division, the virtues and the attitudes that follow the series of paired opposites in 3:11 foster harmony and concord. Using clothing imagery that in all likelihood has a baptismal connotation, Paul writes, "As God's chosen ones, holy and beloved, clothe yourselves with compassion, kindness, humility, meekness, and patience. Bear with one another and, if anyone has a complaint against another, forgive each other; just as the Lord has forgiven you, so you also must forgive" (3:12–13). Moreover, a few verses later he appeals to the imagery of the Church as a body, another image associated with baptism: "And let the peace of Christ rule in your hearts, to which indeed you were called in the one body" (3:15a). Although this body imagery is somewhat removed from the explicit baptismal reference in Colossians 2:11–12, the close association between baptism and the Church as the body of Christ in 1 Corinthians and Ephesians further supports a baptismal reading of the imagery in Colossians

26. N. T. Wright, *The Epistles of Paul to the Colossians and to Philemon: An Introduction and Commentary*, TNTC 12 (Grand Rapids: Eerdmans, 1986), 139–41.

27. Wright puts it well: "[Divisions between these groups] are, ultimately, a denial of the creation of humankind in the image of God" (*Colossians and Philemon*, 140).

3:15 and of the whole flow of the passage leading up to this verse. The baptized must now see their fundamental identity as belonging to the body of Christ.

"And I Will Show You a Still More Excellent Way"

As both 1 Corinthians and Ephesians attest, God has chosen to use baptism to distribute a variety of gifts to those who belong to Christ (1 Cor. 12:28; Eph. 4:11–12). Each of these gifts has its place in the life and ordering of the Church, but for Paul there is one that surpasses them all: love. Shortly after his discussion of baptism and the body of Christ, Paul gives his famous encomium on love (1 Cor. 13) in which he commends to the Corinthians "a still more excellent way" (12:31b). The passage serves to put the Corinthians in their place, reminding them of what matters most. It is to this, the highest gift, that baptism is ultimately ordered. One of the primary consequences of the transgression of Adam and Eve was the fracturing of relationships—between men and women, between human beings and the earth, and, most importantly, between human beings and God (see Gen. 3:9–19). Baptism begins the work of repairing these relationships, uniting us to Christ and, in him, to one another. The task of the baptized is to embody the gift of reconciliation that we have received, working toward harmony through acts of love and forgiveness.

Conclusion

Salvation through Worship

Then everyone who calls on the name of the LORD shall be saved.

—Joel 2:32a

For this is the glory of the human being, to continue and remain permanently in God's service.

—Irenaeus, *Against Heresies* 4.14.1

Baptism is more than a cleansing. It is death and resurrection. Paul himself, speaking in the Letter to the Galatians of the turning point in his life brought about by his encounter with the Risen Christ, describes it with the words: I am dead. At that moment a new life truly begins.

—Benedict XVI, *Saint Paul*

From the beginning of the Bible to the end, water plays a pivotal role in God's saving work. In the Old Testament, it serves as a symbol of life, of death, of freedom, and of purity. In other words, water encompasses and pervades some of the most important aspects of ancient Israel's life. The New Testament takes up and transfigures the power of water by incorporating it into the saving events of Christ's passion, death, and resurrection. By its natural properties, water sustains biological life. Invested with God's saving word, water receives the power to impart eternal life, initiating the baptized into the body of Christ and the cruciform life that membership in that body demands. In closing, rather than summarize each chapter, I would like to offer a synthesis of some of the most important elements of baptism we have considered as well as suggest a few practical ways to remind ourselves of the great gift we have received.

Christ the Center

If one thing is clear from a survey of the New Testament passages relating directly or indirectly to baptism, it is that Christ stands at the center of the sacrament. He is the source of the grace baptism imparts. He is the model of humble submission to God's will. He is the pattern that the life of the baptized is to follow.

The Gospel of John most clearly presents Jesus as the source of living and life-giving water. From Jesus's conversation with the Samaritan woman at the well to his death on the cross to his breathing of the Holy Spirit on the disciples on the day of the resurrection, John repeatedly reminds his readers that Christ is the source of new life. Christ fulfills this role in two ways: by conquering death through his resurrection (John 11:25–26) and by sending the Spirit upon believers after his ascension (16:7). Most of the baptismal passages in the New Testament appeal to at least one of these acts of Christ. In John's Gospel, Jesus's late-night conversation with Nicodemus underscores the need to be reborn of "water and Spirit" (3:5). Embedded in a context rife with explicit baptismal language, this conversation points to the close connection between baptism and reception of the Spirit. The Acts of the Apostles likewise links baptism with the gift of the Spirit. When the Spirit descends upon the apostles at Pentecost and their fellow Jews ask them to explain these extraordinary events, Peter proclaims the gospel of Christ's victory over death and exhorts his listeners to be baptized in his name in order to receive the Holy Spirit. Although there are occasional exceptions to the pattern of water baptism followed by reception of the Spirit, the two are intimately linked throughout Acts. In 1 Corinthians 6, Paul appeals both to Christ's resurrection and to the indwelling of the Holy Spirit in the context of an allusion to baptism. Romans and Colossians also appeal to the resurrection as the source of baptismal life (Rom. 6:3–11; Col. 2:11–12), as does 1 Peter (1 Pet. 1:3; 3:21).

Christ also models for us the humble submission necessary to receive the grace of baptism. We do not administer baptism to ourselves. Rather, we receive it as a gift, and we do so in humble obedience to God's will. Christ perfectly submitted to his Father's will in receiving John's baptism of repentance, even though he had no sins of his own. His messianic anointing at the river Jordan points forward to our own reception of the Spirit through baptism. Perhaps even more importantly, it also foreshadows his perfect gift of self on the cross, which makes the consequent gift of the Spirit possible. The Gospel of Mark particularly draws out the cruciform nature of baptism by recording Jesus's description of his death on the cross as a kind of baptism (Mark 10:38) as well as an act of service (10:45). John, too, brings out Christ's exemplary role through his account of the washing of the disciples' feet at the Last Supper (John 13:1–11). This episode encapsulates Jesus's status as servant and points forward to his ultimate gift of self on the cross. In calling his disciples to imitate him (13:12–15), he does not ask them simply to wash one another's feet in a literal fashion (though such an act is even to this day a beautiful reflection of Jesus's humility). He invites them—and us—to imitate his own humility by dying to self. In this regard, Jesus's action and the deeper reality to which it points set up the pattern of life to which all the baptized are called.

What remains subtle and implicit in Jesus's reply to James and John's request (Mark 10:35–41) becomes explicit in Paul's references to baptism. In Romans 6:1–11 and Colossians 2:11–12, Paul emphasizes that baptism joins us in a mysterious way to the saving events of Christ's death and resurrection. Baptism thus fulfills the Old Testament images of water as the source of both life and death. Moreover, because of the way he describes Christ's gift of self (Gal. 2:19–20) and reminds the Galatians that they have "crucified the flesh with its passions and desires" (5:24), Paul's use of clothing imagery in Galatians 3:27 also implicitly draws on these ideas. His application of such imagery in nonbaptismal contexts (e.g., Rom. 13:11–14) further shows that the death and resurrection of baptism is not a onetime affair but rather establishes the pattern that ought to hold for the whole life of the baptized. It is through this pattern of dying and rising with Christ that we attain to a freedom analogous to the freedom so vividly depicted in the book of Exodus (Rom. 6:17–18).

Unity

Dying to self is one of the keys to unity and reconciliation. It is no coincidence that in 1 Corinthians, a letter addressed to a community racked with internal strife, Paul frequently appeals to baptism and to the cross. In his opening salvo against the divisions plaguing the Corinthian church, Paul asks, "Has Christ been divided? Was Paul crucified for you? Or were you baptized in the name of Paul?" (1 Cor. 1:13). The obvious answer to each of these rhetorical questions is a resounding "No." Christ was crucified for us not so that we might remain divided, but so that we might be united to him and, in him, to one another. One of the keys to this unity is recognizing the beauty of the different gifts that God distributes to the baptized (1 Cor. 12; cf. Eph. 4:8–16). Paul calls the Corinthians to recognize the interdependence of the members of Christ's body rather than see difference as a cause of disunity manifested in arrogance and disdain for others. Moreover, there is no place in the body of Christ for division based on social class, ethnicity, or sex (Gal. 3:28; 1 Cor. 12:12–13; Col. 3:11). Our common baptism gives us equal dignity in Christ and calls us to build one another up, growing in the still more excellent way of love (1 Cor. 13).

A Priestly Vocation

Though not the most obvious or pronounced theme in New Testament passages on baptism, the priestly dimension of the sacrament is an important one. When God freed the Israelites from slavery in Egypt, he called them to himself to be "a kingdom of priests" (Exod. 19:6 ESV). This call followed a passage through the waters of the Red Sea, and in a similar fashion Aaron and his sons were bathed with water as part of their ordination (Exod. 29:1–9; Lev. 8:5–9). Occasionally the New Testament hints at this theme in the context of baptism, indicating that all the baptized—not just those ordained to the ministerial priesthood—have a priestly vocation. First Peter, alluding to Exodus 19, addresses its audience as "a royal priesthood" (1 Pet. 2:9). Hebrews refers to baptism as a washing of the body, drawing on imagery from the priestly ordination rite (Heb. 10:19–22). The mode in which this priestly baptismal vocation is lived out will vary from person to person, based on his or her more particular calling. Nevertheless, all of us are called to offer to God "spotless sacrifices of devotion from the altar of the heart," in the words of St. Leo the Great.[1] In every believer's life, these sacrifices will follow the pattern of

1. Leo the Great, *Sermon* 4.1, in *Sermons*, trans. Jane Patricia Freeland and Agnes Josephine Conway, FC 93 (Washington, DC: Catholic University of America Press, 1996), 25.

Christ's life: dying to oneself so that others might live. We fulfill this priestly vocation every time we follow Christ by denying ourselves (Mark 8:34) in ways both large and small. The priestly dimension of baptism also points to the importance of the sacrament as a gateway to worship.

Salvation through Worship

In one of his sermons on baptism, St. Gregory of Nazianzus describes baptism as "the most beautiful and most magnificent of the gifts of God."[2] St. Gregory's superlatives are probably in part rhetorical flourish, but they underscore the greatness of the gift of baptism. Baptism, however, is not an end but a beginning. The late Norwegian New Testament scholar Nils Dahl once wrote, "As a rite of initiation, baptism can be compared with a door that one must go through to come into a room. The door's significance depends much more on what sort of room it leads into, and on what the difference is between being outside or inside, than on the door's particular appearance and construction."[3] Modifying Dahl's image, we might say that baptism is not simply a door that leads us into a room but rather one that transforms us into a temple fit for God's dwelling (1 Cor. 6:19).[4] In the Old Covenant, the name of the Lord dwelt in the tabernacle and, later, in the temple (Deut. 12:5–6). In the New Covenant, God makes his name dwell within us. This is what it means to be baptized in his name, and the proper response is to worship by calling upon the name of the Lord. In this lies our salvation. The exodus, the paradigmatic image of salvation in the Old Testament, culminates not simply in liberation from slavery—important though such liberation is. Rather, this liberation finds its end in the worship of God, in which we find our true freedom. The New Testament confirms this idea. God created us for himself, to find rest in him by worshiping him.[5] He did so not because he needs our worship but because

2. Gregory of Nazianzus, *Oration* 40.3, in *Festal Orations*, trans. Nonna Verna Harrison (Crestwood, NY: St. Vladimir's Seminary Press, 2008), 100.

3. Nils Alstrup Dahl, "The Concept of Baptism in Ephesians," in *Studies in Ephesians: Introductory Questions, Text- & Edition-Critical Issues, Interpretation of Texts and Themes*, WUNT 131 (Tübingen: Mohr Siebeck, 2000), 413–40, here 416.

4. To qualify Dahl's statement, the appearance of the door does matter to some extent, as the form of the sacrament is an important part of walking through the proper door, as he probably would have agreed.

5. See Augustine, *Confessions* 1.1. For an outstanding recent study of the relationship between worship, repentance, and salvation, see Khaled Anatolios, *Deification through the Cross: An Eastern Christian Theology of Salvation* (Grand Rapids: Eerdmans, 2020).

we do. Only by gazing in adoration on his beauty will we find the fulfillment for which we all long. Baptism makes that fulfillment possible.

"In the Name of the Father and of the Son and of the Holy Spirit"

Most Catholics do not remember their baptism, having had the saving waters poured over their heads as infants. What good, then, is this lengthy meditation on the foundational sacrament? Much, in every way. While it is true that most of us do not remember our own baptism, the Church offers us numerous ways to recall it and opportunities to meditate on it. Each year at the Easter Vigil, when new members are added to God's Church, the rite calls on all the baptized present to renew the commitment that they made—or that their parents and godparents made for them—at their baptism.

Our meditation on the gift of baptism need not be limited to an annual renewal, however. Any time we attend the baptism of a friend or relative, we can remind ourselves of the great gift God has given us in baptism. The rite of baptism for children explicitly calls on the parents and the godparents to renew their baptismal vows, but nothing prevents all those present from doing so silently. Moreover, any time we contemplate Christ's gift of self on the cross, whether through reading Scripture or other spiritual writings or by gazing upon a crucifix, we can also consider the pattern of life into which we have been initiated. Before our eyes we see both the source of our redemption and the model for our life.

Perhaps the simplest and most practical way to recall our baptism is the beautiful Catholic tradition of blessing ourselves with holy water as we mark ourselves with the sign of the cross. In this brief act, both the water and the tracing of the cross on our body recall the form of our baptism. We can even pronounce, either quietly or mentally, the words that were invoked over us at our baptism, "In the name of the Father and of the Son and of the Holy Spirit." In doing so, we are reminded of our call to die to self so that we might live. Moreover, because we perform this act most often upon entering a church, this blessing also reminds us that our baptism was an initiation into an entire life of worship. Dying to self is not self-torture but rather an act of love in which we will find genuine and lasting happiness. By daily imitating and participating in Christ's gift of self, we will gradually fulfill our baptismal vocation and, with the help of God's grace, prepare ourselves for its ultimate fulfillment in the heavenly banquet.

APPENDIX

Infant Baptism

Throughout this study I have deliberately avoided addressing the question of infant baptism for two reasons. First, the biblical evidence regarding the practice of infant baptism is slim and disputed. A few passages in the Acts of the Apostles refer to the conversion of entire households (Acts 16:15, 33; 18:8), and interpreters have suggested that surely some of these households must have included infants. If so, it hardly seems likely that a Roman paterfamilias would leave it to his children to make their own decisions to be baptized once they were old enough (a thoroughly modern position). References to children in some of the Pauline Letters have also been taken to imply that infants received baptism from apostolic times.[1] Some might argue that the admonitions to children, found in the household codes of Colossians and Ephesians, must have addressed children who had attained the age of reason. An obvious reply would be that parents give their children commands even before the children have the capacity to obey them intentionally. It is at least conceivable that Paul would do the same in his churches. Beyond these passages, there is not much by way of evidence for the practice in New Testament times. This is not to say that there are no compelling biblical arguments for infant baptism—only that there is little evidence of the *practice* in the earliest documents.

The second, and perhaps more important, reason for relegating a discussion of infant baptism to an appendix is that I hope the main study will be

1. For a discussion of these and other passages, see W. F. Flemington, *The New Testament Doctrine of Baptism* (London: SPCK, 1964), 130–32.

of use not only to Catholics but also to believers of all Christian traditions, regardless of whether they practice infant baptism or not. I do not expect this brief argument to change the minds of those who are committed to believer's baptism based on their reading of Scripture. I offer it primarily to give Catholics and others open to infant baptism some reasons for the practice. Without in any way pretending to be exhaustive, I would like to consider three different arguments in favor of baptizing infants: the unbroken tradition of the Church, both East and West; the similarities between circumcision and baptism as rites of initiation; and the challenge that the practice of infant baptism poses to Enlightenment emphases on the individual and on choice.

As is widely known, one of the main differences between the Catholic and Protestant traditions is the rejection by the former of the principle of *sola scriptura*. For Catholics, although Scripture is certainly the highest authority, it is not the only authority in matters of theology. Sacred Tradition also plays a crucial role in determining Catholic belief and practice.[2] When it comes to infant baptism, the tradition is early, widespread, and for the most part unbroken.[3] An implicit reference to the practice appears in the writings of St. Justin Martyr in the mid-second century.[4] Some have inferred additional evidence from the *Martyrdom of Polycarp*, the moving account of the death of the great bishop of Smyrna. As he faces his death, St. Polycarp speaks of having served his king and his Savior (i.e., Christ) for eighty-six years.[5] While it is conceivable that Polycarp was baptized around the age of seven and died at the age of ninety-three, it is just as plausible, if not more so, to suggest that he was baptized as an infant and died at the age of eighty-six. If that was the case, given that he was martyred around the middle of the second century, this would put his baptism as an infant squarely in apostolic times. Another allusion to infant baptism appears in the writings of St. Irenaeus in the late second century.[6] Beginning in the third century, some argue against the practice of infant baptism, though not against its validity. Tertullian, for example, recommends that people wait to receive baptism due to the danger of

2. On the relationship between Scripture and Tradition, see *Dei Verbum* (Dogmatic Constitution on Divine Revelation) 7–10.

3. For much in this paragraph, I rely on Flemington, *The New Testament Doctrine of Baptism*, 132–34.

4. Justin Martyr, *First Apology* 15.

5. *Martyrdom of Polycarp* 9.

6. Irenaeus of Lyons, *Against Heresies* 2.22.4. Irenaeus speaks of people from every age group being "born again," a common image for baptism.

sin, an attitude still prevalent at the time of St. Augustine, as we can see in the *Confessions*.[7] Nevertheless, by the time of Augustine the practice was common and widespread, and the Middle Ages witnessed an unbroken tradition in East and West affirming the validity of infant baptism. For Catholics, this unbroken tradition is more than enough to uphold the practice. Nevertheless, it is worthwhile to offer some biblical basis for the practice in addition to the witness of tradition.

Beyond the references to households and children in the New Testament, there is another common argument in favor of infant baptism. Some interpreters extrapolate from Paul's reference to circumcision in Colossians 2:11 to the conclusion that baptism corresponds to circumcision. As circumcision was to the Israelites, so baptism is to the Church. As the Israelite boys were circumcised as infants without their consent, so members of the New Covenant may be initiated even as infants. There are interpretive difficulties with this particular reading of Colossians 2:11. Paul does not explicitly equate baptism with circumcision. Moreover, even if he is speaking indirectly of baptism as corresponding to circumcision, he nevertheless seems to be addressing adults who have come to faith. A similar point could be made with respect to Galatians 3, where Paul implicitly contrasts baptism with circumcision, but some of the same difficulties that apply to Colossians apply here as well. Setting aside the question of whether Paul himself actually presents baptism as the new circumcision, however, it is worth asking a broader question. If in the Old Covenant, God required a rite to be performed on infant boys without their consent—a practice carried on by the Israelites for centuries—then why with the arrival of Christ would he suddenly choose to make an individual's personal decision essential to initiation into his people?[8] Those who favor believer's baptism would no doubt point to the close connection between baptism, faith, and repentance throughout the New Testament. Infants can neither repent nor believe, not yet having attained the age of reason. But if one considers the practice and context of circumcision, a similar argument could be made against circumcision on the eighth day. Circumcision was the induction of infant boys into the people of Israel, but also into a way

7. Tertullian, *On Baptism* 18; Augustine, *Confessions* 1.11.17. It is worth noting that Tertullian speaks of the delay of baptism as "preferable" without condemning the practice of infant baptism.

8. I owe this point to Peter J. Leithart, *The Baptized Body* (Moscow, ID: Canon Press, 2007), 123n13. The entire appendix of Leithart's book, titled "The Sociology of Infant Baptism," is well worth reading.

of life that demanded obedience. The infant boys of ancient Israel were no more capable of obeying God's commandments than are Christian babies of believing in God, and yet this is how God chose to form his people Israel. It seems fitting that the New Covenant would follow a pattern similar to that of the Old. Just as the ancient Israelites inducted their children into a life of obedience and brought them up to observe the commandments, so Christians welcome children into the body of Christ and raise them to embrace the faith of the Church.

Finally, although advocacy of adult believer's baptism preceded the Enlightenment, some arguments against infant baptism have more in common with Enlightenment individualism than with the worldview that shaped the New Testament.[9] I do not intend this as an argument of guilt by association. Despite its problematic treatment of religion, the Enlightenment resulted in many benefits to the human race from which we continue to profit to this day. Nevertheless, the emphasis on the individual and on choice is problematic. Baptism is a gift of God's grace, in no way merited by the one who receives it. What matters most in baptism is God's choice of the person, not the person's choice of baptism. Those who favor believer's baptism no doubt would affirm this point wholeheartedly. Nevertheless, the emphasis on belief and choice at the very least runs the risk of muddying the waters. Moreover, this emphasis can obscure the communal nature of baptism, which in the New Testament is every bit as important as the personal dimension (see 1 Cor. 12). Although tangentially related, here it is worth raising the question of children and adults with severe, even debilitating mental disabilities. Does the emphasis on the individual's acts of repentance and belief exclude those incapable of making such acts, or of articulating them, from the waters of life and the eucharistic table? Such a question challenges not only advocates of believer's baptism but also the widespread eucharistic practice in much of the West, though addressing this issue adequately lies far beyond the scope of this appendix.

Given the long-standing and unbroken tradition of the Church, the pattern of God's dealings with his people Israel with respect to rites of initiation, and the primacy of God's choice in bringing a person into the body of Christ, it seems right and just to welcome infants to the fountain of salvation.

9. See again Leithart, *The Baptized Body*, 121–24.

Suggested Resources

Beasley-Murray, G. R. *Baptism in the New Testament*. Grand Rapids: Eerdmans, 1962. Though first published sixty years ago, this work remains the most exhaustive study of the subject in the New Testament. A Baptist, Beasley-Murray makes a lengthy argument in favor of believer's baptism. Nevertheless, his work has much of value for those who affirm infant baptism.

Daniélou, Jean. *The Bible and the Liturgy*. Notre Dame, IN: University of Notre Dame Press, 1956. This classic study offers a good summary of the types the Church Fathers used to interpret the Church's various liturgical practices and rites.

Gregory of Nazianzus. *Festal Orations*. Translated by Nonna Verna Harrison. Crestwood, NY: St. Vladimir's Seminary Press, 2008. This little volume includes St. Gregory's eloquent homilies on the sacrament of baptism and on Christ's own baptism.

Jensen, Robin Margaret. *Living Water: Images, Symbols, and Settings of Early Christian Baptism*. Supplements to Vigiliae Christianae 105. Leiden: Brill, 2011. This is a fascinating study of the architectural and artistic design of baptismal fonts and how they reflect the early Church's theology of baptism.

Leithart, Peter J. *The Priesthood of the Plebs: A Theology of Baptism*. Eugene, OR: Wipf & Stock, 2003. This bold and learned book by Reformed theologian Peter Leithart argues for an Old Testament priestly typology as essential for understanding Christian baptism.

Thate, Michael J., Kevin J. Vanhoozer, and Constantine R. Campbell, eds. *"In Christ" in Paul: Explorations in Paul's Theology of Union and Participation*. WUNT 2/384. Tübingen: Mohr Siebeck, 2014. Not directly related to baptism, this collection of essays explores a crucial aspect of Paul's theology that finds its roots in baptism.

Selected Bibliography

Allison, Dale C., Jr. *Studies in Matthew: Interpretation Past and Present.* Grand Rapids: Baker Academic, 2005.

Anatolios, Khaled. *Deification through the Cross: An Eastern Christian Theology of Salvation.* Grand Rapids: Eerdmans, 2020.

Anderson, Bernhard W. "Exodus Typology in Second Isaiah." In *Israel's Prophetic Heritage: Essays in Honor of James Muilenburg*, edited by B. W. Anderson and W. Harrelson, 177–95. New York: Harper & Brothers, 1962.

Aune, David E., ed. *Rereading Paul Together: Protestant and Catholic Perspectives on Justification.* Grand Rapids: Baker Academic, 2006.

Barber, Michael P., and John A. Kincaid. "Cultic Theosis in Paul and Second Temple Judaism." *JSPHL* 5, no. 2 (2015): 237–56.

Barclay, John M. G. "Mirror-Reading a Polemical Letter: Galatians as a Test Case." *JSNT* 10 (1987): 73–93.

Barth, Markus. *Die Taufe—Ein Sakrament? Ein exegetischer Beitrag zum Gespräch über die kirchliche Taufe.* Zürich: Evangelischer A.G. Zollikon, 1951.

Bauckham, Richard J. *Gospel of Glory: Major Themes in Johannine Theology.* Grand Rapids: Baker Academic, 2015.

Beasley-Murray, G. R. *Baptism in the New Testament.* Grand Rapids: Eerdmans, 1962.

Benedict XVI. *Jesus of Nazareth: From the Baptism in the Jordan to the Transfiguration.* Translated by Adrian J. Walker. New York: Doubleday, 2007.

———. *Saint Paul.* Translated by L'Osservatore Romano. Vatican City: Libreria Editrice Vaticana, 2009.

Berman, Joshua A. *Inconsistency in the Torah: Ancient Literary Convention and the Limits of Source Criticism.* Oxford: Oxford University Press, 2017.

Blenkinsopp, Joseph. "The Structure of P." *CBQ* 38 (1976): 275–92.

Brooks, Oscar S. "1 Peter 3:21—The Clue to the Literary Structure of the Epistle." *NovT* 16 (1974): 290–305.

Childs, Brevard S. *Myth and Reality in the Old Testament.* SBT 27. London: SCM, 1960.

Coloe, Mary L. *God Dwells with Us: Temple Symbolism in the Fourth Gospel.* Collegeville, MN: Liturgical Press, 2001.

Connell, Martin. "Clothing the Body of Christ: An Inquiry about the Letters of Paul." *Worship* 85 (2011): 128–46.

Cross, F. L. *1 Peter: A Paschal Liturgy*. London: Mowbray, 1954.

Crossan, John Dominic. *The Historical Jesus: The Life of a Mediterranean Peasant*. San Francisco: HarperCollins, 1991.

Cullmann, Oscar. *Baptism in the New Testament*. Translated by J. K. S. Reid. London: SCM, 1964.

———. *Early Christian Worship*. Translated by A. Stewart Todd and James B. Torrance. SBT 10. London: SCM, 1953.

Dahl, Nils Alstrup. "The Concept of Baptism in Ephesians." In *Studies in Ephesians: Introductory Questions, Text- & Edition-Critical Issues, Interpretation of Texts and Themes*, 413–40. WUNT 131. Tübingen: Mohr Siebeck, 2000.

Daniélou, Jean. *The Bible and the Liturgy*. Notre Dame, IN: University of Notre Dame Press, 1956.

DiFransico, Lesley R. *Washing Away Sin: An Analysis of the Metaphor in the Hebrew Bible and Its Influence*. BTS 23. Leuven: Peeters, 2016.

DiPaolo, Lawrence, Jr. "Images of Water in the Psalms." *The Bible Today* 53 (2015): 207–12.

Dunn, James D. G. "Baptism as Metaphor." In *Baptism, the New Testament and the Church: Historical and Contemporary Studies in Honour of R. E. O. White*, edited by Stanley E. Porter and Anthony R. Cross, 294–310. JSNTSup 171. Sheffield, UK: Sheffield Academic, 1999.

———. *The Theology of Paul the Apostle*. Grand Rapids: Eerdmans, 1998.

Estes, Joel D. "Calling On the Name of the Lord: The Meaning and Significance of ἐπικαλέω in Romans 10:13." *Themelios* 41 (2016): 20–36.

Eubank, Nathan. *Wages of Cross-Bearing and Debt of Sin: The Economy of Heaven in Matthew's Gospel*. BZNW 196. Berlin: de Gruyter, 2013.

Fee, Gordon D. "Christology and Pneumatology in Romans 8:9–11—and Elsewhere: Some Reflections on Paul as a Trinitarian." In *Jesus of Nazareth: Lord and Christ; Essays on the Historical Jesus and New Testament Christology*, edited by Joel B. Green and Max Turner, 312–31. Grand Rapids: Eerdmans, 1994.

Ferda, Tucker S. "John the Baptist, Isaiah 40, and the Ingathering of the Exiles." *JSHJ* 10 (2012): 154–88.

Flemington, W. F. *The New Testament Doctrine of Baptism*. London: SPCK, 1964.

Freedman, David Noel, ed. *Anchor Bible Dictionary*. 6 vols. New York: Doubleday, 1992.

Gieschen, Charles A. "The Divine Name in Holy Baptism." In *All Theology Is Christology: Essays in Honor of David P. Scaer*, edited by Dean O. Wenthe et al., 67–77. Fort Wayne: Concordia Theological Seminary Press, 2000.

———. "Sacramental Theology in the Book of Revelation." *CTQ* 67 (2003): 149–74.

Gorman, Michael J. *Apostle of the Crucified Lord: A Theological Introduction to Paul and His Letters*. 2nd ed. Grand Rapids: Eerdmans, 2017.

———. *Cruciformity: Paul's Narrative Spirituality of the Cross*. Grand Rapids: Eerdmans, 2001.

Gregory of Nazianzus. *Festal Orations*. Translated by Nonna Verna Harrison. Crestwood, NY: St. Vladimir's Seminary Press, 2008.

Gunkel, Hermann. *Schöpfung und Chaos in Urzeit und Endzeit*. Göttingen: Vandenhoeck & Ruprecht, 1921.

Gupta, Nijay K. *Worship That Makes Sense to Paul: A New Approach to the Theology and Ethics of Paul's Cultic Metaphors*. BZNW 175. Berlin: de Gruyter, 2010.

Hart, David Bentley. *Atheist Delusions: The Christian Revolution and Its Fashionable Enemies*. New Haven: Yale University Press, 2009.

Hartman, Lars. *"Into the Name of the Lord Jesus": Baptism in the Early Church*. SNTW. Edinburgh: T&T Clark, 1997.

———. "Usages—Some Notes on the Baptismal Name-Formulae." In *Ablution, Initiation, and Baptism: Late Antiquity, Early Judaism, and Early Christianity*, edited by David Hellholm et al., 1:397–413. 3 vols. BZNW 176. Berlin: de Gruyter, 2011.

Hays, Richard B. *The Moral Vision of the New Testament: Community, Cross, New Creation; A Contemporary Introduction to New Testament Ethics*. San Francisco: HarperSanFrancisco, 1996.

———. *Reading Backwards: Figural Christology and the Fourfold Gospel Witness*. Waco: Baylor University Press, 2014.

Hill, David. "On Suffering and Baptism in 1 Peter." *NovT* 18 (1976): 181–89.

Huizenga, Leroy Andrew. *The New Isaac: Tradition and Intertextuality in the Gospel of Matthew*. NovTSup 131. Leiden: Brill, 2009.

Jensen, Robin Margaret. *Living Water: Images, Symbols, and Settings of Early Christian Baptism*. Supplements to Vigiliae Christianae 105. Leiden: Brill, 2011.

Jipp, Joshua W. *The Messianic Theology of the New Testament*. Grand Rapids: Eerdmans, 2020.

Josephus. *Josephus*. Translated by Henry St. J. Thackeray et al. 10 vols. LCL. Cambridge, MA: Harvard University Press, 1926–65.

Kingsbury, Jack Dean. *The Christology of Mark's Gospel*. Philadelphia: Fortress, 1983.

Kinzer, Mark. "Temple Christology in the Gospel of John." In *Society of Biblical Literature Seminar Papers* 27, edited by David Lull, 447–64. Missoula, MT: Scholars Press, 1988.

Klawans, Jonathan. *Impurity and Sin in Ancient Judaism*. New York: Oxford University Press, 2000.

———. *Purity, Sacrifice, and the Temple: Symbolism and Supersessionism in the Study of Ancient Judaism*. Oxford: Oxford University Press, 2006.

Leithart, Peter J. *The Baptized Body*. Moscow, ID: Canon Press, 2007.

———. *Delivered from the Elements of the World: Atonement, Justification, Mission*. Downers Grove, IL: IVP Academic, 2016.

———. *The Priesthood of the Plebs: A Theology of Baptism*. Eugene, OR: Wipf & Stock, 2003.

Levenson, Jon D. *The Death and Resurrection of the Beloved Son*. New Haven: Yale University Press, 1993.

———. *Resurrection and the Restoration of Israel: The Ultimate Victory of the God of Life*. New Haven: Yale University Press, 2006.

———. *Sinai and Zion: An Entry into the Jewish Bible*. San Francisco: Harper & Row, 1987.

Martin, Troy W. "Apostasy to Paganism: The Rhetorical Stasis of the Galatian Controversy." *JBL* 114 (1995): 437–61.

———. "The Covenant of Circumcision (Genesis 17:9–14) and the Situational Antitheses in Galatians 3:28." *JBL* 122 (2003): 111–25.

Meier, John P. *A Marginal Jew: Rethinking the Historical Jesus*. 5 vols. AYBRL. New Haven: Yale University Press, 1991–2016.

Millar, J. Gary. *Calling On the Name of the Lord: A Biblical Theology of Prayer*. New Studies in Biblical Theology 38. Downers Grove, IL: InterVarsity, 2016.

Moffitt, David M. *Atonement and the Logic of Resurrection in the Epistle to the Hebrews*. NovTSup 141. Leiden: Brill, 2011.

Morales, Isaac Augustine. "Baptism and Union with Christ." In *"In Christ" in Paul: Explorations in Paul's Theology of Union and Participation*, edited by Michael J. Thate, Kevin J. Vanhoozer, and Constantine R. Campbell, 156–79. WUNT 2/384. Tübingen: Mohr Siebeck, 2014.

———. "Baptism, Holiness, and Resurrection Hope in Romans 6." *CBQ* 83 (2021): 466–81.

———. "Washed, Sanctified, Justified: 1 Corinthians 6 and Baptismal Participation in Christ." In *A Scribe Trained for the Kingdom of Heaven: Essays on Christology and Ethics in Honor of Richard B. Hays*, edited by David M. Moffitt and Isaac Augustine Morales, 91–108. Lanham, MD: Fortress Academic, 2021.

Morales, L. Michael. *Who Shall Ascend the Mountain of the Lord? A Biblical Theology of the Book of Leviticus*. New Studies in Biblical Theology. Downers Grove, IL: InterVarsity, 2015.

Morales, Rodrigo J. "Baptism, Unity, and Crucifying the Flesh." In *A Man of the Church: Honoring the Theology, Life, and Witness of Ralph del Colle*, edited by Michel René Barnes, 249–62. Eugene, OR: Wipf & Stock, 2012.

———. "A Liturgical Conversion of the Imagination: Worship and Ethics in 1 Corinthians." *Letter and Spirit* 5 (2009): 103–24.

———. *The Spirit and the Restoration of Israel: New Exodus and New Creation Motifs in Galatians*. WUNT 2/282. Tübingen: Mohr Siebeck, 2010.

Nelson, Richard D. *Raising Up a Faithful Priest: Community and Priesthood in Biblical Theology*. Louisville: Westminster John Knox, 1993.

Oancea, C. "*Chaoskampf* in the Orthodox Baptism Ritual." *AcT* 37 (2017): 125–42.

Ouspensky, Leonid, and Vladimir Lossky. *The Meaning of Icons*. 2nd ed. Crestwood, NY: St. Vladimir's Seminary Press, 1982.

Petersen, David L. "The Yahwist on the Flood." *VT* 26 (1976): 438–46.

Ratzinger, Joseph. *Introduction to Christianity*. Translated by J. R. Foster and Michael J. Miller. San Francisco: Ignatius, 2004.

———. *The Spirit of the Liturgy*. Translated by John Saward. San Francisco: Ignatius, 2000.

Seitz, Christopher R. *Word without End: The Old Testament as Abiding Theological Witness*. Grand Rapids: Eerdmans, 1998.

Sklar, Jay. "Sin and Impurity: Atoned or Purified? Yes!" In *Perspectives on Purity and Purification in the Bible*, edited by Baruch J. Schwartz et al., 18–31. London: T&T Clark, 2008.

———. *Sin, Impurity, Sacrifice, Atonement: The Priestly Conceptions*. Hebrew Bible Monographs 2. Sheffield, UK: Sheffield Phoenix, 2005.

Spoelstra, Joshua Joel. *Life Preservation in Genesis and Exodus: An Exegetical Study of the* Tēbâ *of Noah and Moses*. CBET. Leuven: Peeters, 2020.

Strauss, Mark. *The Davidic Messiah in Luke-Acts: The Promise and Its Fulfillment in Lukan Christology*. Sheffield, UK: Sheffield Academic, 1995.

Streett, R. Alan. *Caesar and the Sacrament: Baptism—a Rite of Resistance*. Eugene, OR: Cascade Books, 2018.

Thate, Michael J., Kevin J. Vanhoozer, and Constantine R. Campbell, eds. *"In Christ" in Paul: Explorations in Paul's Theology of Union and Participation*. WUNT 2/384. Tübingen: Mohr Siebeck, 2014.

Thiessen, Matthew. *Jesus and the Forces of Death: The Gospels' Portrayal of Ritual Impurity within First-Century Judaism*. Grand Rapids: Baker Academic, 2020.

Trevaskis, Leigh M. *Holiness, Ethics and Ritual in Leviticus*. Sheffield, UK: Sheffield Phoenix, 2011.

Tsumura, David Toshio. *Creation and Destruction: A Reappraisal of the* Chaoskampf *Theory in the Old Testament*. Winona Lake, IN: Eisenbrauns, 2005.

Turner, Kenneth J. *The Death of Deaths in the Death of Israel: Deuteronomy's Theology of Exile*. Eugene, OR: Wipf & Stock, 2010.

Wagner, J. Ross. *Heralds of the Good News: Isaiah and Paul in Concert in the Letter to the Romans*. Leiden: Brill, 2002.

Wenham, Gordon J. "Sanctuary Symbolism in the Garden of Eden Story." In *I Studied Inscriptions from before the Flood: Ancient Near Eastern, Literary, and Linguistic Approaches to Genesis 1–11*, edited by Richard S. Hess and David Toshio Tsumura, 399–404. Winona Lake, IN: Eisenbrauns, 1994.

Westfall, Cynthia Long. "The Relationship between the Resurrection, the Proclamation to the Spirits in Prison and Baptismal Regeneration: 1 Peter 3.19–22." In *Resurrection*, edited by Stanley E. Porter, Michael A. Hayes, and David Tombs, 106–35. JSNTSup 186. Sheffield, UK: Sheffield Academic, 1999.

Willis, John T. *Images of Water in Isaiah*. Lanham, MD: Lexington Books, 2017.

Wrede, William. *The Messianic Secret*. Translated by J. C. G. Greig. London: James Clarke, 1971.

Wright, David P. "The Spectrum of Priestly Impurity." In *Priesthood and Cult in Ancient Israel*, edited by Gary A. Anderson and Saul M. Olyan, 150–81. JSOTSup 125. Sheffield, UK: Sheffield Academic, 1991.

Subject Index

Scripture and Other Ancient Sources Index

New Testament

Matthew

Mark

Luke

John

Acts

Romans

1 Corinthians

2 Corinthians

Galatians

Ephesians

www.ingramcontent.com/pod-product-compliance
Lightning Source LLC
LaVergne TN
LVHW101321110826
845152LV00011B/25

* 9 7 8 1 5 4 0 9 6 5 6 5 3 *